Accounting for Agent Heterogeneity in Market and Policy Analysis

Konstantinos Giannakas

Book one

Center for Agricultural & Food Industrial Organization

University of Nebraska-Lincoln

January 2019

Front cover image:
Drawing inspired by a group of ten marble figures from the early Cycladic period.
Created by Protoleum™, Copyright © 2011-2019 by Protoleum™, Athens, Greece
www.joingreekart.com

ISBN: 978-1-60962-142-1 paperback

doi:10.13014/K2416V8V
https://doi.org/10.13014/K2416V8V

Donation and download page at:
http://www.theheterogeneitybook.com/

Suggested citation:

Giannakas K. *Accounting for Agent Heterogeneity in Market and Policy Analysis*. eBook one, Center for Agricultural & Food Industrial Organization, University of Nebraska-Lincoln. January 2019, doi:10.13014/ K2416V8V.

Zea Books are published by the University of Nebraska–Lincoln Libraries.

Electronic (pdf) editions published online at
https://digitalcommons.unl.edu/zeabook/

Print editions sold at
ttp://www.lulu.com/spotlight/unllib

UNL does not discriminate based upon any protected status.
Please go to unl.edu/nondiscrimination

University of Nebraska
Lincoln

To Tala, Ritsa & Christos

Acknowledgements

This book and its author have benefited greatly from the interaction with, and assistance of a number of individuals and organizations. Special thanks go to my longtime colleague and research collaborator, Murray Fulton, for the (many) stimulating conversations and useful comments and suggestions at different stages of this project. The book also benefited from intellectually stimulating interactions with our distinguished colleagues and members of the external advisory board of the Center for Agricultural & Food Industrial Organization-Policy Research Group (CAFIO-PRG), Julian Alston, Nicholas Kalaitzandonakes, Jayson Lusk and Ian Sheldon; CAFIO-PRG colleagues and collaborators; my graduate students; and anonymous reviewers of my journal articles whose challenging comments and suggestions shaped this line of research and the content of this book.

Funding from the National Institute of Food and Agriculture of the U.S. Department of Agriculture through its Policy Research Centers Program supported the development of the new policy analysis framework and it is gratefully acknowledged.

The support by the Department of Agricultural Economics, the College of Agricultural Sciences and Natural Resources (CASNR), the Agricultural Research Division, and the Institute of Agriculture and Natural Resources at the University of Nebraska-Lincoln has been strong, continuous and important for the timely development and successful completion of this project.

I would also like to express my gratitude to Protoleum™ for its no-cost licensing of the magnificent drawing of the Cycladic figurines gracing the cover page and website of my book; my wonderful sister Dr. Eri Giannaka for the pro bono design and development of the website of this book; Kara Heideman for her assistance with the promotion of this book through social media; my student Dr. Imran Meerza for superb research assistance; Barbara Soderlin and the NU Foundation for their help with the Astir CASNR Emergency Student Aid Fund, established in 2015 with the Christmas and birthday gift money of my, then, 13-year-old daughter Ritsa.

Last but not least, I would like to thank my wife Tala and my children Ritsa and Christos for their patience, love, support, and for making life wonderful.

Working on this book has been a challenging and edifying endeavor. I hope you find it useful and stimulating.

K.G.

Table of Contents

Accounting for Agent Heterogeneity in Market and Policy Analysis

This book presents a multi-market framework of market and policy analysis that explicitly accounts for the empirically relevant heterogeneity in consumer preferences and producer characteristics. The explicit consideration of consumer and producer heterogeneity represents a significant departure from the representative consumer and producer that have been at the center of most of the literature on market and policy analysis, and enables the distributional impacts of changes in market conditions and policies to be fully identified. The framework is used to analyze the system-wide market and welfare impacts of a number of changes in market conditions (like changes in consumer preferences, costs and market structure) and policies (like subsidies and taxes) on one of the products in the system. Consistent with a priori expectations, the use of the framework unveils impacts masked by the conventional market and policy analysis.

Introduction

This book discusses the importance of agent heterogeneity in the increasingly industrialized agri-food system and presents a novel, empirically relevant, integrated, multi-market framework of market and policy analysis that explicitly accounts for consumer and producer heterogeneity. In particular, this new analytical framework can account for heterogeneity in consumer preferences or/and incomes; heterogeneous producers (producers differing in their efficiency and net returns associated with the production of different crops due to differences in education, experience, location and quality of land, management skills, technology adopted etc.); imperfectly competitive input suppliers, processors or/and retailers; and links and interactions between the agri-food supply channels of interest (i.e., markets of the reference/regulated product and its relevant substitute products and services).

The new market and policy analysis framework is based on various models of heterogeneous agents (producers and/or consumers) and imperfectly competitive firms developed by the author and his colleagues and students over the past twenty years. These models have been used to analyze: the market and welfare effects of genetically modified products under different regulatory and labeling regimes (Giannakas and Fulton, 2002; Fulton and Giannakas, 2004; Giannakas and Yiannaka, 2004, 2006, 2008; Veyssiere and Giannakas, 2006; Plastina and Giannakas, 2007; Lassoued and Giannakas, 2010; Giannakas, 2016); the market for organic products (Giannakas, 2002a; Giannakas and Yiannaka, 2006); the enforcement of intellectual property rights (Giannakas, 2002b); the effect of cooperatives in agricultural markets (Fulton and Giannakas, 2001, 2012, 2013; Giannakas and Fulton, 2005; Drivas and Giannakas, 2009, 2010; Giannakas, Fulton and Sesmero, 2016); conservation compliance on highly erodible lands (Giannakas and Kaplan, 2005); the economic effects of purity standards in food labeling laws (Giannakas et al., 2011); consumer demand for quality-differentiated products (Giannakas, 2011); the market and welfare effects of country-of-origin-labeling (Plastina, Giannakas and Pick, 2011); the impact of fair trade on agricultural producers (Omidvar and Giannakas, 2015); the market and welfare effects of renewable portfolio standards in the U.S. electricity sector (Bhattacharya, Giannakas and Schoengold, 2017); the market and welfare effects of food nanotechnology innovations (Tran, Yiannaka and Giannakas, 2018) and the economic impacts of mandatory labeling of products of food nanotechnology (Tran, Yiannaka and Giannakas, 2019); the economic effects of, and optimal policy response to food fraud in the form of food adulteration and mislabeling (Meerza, Giannakas and Yiannaka, 2018, 2019); the economic impacts and optimal design of crop insurance (Mavroutsikos, Giannakas and Walters, 2018); and the effect of innovation and policy on food security (Giannakas and Yiannaka, 2018).

The research presented here integrates this accumulated knowledge and experience into an empirically relevant market and policy analysis framework that can be adapted to encompass all relevant segments/participants in the agri-food system. The development of this new framework of analysis was funded by the U.S. Department of Agriculture's Policy Research Centers Program under award number 2012-70002-19387.

Once the general framework of analysis has been developed, it is used to analyze the market and welfare impacts of changes in market conditions (like consumer preferences, costs and market structure) and standard, textbook policy mechanisms like input and output subsidies and taxes. In addition to deriving the effects of these market changes and policies on the different consumer and producer groups (and comparing the results to those of the traditional analysis), the analysis of these market changes and policy mechanisms demonstrates how the proposed framework can be utilized in market and policy analysis.

Novelty, Relevance & Significance

The explicit consideration of consumer and producer heterogeneity in market and policy research represents a significant departure from the "representative consumer" and "representative producer" that have been the foundation of most of the literature on market and policy analysis, while accounting for the presence of imperfect competition in the agri-food system represents a departure from the perfectly competitive market structures analyzed in many market and policy studies. Indeed, through its reliance on the conventional models of representative consumers and producers, traditional market and policy analysis has (implicitly or explicitly) assumed a homogeneous response to, and impacts from, various changes and policies affecting the agri-food marketing system.

It is well-known, however, that both consumers and producers are highly heterogeneous groups and that this heterogeneity is expressed through highly diverse demands for and supplies of products, programs, services, and policies. In this context, the traditional focus on representative consumers and/or producers prevents both the determination of the effects of different market changes and policies on different consumer and producer groups as well as the understanding of the widely different positions held by seemingly similar groups in policy negotiations.

These assumptions of the traditional market and policy analysis are becoming particularly questionable in the contemporary agri-food system. Retailing, processing and key input supply sectors (e.g., seeds and chemicals) are now highly concentrated, while there has been a recognition that consumers and producers are anything but homogenous, particularly when it comes to the consumption and production of an increasing range of product qualities and types. In addition, the presence of differentiated products leads to departures from perfect competition, thus linking concentration to product differentiation (Sexton, 2013).

The presence of oligopoly and oligopsony power has been shown to lead to significant efficiency losses and distributional impacts between agribusiness firms, producers and consumers (Sexton, 2000). The introduction of heterogeneous consumers and producers generates differentiated demands for and supplies of products and services, which, in turn, affect the response to policy changes and the impact of the response on individual welfare.

While a large number of recent market studies of various segments of the agri-food system have moved past the representative consumer and producer frameworks and have incorporated consumer (mainly) and producer heterogeneity in their analyses, the relevant adjustment rate in policy studies has been significantly lower. This is happening at the same time that the policy debate includes protests against the diverse impacts of policies on producers such as the concentration of most of agricultural support to a small number of large farms. Consumers also seem to have widely differing views on the role of new technology (e.g., biotechnology, nanotechnology) in food production as well as the optimal regulatory response to products of these technologies.

Recognizing 1) the increasing industrialization of the agri-food system (characterized, at least in part, by a move from commodities to differentiated products and an increased vertical coordination from "lab to fork" (Boehlje, 1996)); 2) that this fundamental transformation of the agri-food system makes the consumer and producer differentiating attributes and idiosyncrasies critical in understanding its increasingly complex workings; and 3) that such an understanding is imperative both for the analysis of the economic impacts of market changes and policies and the design of mechanisms that can achieve certain policy objectives in a more efficient manner, the proposed framework of analysis allows market and policy research to explicitly account for critical elements of this transformed environment.

As mentioned earlier, the explicit consideration of consumer and producer heterogeneity represents a significant departure from the "representative consumer" and "representative producer" that have been at the epicenter of most of the literature on market and policy analysis, while accounting for the presence of imperfect competition in the agri-food system represents a departure from the perfectly competitive markets analyzed in many market and policy studies. In addition, the focus on the links and interactions between the reference/regulated products and their close but imperfect substitutes (the number of which has been growing rapidly in the increasingly industrialized agri-food system; see Giannakas (2011)) is a departure from both the general equilibrium and the partial equilibrium approaches employed extensively in policy analysis. Specifically, our framework is neither a general equilibrium nor a partial equilibrium in the sense that it does not focus either on the whole economy or a single market. Instead, *it is a flexible, multi-market framework that can be adapted to analyze any number of supply channels of interest* – i.e., any number of products along with their substitute products and services.

While equilibrium models and equilibrium displacement models also recognize the interdependence of markets and are able to capture how a policy intervention in one market affects both this market and other markets, these models have often assumed perfectly competitive market structures (although the impact of market power has also been examined – see, for instance, Holloway (1991) and Alston et al. (1997)) and have typically examined homogeneous products demanded and supplied by representative consumers and representative producers (for an extensive review of this literature, see Wohlgenant (2011)).

In addition to enhancing the empirical relevance of market and policy analysis by allowing the research to account for key elements of the increasingly industrialized agri-food system, the explicit consideration of consumer and producer heterogeneity enables the analysis to disaggregate these interest groups and determine the effects of different market changes and policies on different consumers and producers (e.g., consumers of different products, low- versus high-income consumers, more- versus less-efficient producers, etc.). *Better measures (and understanding) of the market and welfare effects of a policy can lead to improved policy design, enhanced efficiency, increased effectiveness, and reduced policy failures.*

Book Structure

The rest of this book is structured as follows. Section I focuses on the development of the new multi-market framework of analysis. The decisions and welfare of heterogeneous consumers are considered first, followed by the decisions and welfare of heterogeneous producers, and imperfectly competitive middlemen and input suppliers. This section concludes with alternative considerations, market arrangements and organizational forms that can be analyzed with proper adaptations of our framework of analysis. Section II utilizes our integrated methodological framework to analyze the system-wide market and welfare impacts of changes in (a) consumer preferences, (b) market power of middlemen and input suppliers, and (c) the cost structure on input suppliers. This section concludes with a discussion of alternative market considerations and firm strategies that can be (and, many, have been) analyzed using this framework. Following a similar structure, Section III utilizes our integrated framework to analyze (a) a textbook output (producer/consumer) subsidy under perfect competition, (b) demand-affecting policies (like a consumption tax) under imperfect competition, and (c) supply-affecting policies (like an input subsidy) under imperfect competition. This section concludes with a discussion of other important food and environmental policies that can be (and have been) analyzed using our market and policy analysis framework. The sections focusing on the different market changes and policies have a similar structure and level of explanation to ensure that (i) each analysis can stand alone and (ii) the interested reader can easily identify the similarities and differences in the market and welfare impacts of these changes in the economic environment. The empirical implementation of our framework is also discussed before the final section summarizes and concludes this book.

I. Framework of Analysis

This section focuses on the development of our integrated, multi-market framework of market and policy analysis. Figure I.1. depicts a typical supply chain from lab to fork. Agricultural producers produce the farm product using inputs provided by the input suppliers. The farm product is then procured by middlemen (food processors and retailers) who produce the food product and sell it to consumers.

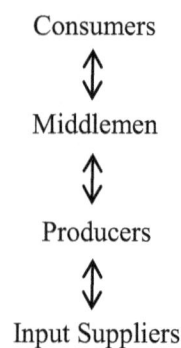

Consumers

⇅

Middlemen

⇅

Producers

⇅

Input Suppliers

Figure I.1. A Typical Supply Chain

The framework considers the vertical relationships in this supply chain as well as the horizontal and diagonal relationships between the various segments of this supply chain and the supply chain of its substitute products, i.e., products that are linked in the demand and supply stages of the different marketing systems.[1] We begin by considering the consumption decisions of heterogeneous consumers and derive the demands for the different products and theory-consistent measures of the welfare of the different consumers involved. This part also compares the consumer welfare measures derived using our framework with the standard consumer surplus measures derived in the literature. Once the consumer problem has been analyzed, we move to the analysis of the production decisions of heterogeneous agricultural producers, the derivation of farm product supplies and input

---

[1] The term "diagonally related markets" refers to markets at different stages of different supply channels. An example of diagonally related markets would be the final consumer market for a product and the producer (or input) market for its substitute.

demands, and the welfare of these producers. Similar to the consumer case, the welfare measures derived using our framework are compared to the standard producer surplus measures derived in the literature. Once the different demand and supply schedules have been derived, we consider the optimization problems of imperfectly competitive middlemen and input suppliers in the relevant supply channels and derive the system-wide equilibrium conditions. The advantages of utilizing this framework for the analysis of the welfare impacts of market and policy changes are discussed before the final part of this section presents alternative relevant formulations of the consumer, producer, middlemen and input supplier models that can be accommodated by our framework of analysis.

I.1. Consumers

Consumers are assumed to have a choice between three products: the reference/regulated product (i.e., the product in the supply chain of which market changes are studied in Section II and which is subsidized and taxed in Section III below) and its lower- and higher-quality substitutes. Consumers buy, at most, one unit of their chosen product and differ in the strength of their preference for the different food products. Let $\alpha \in [0,1]$ be the attribute that differentiates consumers with greater αs corresponding to stronger consumer preference for quality. Assuming that the unit consumption of the products in question represents a small share of the total consumer budget, the consumer utility function can be written as:

$$U_{rg} = U - p_{rg}^c + \lambda\alpha \quad \text{if a unit of the reference product is consumed}$$
$$U_{hs} = U - p_{hs}^c + \mu\alpha \quad \text{if a unit of the high quality substitute is consumed}$$
$$U_{ls} = U \quad \text{if a unit of the low quality substitute is consumed} \quad (I.1)$$

where U is a base level of utility associated with the consumption of these products; p_{rg}^c and p_{hs}^c are the consumer prices of the reference product (rg) and its high quality substitute (hs), respectively; α reflects differences in the consumer valuation of the differentiating attribute of these products (i.e., quality); and λ and μ are preference parameters/utility enhancement factors associated with the consumption of the reference product and its high quality substitute, respectively. To capture the quality difference between the *hs* and the *rg* products, it is assumed that $\mu > \lambda$ with $(\mu - \lambda)\alpha$ capturing the valuation of the quality differential between these products by the consumer with differentiating attribute α – the greater is α, the greater the consumer valuation of the perceived quality difference between the two products.[2]

In addition to reflecting the utility associated with the low quality substitute product, U_{ls} can also be viewed as reflecting a reservation level of utility – i.e., the utility consumers would receive if they chose to consume neither the reference product nor its high quality substitute. For simplicity (and without loss of generality), in what follows, our analysis treats U_{ls} as the consumer reservation level of utility and focuses on the markets for the reference product and its high quality substitute. In addition to saving on notation, such a formulation enables us to account for consumer entry and/or exit from the markets under consideration.

In this context, the consumer choice/consumption decision depends on the relationship between U_{rg}, U_{hs} and U_{ls}. More specifically, the consumer with differentiating attribute:

$$\alpha_{ls} : U_{ls} = U_{rg} \Rightarrow \alpha_{ls} = \frac{p_{rg}^c}{\lambda} \tag{I.2}$$

is indifferent between consuming a unit of the reference product and not consuming any of these products – the utility associated with these alternatives is the same. Similarly, the consumer with differentiating characteristic:

$$\alpha_{rg} : U_{rg} = U_{hs} \Rightarrow \alpha_{rg} = \frac{p_{hs}^c - p_{rg}^c}{\mu - \lambda} \tag{I.3}$$

is indifferent between consuming a unit of the reference product and a unit of its higher quality substitute. Consumers with a strong preference for quality (i.e., consumers with $\alpha \in (\alpha_{rg}, 1]$) prefer the higher quality substitute, consumers with $\alpha \in (\alpha_{ls}, \alpha_{rg})$ prefer the

---

[2] For the relationship of our model with the classical models of vertical product differentiation and its suitability for studies of the agri-food marketing system, see Giannakas (2011).

reference product, while consumers with $\alpha \in [0, \alpha_{ls}]$ consume neither of these two products. Figure I.2 graphs U_{rg}, U_{hs} and U_{ls} and illustrates the consumer decisions in consumer utility space.

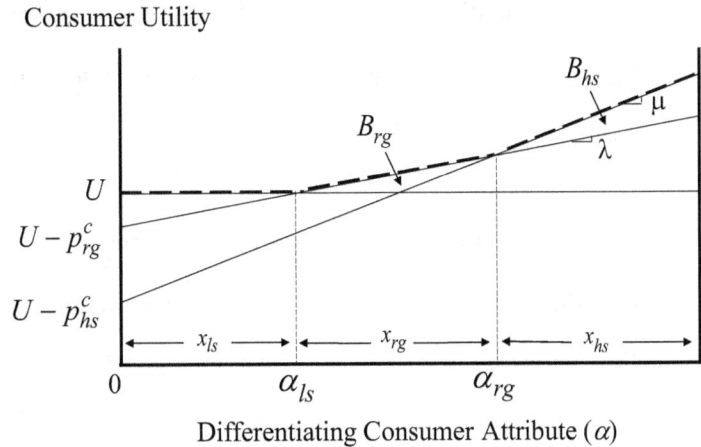

Figure I.2. Consumption Decisions and Welfare

When consumers are uniformly distributed between the polar values of α,[3] $1 - \alpha_{rg}$ determines the share of the high quality substitute product in total consumption, x_{hs}. The consumption share of the reference product, x_{rg}, is given by $\alpha_{rg} - \alpha_{ls}$. Normalizing the mass of consumers at unity, x_{hs} and x_{rg} give the consumer demands for the high quality substitute and the reference products, respectively. Mathematically, x_{hs} and x_{rg} can be written as:

$$x_{hs} = \frac{\mu - \lambda - p_{hs}^c + p_{rg}^c}{\mu - \lambda} \tag{I.4}$$

$$x_{rg} = \frac{\lambda p_{hs}^c - \mu p_{rg}^c}{\lambda(\mu - \lambda)} \tag{I.5}$$

---

[3] The implications of relaxing this assumption to allow for a concentration of consumers at the ends of the spectrum (i.e., zero and one) are straight forward and are discussed throughout this section.

- 12 -

From equations (I.4) and (I.5) it follows that the demand for the high quality substitute (reference) product falls with an increase in its price and/or a decrease (increase) in the strength of the consumer preference for quality,[4] and rises as the price of the reference (high quality substitute) product increases. If p_{rg}^c were greater than p_{hs}^c, the utility curve U_{rg} would lie underneath U_{hs} for all consumers ($\forall \alpha$), the reference product would be driven out of the market, and the demand for the high quality substitute would be:

$$x_{hs} = 1 - \alpha'_{ls} = \frac{\mu - p_{hs}^c}{\mu} \qquad \text{where } \alpha'_{ls} : U_{hs} = U_{ls} \qquad (I.6)$$

On the other hand, if the price premium of the high quality substitute, $p_{hs}^c - p_{rg}^c$, exceeded the valuation of the quality difference between the two products for all consumers, μ-λ, the utility curve U_{hs} would lie underneath U_{rg} for all consumers, and it would be the high quality substitute priced out of the market. The demand for the reference product would then be:

$$x_{rg} = 1 - \alpha_{ls} = \frac{\lambda - p_{rg}^c}{\lambda} \qquad (I.7)$$

Figure I.3 graphs the inverse demand curves for the reference product and its high quality substitute (shown as D_{rg} and D_{hs}, respectively) in the familiar price-quantity space when the prices and preference parameters are such that the two products co-exist in the market. The inverse demand curves (derived from equations (I.4) and (I.5)) are given by:

$$p_{rg}^c = \frac{\lambda}{\mu}\left[p_{hs}^c - (\mu - \lambda)x_{rg}\right] \qquad (I.8)$$

$$p_{hs}^c = p_{rg}^c + \mu - \lambda - (\mu - \lambda)x_{hs} \qquad (I.9)$$

and illustrate the interdependence between the markets for the two products – the price and preference parameters associated with the consumption of a product are direct arguments in the demand for its substitute.

---

[4] An increase in the consumer preference for quality can occur due to an increase in μ and/or a reduction in λ.

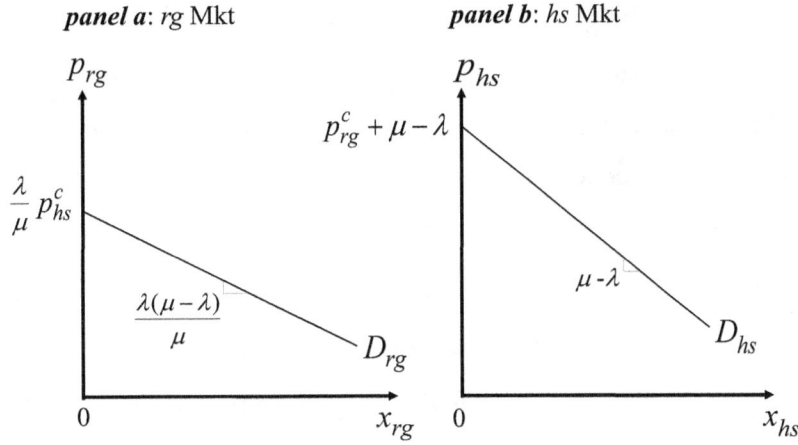

Figure I.3. Consumer Demands for the Reference (*rg*) and High Quality Substitute (*hs*) Products

Before concluding this section, it should be pointed out that, in addition to enabling the derivation of the market shares and consumer demands for the different products, the heterogeneous consumer framework of analysis outlined above also enables us to derive theory-consistent measures of consumer welfare. Since the expressions in equation (I.1) are direct measures of the utility associated with the consumption of the different products for the consumer with differentiating attribute α, the area under the effective (bold dashed kinked) utility curve in Figure I.2 shows the welfare of the different consumers. The welfare of consumers of the regulated product (U_{rg}^*), the high quality substitute (U_{hs}^*), and those staying out of the markets for these products (U_{ls}^*), is given by

$$U_{rg}^* = \int_{\alpha_{ls}}^{\alpha_{rg}} U_{rg}\, d\alpha = Ux_{rg} + \frac{1}{2}\lambda x_{rg}^2 = \left[U + \frac{\lambda p_{hs}^c - \mu p_{rg}^c}{2(\mu-\lambda)}\right]\frac{\lambda p_{hs}^c - \mu p_{rg}^c}{\lambda(\mu-\lambda)} \qquad (I.10)$$

$$U_{hs}^* = \int_{\alpha_{rg}}^{1} U_{hs}\, d\alpha = (U+\lambda x_{rg})x_{hs} + \frac{1}{2}\mu x_{hs}^2 =$$

$$= \left[U + \frac{\mu(\mu-\lambda)+(2\lambda-\mu)p_{hs}^c - \mu p_{rg}^c}{2(\mu-\lambda)}\right]\frac{(\mu-\lambda)-p_{hs}^c + p_{rg}^c}{\mu-\lambda} \qquad (I.11)$$

$$U_{ls}^* = \int_{0}^{\alpha_{ls}} U_{ls}\, d\alpha = U\alpha_{ls} = \frac{Up_{rg}^c}{\lambda} \qquad (I.12)$$

Aggregate consumer welfare is given by the summation of U_{rg}^*, U_{hs}^* and U_{ls}^*. Obviously, if the distribution of consumers is not uniform, but is, for instance, skewed to the left (i.e., the probability mass is shifted towards one), the greater is the number of consumers with relatively strong preference for quality, the greater is the market share of the high quality substitute product, and the greater the welfare of the consumers of this product, U_{hs}^*.

Finally, it is important to note that there is a direct correspondence between the consumer welfare measures presented above and the surplus measures derived from the consumer demand schedules presented in Figure I.3. Specifically, while the U_{rg}^* and U_{hs}^* in equations (I.10) and (I.11) measure the total welfare of consumers of the regulated product and its high quality substitute (i.e., the areas under the U_{rg} and U_{hs} curves in Figure I.2), the surplus measures derived from the demand curves in Figure I.3 correspond to the benefit received from the consumption of the two goods *relative* to their next best alternative. Thus, for given prices p_{hs}^c and p_{rg}^c, the consumer surplus measures CS_{rg} and CS_{hs} that could be calculated in Figure I.3 are equal to areas B_{rg} and B_{hs} in Figure I.2, where

$$CS_{rg} = B_{rg} = \int_{\alpha_{ls}}^{\alpha_{ls}'} \left(U_{rg} - U \right) d\alpha + \int_{\alpha_{ls}'}^{\alpha_{rg}} \left(U_{rg} - U_{hs} \right) d\alpha = \frac{1}{2}\left(\frac{\lambda}{\mu} p_{hs}^c - p_{rg}^c \right) x_{rg} = \frac{1}{2} \frac{\left(\lambda p_{hs}^c - \mu p_{rg}^c \right)^2}{\mu\lambda(\mu - \lambda)}$$

and

$$CS_{hs} = B_{hs} = \int_{\alpha_{rg}}^{1} (U_{hs} - U_{rg}) d\alpha = \frac{1}{2}(p_{rg}^c + \mu - \lambda - p_{hs}^c)x_{hs} = \frac{1}{2} \frac{(p_{rg}^c + \mu - \lambda - p_{hs}^c)^2}{(\mu - \lambda)}.$$

I.2. Producers

Our framework also assumes that producers differ in the net returns they receive from different crops due to differences in such things as age, education, experience, management skills, location and quality of land, and technology adopted. Let $A \in [0,1]$ be the attribute that differentiates producers, with higher values of A corresponding to less efficient producers. Producers, in our case, have the choice between the reference product, its higher-quality substitute and an alternative crop, and their net return function is given by:

$$NR_{rg} = p_{rg}^f - w_{rg} - \gamma A \quad \text{if a unit of reference product is produced}$$
$$NR_{hs} = p_{hs}^f - w_{hs} - \delta A \quad \text{if a unit of high quality substitute is produced}$$
$$NR_a = 0 \quad \text{if a unit of alternative crop is produced} \quad \text{(I.13)}$$

where p_i^f is the producer price of product i ($i = rg, hs$); w_i are the production costs that are outside the control of the farmer; A is the differentiating producer attribute (efficiency, in our case); and γ and δ are cost enhancement factors associated with the production of the reference product and its high quality substitute, respectively. To ensure a non-negative relationship between quality and costs of production, we assume that $\delta > \gamma$ with $(\delta - \gamma)A$ capturing the difference in the costs of producing the two products for the producer with differentiating attribute A. To save on notation, the returns to the production of the alternative crop have been normalized to zero.

In this context, the producer decision is determined by the relationship between NR_{rg}, NR_{hs} and NR_a. More specifically, the producer with differentiating attribute:

$$A_{hs} : NR_{hs} = NR_{rg} \Rightarrow A_{hs} = \frac{(p_{hs}^f - w_{hs}) - (p_{rg}^f - w_{rg})}{\delta - \gamma} \quad \text{(I.14)}$$

is indifferent between producing a unit of the reference product and its higher quality substitute – the net returns associated with the production of these crops are the same. Similarly, the producer with differentiating characteristic:

$$A_{rg} : NR_{rg} = 0 \Rightarrow A_{rg} = \frac{p_{rg}^f - w_{rg}}{\gamma} \quad \text{(I.15)}$$

is indifferent between producing a unit of the reference product and a unit of the alternative crop. More efficient producers (i.e., producers with $A \in [0, A_{hs}))$ prefer to produce the higher quality substitute, producers with $A \in (A_{hs}, A_{rg})$ prefer to produce the reference crop, while producers with $A \in (A_{rg}, 1]$ produce the alternative crop. Figure I.4 graphs NR_{rg}, NR_{hs} and NR_a and illustrates the producer decisions in the net returns space.

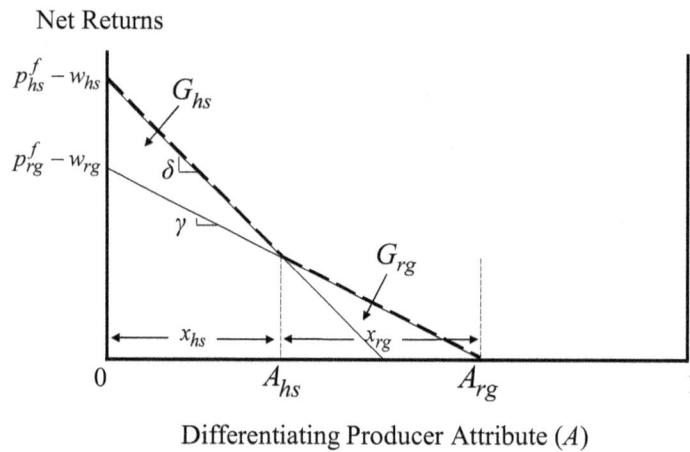

Figure I.4. Producer Decisions and Welfare

When producers are uniformly distributed between the polar values of A, A_{hs} determines the share of the high quality substitute crop in total production, x_{hs}.[5] The production share of the reference product, x_{rg}, is given by $A_{rg} - A_{hs}$. Normalizing the mass of producers at unity, x_{hs} and x_{rg} give the supplies of the high quality substitute and the reference crops, respectively. Mathematically, x_{hs} and x_{rg} can be written as:

$$x_{hs} = \frac{(p_{hs}^f - w_{hs}) - (p_{rg}^f - w_{rg})}{\delta - \gamma} \tag{I.16}$$

___

[5] The implications of relaxing this assumption to allow for a concentration of producers at the ends of the spectrum (i.e., zero and one) are straight forward and are discussed throughout this section.

$$x_{rg} = \frac{\delta(p_{rg}^f - w_{rg}) - \gamma(p_{hs}^f - w_{hs})}{\gamma(\delta - \gamma)} \tag{I.17}$$

The greater is the farm price of a product and/or the lower is the cost associated with its production, the greater is its production share (and quantity supplied). If $p_{hs}^f - w_{hs}$ were smaller than $p_{rg}^f - w_{rg}$, the net returns curve NR_{hs} would lie underneath NR_{rg} for all producers ($\forall A$), the high quality substitute would be driven out of the market and the supply of the regulated product would be:

$$x_{rg} = A_{rg} = \frac{p_{rg}^f - w_{rg}}{\gamma}$$

On the other hand, if the difference $p_{hs}^f - w_{hs}$ exceeded $\frac{\delta(p_{rg}^f - w_{rg})}{\gamma}$, the net returns curve NR_{rg} would lie underneath NR_{hs} for all producers, and the regulated product would be priced out of the market. The supply of the high quality substitute would then be:

$$x_{hs} = A_{hs}' = \frac{p_{hs}^f - w_{hs}}{\delta} \qquad \text{where } A_{hs}' : NR_{hs} = 0$$

Figure I.5 graphs the inverse supply curves for the reference and high quality substitute crops (shown as S_{rg} and S_{hs}, respectively) in the familiar price-quantity space when the prices and cost/efficiency parameters are such that the different crops co-exist in the market. The inverse supply curves (derived from equations (I.16) and (I.17)) are given by:

$$p_{rg}^f = w_{rg} + \frac{\gamma}{\delta}(p_{hs}^f - w_{hs}) + \frac{\gamma(\delta - \gamma)}{\delta} x_{rg} \tag{I.18}$$

$$p_{hs}^f = w_{hs} + (p_{rg}^f - w_{rg}) + (\delta - \gamma)x_{hs} \tag{I.19}$$

and illustrate the interdependence between the two markets – the price and cost/efficiency parameters associated with the production of a crop are direct arguments in the supply of its substitute.

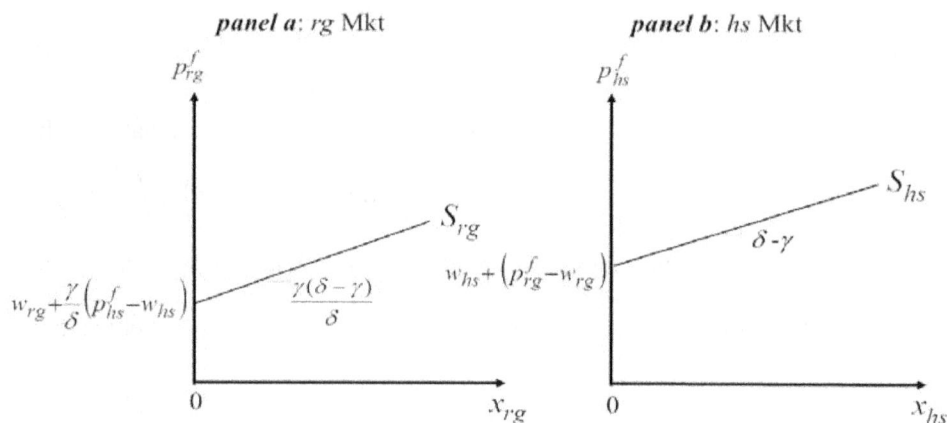

Figure I.5. Farm Supplies of Reference (*rg*) and High Quality Substitute (*hs*) Products

Equations (I.16) and (I.17) can also be used to derive the demands for the inputs used in the production of the reference product and its high quality substitute. Specifically, in the case of a fixed proportions technology in the production of the crops under consideration,[6] the input demands for the reference and high quality substitute crop production are, respectively:

$$w_{rg} = \left[p_{rg}^f - \frac{\gamma}{\delta}(p_{hs}^f - w_{hs}) \right] - \frac{\gamma(\delta - \gamma)}{\delta} x_{rg} \tag{I.20}$$

$$w_{hs} = p_{hs}^f - (p_{rg}^f - w_{rg}) - (\delta - \gamma)x_{hs} \tag{I.21}$$

Figure I.6 graphs these input demands. Similar to the demand and supply schedules derived earlier, the prices and cost parameters in a market have a direct effect on the input demand for the substitute.

---

[6] For a variant of our framework modeling a variable proportions technology see the study on the future of agricultural cooperatives by Fulton and Giannakas (2013). The implications of a variable proportions technology are also discussed by Giannakas and Yiannaka (2018) in their study of the role of agricultural biotechnology in the fight against malnutrition and hunger.

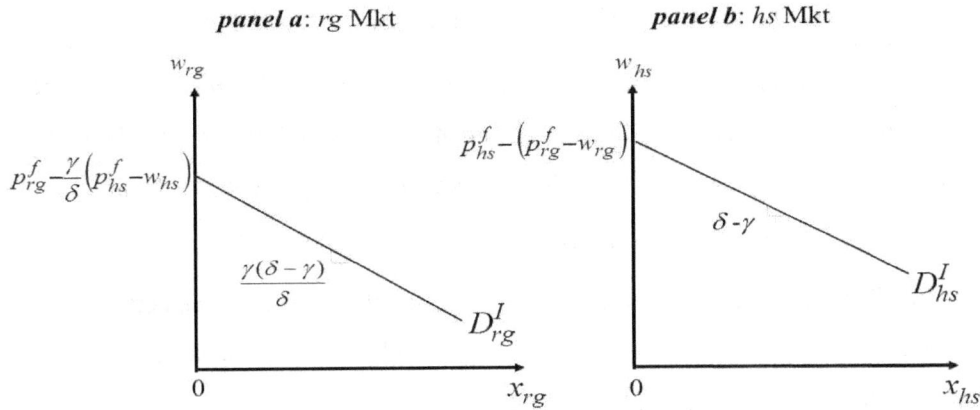

panel a: *rg* Mkt

w_{rg}

$p_{rg}^f - \frac{\gamma}{\delta}\left(p_{hs}^f - w_{hs}\right)$

$\frac{\gamma(\delta-\gamma)}{\delta}$

D_{rg}^I

0 x_{rg}

panel b: *hs* Mkt

w_{hs}

$p_{hs}^f - \left(p_{rg}^f - w_{rg}\right)$

$\delta - \gamma$

D_{hs}^I

0 x_{hs}

Figure I.6. Input Demands from Reference (*rg*) and High Quality Substitute (*hs*) Producers

Before concluding this section, it should be pointed out that, in addition to enabling the derivation of the input demands and supplies of the different products, the heterogeneous producer framework outlined above also enables us to derive theory-consistent measures of producer welfare. In particular, since the expressions in equation (I.13) are direct measures of the net returns associated with the production of the different products (i.e., price minus the costs associated with the unit production of a product), the area under the effective (bold dashed kinked) net returns curve in Figure I.4 shows the welfare of the different producers. Specifically, the welfare of producers of the reference product (NR_{rg}^*) and the high quality substitute (NR_{hs}^*) are given by:

$$NR_{rg}^* = \int_{A_{hs}}^{A_{rg}} NR_{rg} d\alpha = \frac{1}{2}(p_{rg}^f - w_{rg} - \gamma x_{hs})x_{rg} = \frac{\left[\delta(p_{rg}^f - w_{rg}) - \gamma(p_{hs}^f - w_{hs})\right]^2}{2\gamma(\delta-\gamma)^2} \tag{I.22}$$

$$NR_{hs}^* = \int_0^{A_{hs}} NR_{hs} d\alpha = (p_{hs}^f - w_{hs} - \frac{1}{2}\delta x_{hs})x_{hs} =$$

$$= \frac{\left[(\delta-2\gamma)(p_{hs}^f - w_{hs}) + \delta(p_{rg}^f - w_{rg})\right]\left[(p_{hs}^f - w_{hs}) - (p_{rg}^f - w_{rg})\right]}{2(\delta-\gamma)^2} \tag{I.23}$$

Aggregate producer welfare is given by the summation of NR_{rg}^* and NR_{hs}^*. If the distribution of producers is not uniform but is, for instance, skewed to the right (i.e., the probability mass has shifted towards zero), the greater is the number of relatively more efficient producers, the greater is the production share of the high quality substitute product and the greater the welfare of the producers of this product, NR_{hs}^*.

Finally, it is important to note that there is a direct correspondence between the producer welfare measures presented above and the producer surplus measures derived from the supply schedules presented in Figure I.5. Specifically, while NR_{rg}^* and NR_{hs}^* in equations (I.22) and (I.23) measure the total net returns of producers of the regulated product and its high quality substitute (i.e., the areas under NR_{rg} and NR_{hs} in Figure I.4), the surplus measures from the supply curves in Figure I.5 correspond to the surplus generated from the production of a product over and above its next best alternative. As a result, for given prices p_{hs}^f, p_{rg}^f, w_{rg} and w_{hs}, the producer surplus measures PS_{rg} and PS_{hs} that could be calculated in Figure I.5 are equal to areas G_{rg} and G_{hs} in Figure I.4, where:

$$PS_{rg} = G_{rg} = \int_{A_{hs}}^{A_{rg}} \left(\Pi_{rg} - \Pi_{hs} \right) d\alpha = \frac{1}{2} \left[\left(p_{rg}^f - w_{rg} \right) - \frac{\gamma}{\delta} \left(p_{hs}^f - w_{hs} \right) \right] x_{rg} = \frac{\left[\delta \left(p_{rg}^f - w_{rg} \right) - \gamma \left(p_{hs}^f - w_{hs} \right) \right]^2}{2 \delta \gamma (\delta - \gamma)}$$

and

$$PS_{hs} = G_{hs} = \int_{0}^{A_{hs}} \left(\Pi_{hs} - \Pi_{rg} \right) d\alpha = \frac{1}{2} \left[\left(p_{hs}^f - w_{hs} \right) - \left(p_{rg}^f - w_{rg} \right) \right] x_{hs} = \frac{\left[\left(p_{hs}^f - w_{hs} \right) - \left(p_{rg}^f - w_{rg} \right) \right]^2}{2 (\delta - \gamma)}.$$

I.3. Middlemen and Input Suppliers

Depending on the structure of the relevant supply channel, middlemen (e.g., processors and/or retailers) can exercise market power both when procuring the farm product from producers and when selling the processed food product to consumers (Sexton, 2000, 2013). Facing the demand and supply schedules presented in equations (I.8), (I.9), (I.18) and (I.19), the profit-maximizing middlemen find it optimal to produce the quantity determined by the equality of the associated "marginal revenues" and "marginal outlays" and charge the maximum price consumers are willing to pay for this quantity (determined by the point on the demand curve that corresponds to the produced output) while offering producers the minimum price that would induce them to supply the necessary quantity of the farm product (given by the corresponding point of the relevant supply curve).[7]

To capture this behavior, the framework uses the parameters θ_i^b and θ_i^s, where $i \in \{rg, hs\}$, b refers to buyers and s refers to sellers. These parameters determine the location of the relevant "marginal revenue" and "marginal outlay" curves, and capture the degree to which output is restricted when procuring the farm product from producers and when selling the processed food product to consumers.[8] Figure I.7 graphs the profit-maximizing decisions of the middlemen in the markets for the reference product and its high quality substitute.

---

[7] When determining marginal revenue and marginal outlay, it is assumed that marginal costs of processing are zero.

[8] The θ parameters are often referred to as conjectural variation elasticities and are assumed to take values between zero and one. A value of $\theta =1$ corresponds to a monopoly/monopsony; a value of $\theta =0$ reflects either a perfectly competitive market structure or oligopolistic price competition à la Bertrand; while a value of $\theta \in (0,1)$ corresponds to various oligopolistic/ oligopsonistic market structures (Perloff, Karp and Golan, 2007). The θ parameters have also been used to model firm behavior and to capture market power in equilibrium displacement models (Holloway, 1991; Sexton, 2000).

panel a: *rg* Mkt   **panel b**: *hs* Mkt

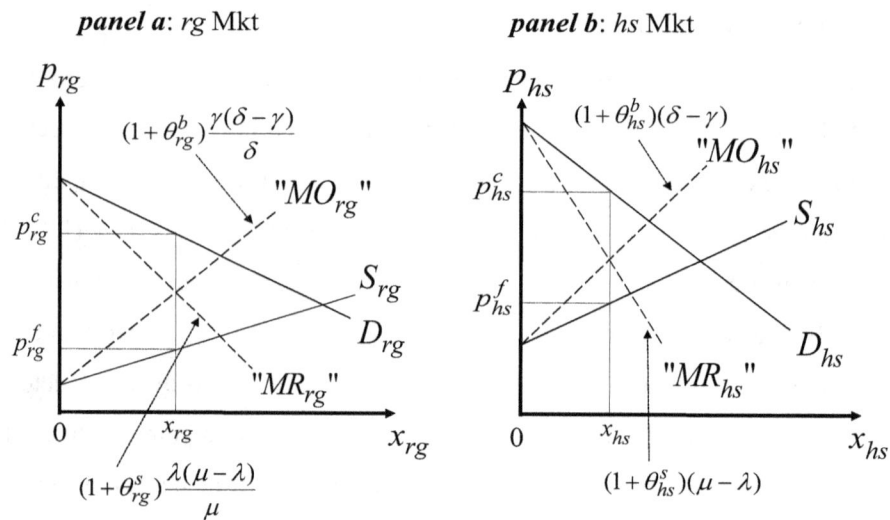

Figure I.7. Determination of Consumer and Producer Prices and Output by Processors/ Retailers with Oligopolistic and Oligopsonistic Market Power

Market structure also plays a role in the supply of farm inputs. Following the approach adopted in the case of middlemen and using the output restriction parameters θ_{rg}^I and θ_{hs}^I, the location of the relevant "marginal revenue" curves for the input suppliers is determined. To focus the analysis on the activities downstream of the input suppliers, it is assumed that the input suppliers face constant marginal costs. Figure I.8 graphs the profit-maximizing decisions of the input suppliers in the *rg* and *hs* markets.

panel a: *rg* Input Mkt   **panel b**: *hs* Input Mkt

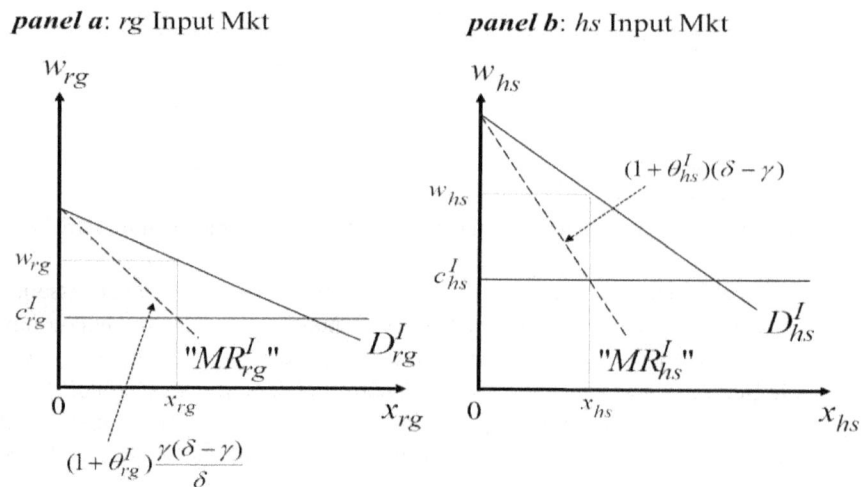

Figure I.8. Determination of Farm Input Prices and Output by Oligopolistic Input Suppliers

I.4. Market Equilibrium

Given the demand and supply schedules presented in equations (I.8), (I.9), (I.18), and (I.19), and the output restriction parameters (the θs), we can determine the equilibrium prices and quantities in the reference and substitute product and input markets. Specifically, solving the following 14 equations simultaneously gives the equilibrium values for the consumer and farm prices of the reference good, the consumer and farm prices of the substitute good, the input prices for the reference and substitute good, and the output of the regulated and substitute goods (the model also determines four marginal revenues and two marginal outlays).

$$p_{rg}^{c} = \frac{\lambda}{\mu}\left[p_{hs}^{c} - (\mu - \lambda)x_{rg}\right]$$

$$p_{hs}^{c} = p_{rg}^{c} + \mu - \lambda - (\mu - \lambda)x_{hs}$$

$$p_{rg}^{f} = w_{rg} + \frac{\gamma}{\delta}(p_{hs}^{f} - w_{hs}) + \frac{\gamma(\delta - \gamma)}{\delta}x_{rg}$$

$$p_{hs}^{f} = w_{hs} + (p_{rg}^{f} - w_{rg}) + (\delta - \gamma)x_{hs}$$

$$MR_{rg}^{b} = \frac{\lambda}{\mu}\left[p_{hs}^{c} - (1 + \theta_{rg}^{b})(\mu - \lambda)x_{rg}\right]$$

$$MR_{hs}^{b} = p_{rg}^{c} + \mu - \lambda - (1 + \theta_{hs}^{b})(\mu - \lambda)x_{hs}$$

$$MO_{rg}^{s} = w_{rg} + \frac{\gamma}{\delta}(p_{hs}^{f} - w_{hs}) + (1 + \theta_{rg}^{s})\frac{\gamma(\delta - \gamma)}{\delta}x_{rg}$$

$$MO_{hs}^{s} = w_{hs} + (p_{rg}^{f} - w_{rg}) + (1 + \theta_{hs}^{s})(\delta - \gamma)x_{hs}$$

$$MR_{rg}^{I} = \left[p_{rg}^{f} - \frac{\gamma}{\delta}(p_{hs}^{f} - w_{hs})\right] - (1 + \theta_{rg}^{I})\frac{\gamma(\delta - \gamma)}{\delta}x_{rg}$$

$$MR_{hs}^{I} = p_{hs}^{f} - (p_{rg}^{f} - w_{rg}) - (1 + \theta_{hs}^{I})(\delta - \gamma)x_{hs}$$

$$MR_{rg}^{b} = MO_{rg}^{s} \quad MR_{hs}^{b} = MO_{hs}^{s} \quad MR_{rg}^{I} = MC_{rg} \quad MR_{hs}^{I} = MC_{hs}$$

The mathematical expressions for the equilibrium prices and quantities in each market, conditional on the equilibrium prices in the other horizontal, vertical and diagonal markets, are as follows:

$$p_{rg}^c = \frac{\lambda}{\mu}\left\{\frac{p_{hs}^c\left[\theta_{rg}^s\frac{\lambda(\mu-\lambda)}{\mu}+(1+\theta_{rg}^b)\frac{\gamma(\delta-\gamma)}{\delta}\right]+(\mu-\lambda)\left[w_{rg}+\frac{\gamma}{\delta}(p_{hs}^f-w_{hs})\right]}{(1+\theta_{rg}^s)\frac{\lambda(\mu-\lambda)}{\mu}+(1+\theta_{rg}^b)\frac{\gamma(\delta-\gamma)}{\delta}}\right\} \qquad (I.24)$$

$$p_{rg}^f = \frac{\left[w_{rg}+\frac{\gamma}{\delta}(p_{hs}^f-w_{hs})\right]\left[(1+\theta_{rg}^s)\frac{\lambda(\mu-\lambda)}{\mu}+\theta_{rg}^b\frac{\gamma(\delta-\gamma)}{\delta}\right]+\frac{\lambda\gamma(\delta-\gamma)}{\mu\delta}p_{hs}^c}{(1+\theta_{rg}^s)\frac{\lambda(\mu-\lambda)}{\mu}+(1+\theta_{rg}^b)\frac{\gamma(\delta-\gamma)}{\delta}} \qquad (I.25)$$

$$p_{hs}^c = \frac{(p_{rg}^c+\mu-\lambda)\left[\theta_{hs}^s(\mu-\lambda)+(1+\theta_{hs}^b)(\delta-\gamma)\right]+(\mu-\lambda)\left[w_{hs}+(p_{rg}^f-w_{rg})\right]}{(1+\theta_{hs}^s)(\mu-\lambda)+(1+\theta_{hs}^b)(\delta-\gamma)} \qquad (I.26)$$

$$p_{hs}^f = \frac{\left[w_{hs}+(p_{rg}^f-w_{rg})\right]\left[(1+\theta_{hs}^s)(\mu-\lambda)+\theta_{hs}^b(\delta-\gamma)\right]+(\delta-\gamma)(p_{rg}^c+\mu-\lambda)}{(1+\theta_{hs}^s)(\mu-\lambda)+(1+\theta_{hs}^b)(\delta-\gamma)} \qquad (I.27)$$

$$w_{rg} = \frac{\theta_{rg}^I\left[p_{rg}^f-\frac{\gamma}{\delta}(p_{hs}^f-w_{hs})\right]+c_{rg}^I}{(1+\theta_{rg}^I)} \qquad (I.28)$$

$$w_{hs} = \frac{\theta_{hs}^I\left[p_{hs}^f-(p_{rg}^f-w_{rg})\right]+c_{hs}^I}{(1+\theta_{hs}^I)} \qquad (I.29)$$

$$x_{rg} = \frac{\frac{\lambda}{\mu}p_{hs}^c-\left[w_{rg}+\frac{\gamma}{\delta}(p_{hs}^f-w_{hs})\right]}{(1+\theta_{rg}^s)\frac{\lambda(\mu-\lambda)}{\mu}+(1+\theta_{rg}^b)\frac{\gamma(\delta-\gamma)}{\delta}} \qquad (I.30)$$

$$x_{hs} = \frac{p_{rg}^c+\mu-\lambda-\left[w_{hs}+(p_{rg}^f-w_{rg})\right]}{(1+\theta_{hs}^s)(\mu-\lambda)+(1+\theta_{hs}^b)(\delta-\gamma)} \qquad (I.31)$$

The expressions in equations (I.24)-(I.31) nicely capture the interdependence between the different markets with the price, cost, preference and market power parameters in one market showing up as direct arguments in the equilibrium expressions for the prices and quantities in its substitute market. As demonstrated in the analysis that follows, the nature of the interdependence of markets captured by the expressions above provides valuable insights on the mechanism through which a market or policy change affects the different vertically, horizontally and diagonally related markets. To reflect their nature, in what follows these equilibrium expressions are referred to as market reaction functions.

Solving the equations for the equilibrium prices simultaneously allows the expression of the output and input prices as functions of the exogenous variables of the model (i.e., preference, cost and market power parameters). Substituting these prices into the expressions for the equilibrium quantities provides the expression of all equilibrium conditions as functions of the exogenous variables of the model (i.e., the reduced form equations). The system-wide equilibrium conditions are graphed in Figure I.9.

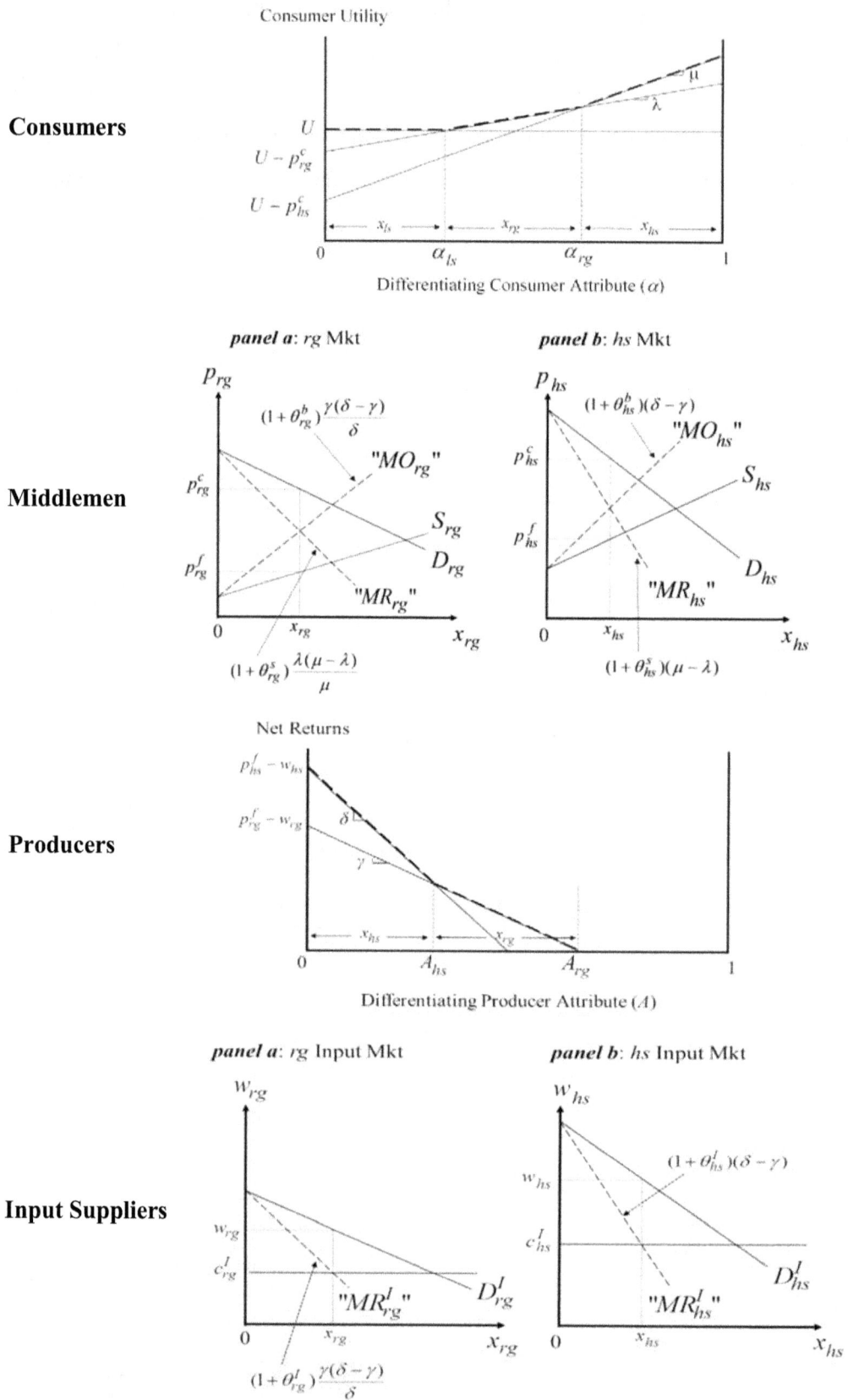

Figure I.9. System-Wide Equilibrium Conditions

I.5. Welfare Analysis

With the equilibrium prices and quantities derived, the economic welfare of the various agents in the system can be determined. The gross profits of the middlemen are determined by multiplying the difference between the buying price and selling price by the quantity sold, while the gross profits of the input suppliers are determined by multiplying the difference between the selling price and marginal cost by the quantity sold (net profits can be calculated from gross profits by subtracting fixed costs). Consumer utility and producer net returns can be determined as outlined above by using the utility and net return expressions presented in equations (I.10)-(I.12), and equations (I.22) and (I.23), respectively.

As will be shown in the next sections, the equilibrium model derived above can be used to determine the impact of market changes and policy interventions. One of the key issues addressed in the literature is the measurement of the change in economic welfare resulting from market changes and policy interventions in linked markets. A key conclusion from the literature is that the aggregate welfare impact can be measured in the market where the market or policy shock is introduced using general equilibrium demand and supply curves (see Buse (1958), Thurman and Wohlgenant (1989), Thurman (1991), Panzar and Willig (1978) and Just and Hueth (1979)).[9] In addition, as Thurman (1991) points out, when two markets are linked in both supply and demand, as is the case in the multi-market framework presented in this book, the aggregate welfare impact can only be obtained if both the general equilibrium supply and demand curves are used to calculate the change in total economic surplus.

It is important to note, however, that the aggregate welfare impacts determined from general equilibrium demand and supply curves are net impacts and do not separate out the effects on each of the various groups (e.g., consumers, producers, middlemen,

---

[9] A general equilibrium curve shows the relationship between the price of a good and the quantity consumed/produced of that good when the rest of the prices that are arguments in the curve are allowed to adjust according to equilibrium conditions in their respective markets. Thus, the general equilibrium demand curve for the regulated good does not hold the price of the substitute good constant, but instead allows the price of that good to change according to the supply and demand equilibrium in that market.

input suppliers). The distributional impacts of a policy can be determined in equilibrium models by calculating the welfare changes in each market; this is done by integrating under the appropriate demand and supply curves (Just, Hueth and Schmitz, 1982). To do so, however, requires the supply and demand curves in each market.

The conclusions outlined above apply, of course, to the model developed in this book. Thus, the aggregate welfare changes can be determined either by the use of general equilibrium supply and demand curves, or by calculating the welfare changes in each market and then aggregating the results. In our case, of course, the aggregate welfare results can also be calculated by directly determining the utility and net returns as outlined in equations (I.10)-(I.12) and (I.22)-(I.23), and then aggregating these measures.

While it is relatively easy to estimate the distributional impacts of a market change or policy intervention using supply and demand curves if it is assumed consumers and producers are homogeneous, this is much more difficult to do when consumer and producer heterogeneity are explicitly taken into account. The reason is that different agents react to the regulation in different ways and thus experience different gains or losses, and these differential impacts need to be determined on an individual basis. For instance, in the case of increased middlemen market power or a consumption tax, some consumers (producers) that were originally consuming (producing) the reference/regulated good switch their consumption (production) to the substitute good. To be able to properly allocate the benefits and costs to individual consumers (producers), it is necessary to keep track of which product they are consuming (producing). The utility and net return framework outlined above allows us to do this.

I.6. Alternative Considerations and Model Formulations

Consumer Heterogeneity

While our analysis focuses on quality- (or vertically-) differentiated products (i.e., products that are uniformly quality- and, thus, utility-ranked by consumers; see Giannakas (2011)), the framework can be easily adapted to study markets of horizontally- (or variety-) differentiated products (i.e., markets where consumers are alike in their basic willingness to pay for a product but differ in the product characteristics they consider important; see Gabszewicz and Thisse (1992) and Mérel and Sexton (2011)). Hybrid markets of both vertical and horizontal product differentiation can also be studied using this framework. Examples of models accommodating this consumer preference structure (and heterogeneity) include those developed and utilized to study the market and welfare impacts of consumer-oriented second generation GM products (Giannakas and Yiannaka, 2008) and quality-enhancing product innovation activity by consumer cooperatives (Drivas and Giannakas, 2010). Finally, the framework can be adapted to study cases in which the relevant/important differentiating consumer attribute is income (rather than preferences; see Tirole (1988), pp. 96-97, and Giannakas and Yiannaka (2018)). Once the relevant demand schedules (and welfare measures) for these cases have been derived, the rest of the framework structure (and links between markets) are similar to those presented in this book.

Producer Heterogeneity

Similar to the consumer case, our framework can be adapted to accommodate a wide array of sources of producer heterogeneity. Thus, in addition to producer efficiency and costs of production, alternative sources of heterogeneity that can be relevant determinants of producer behavior and modeled using our framework's structure include the producers' physical location (Greenhut, Norman and Hung, 1987), ideology and commitment to different organizations (Fulton and Giannakas, 2001, 2013), observability of their actions (Giannakas, 2002b; Giannakas and Kaplan, 2005; Meerza, Giannakas and Yiannaka, 2018, 2019), personal goals and objectives (Giannakas, Fulton and Sesmero, 2016), and level of risk aversion (Mavroutsikos, Giannakas and Walters, 2018). Once the relevant supply schedules (and welfare measures) for these cases have been derived, the rest of the framework structure (and links between markets) are similar to those presented in this book.

Market Structure, Organizational Forms & Trade

In addition to capturing different forms of consumer and producer heterogeneity, the framework can also accommodate a wide range of other market arrangements and forms of strategic interaction among the key actors in the relevant supply channels. For instance, it is possible to disaggregate the middlemen and consider relevant successive or bilateral monopoly/oligopoly situations between processors and retailers (see Waterson (1984)); strategic and extensive (i.e., sequential) price or quantity competition between relevant middlemen or/and input suppliers under different objectives and/or information structures could also be modeled. Examples of game-theoretic models of strategic interactions in pure and mixed oligopolies and oligopsonies that have been developed in the context of our framework include Fulton and Giannakas (2001), Giannakas and Fulton (2005), Veyssiere and Giannakas (2006), and Drivas and Giannakas (2008, 2010).

Our framework is also equipped (and has been used) to study collective action institutions like cooperative organizations. In addition to operating in markets for (quality- and variety-) differentiated products (facing, this way, significant heterogeneity in the consumer valuation of, and willingness-to-pay for their products), cooperatives face significant member heterogeneity and, while they normally focus on maximizing the welfare of their members, they, more often than not, find themselves competing with profit-maximizing investor-owned firms in imperfectly competitive markets of the sort modeled in our framework. In addition to capturing the essence of the aforementioned environment (i.e., consumer and producer heterogeneity, market power and different objectives of the firms involved), our framework enables the distinction between members and non-members of the cooperative(s) and changes in the membership due to different policies and strategies of the cooperative and its rivals. Examples of cooperative studies using adaptations of our framework of analysis include the study of the impact of different types of cooperative organizations on (product and process) innovation activity in oligopolistic and oligopsonistic markets (Giannakas and Fulton, 2005; Drivas and Giannakas, 2008, 2010); the impact of member commitment on market outcomes (Fulton and Giannakas, 2001); horizon and free-rider problems in cooperative organizations (Fulton and Giannakas, 2012; Giannakas, Fulton and Sesmero, 2016); and the future of agricultural cooperatives (Fulton and Giannakas, 2013).

Finally, it is important to note that, while our formulation assumes that domestic agricultural producers supply both the regulated and the substitute products, the model can be modified to analyze cases where the high quality substitute and/or part of the regulated product are imported from the international market, for instance. Similarly, the heterogeneous consumer framework can be adapted to model either consumer behavior in different countries or the behavior of (heterogeneous) consumers in the world market for these products. Examples of studies utilizing variants of our framework in a multi-market trade context include Veyssiere and Giannakas (2006), Plastina, Giannakas and Pick (2011) and Giannakas and Yiannaka (2018).

II. Market Analysis

This part of the book utilizes the methodological framework developed in Section I to analyze the market and (disaggregated) welfare impacts of changes in important determinants of market behavior and outcomes (and key exogenous parameters of our model) like consumer preferences, market structure at different stages of the supply channel of interest, and cost structure. In particular, the following sections focus on the analysis of:

1. Changes in the consumer preferences for the good under study
2. Changes in the oligopolistic and/or oligopsonistic power of middlemen
3. Changes in the oligopolistic power of input suppliers
4. Changes in the cost structure of input suppliers

While the impact of these changes can be derived mathematically through the differentiation of the equilibrium conditions with respect to the parameters of interest (λ, the different θs, and c_{rg}^{I}), our main focus here is on analyzing the impact of these changes on the market in which they occur and carefully tracing the effects on the vertically, horizontally and diagonally related markets. As noted earlier, the market reaction functions in equations (I.24)-(I.31) are uniquely equipped to assist in this endeavor.

II.1. Changes in Consumer Preferences

To determine the system-wide market and welfare impacts of a change in consumer preferences for the good under study, we compare and contrast the equilibrium prices, quantities, and welfare of the interest groups involved before and after the change in consumer preferences. Such a change in consumer preferences can be the outcome of new information about the product, changes in its quality characteristics, quality-enhancing product innovation activity, advertising, and lifestyle changes. As noted earlier, our main focus here is on discussing the impact on the market in which the change occurs and carefully tracing its effects on the vertically, horizontally and diagonally related markets.

The expressions in equations (I.24)-(I.31) capture the interdependence between the markets for the reference product and its substitute as the price, cost, and preference parameters in a market are direct arguments in the equilibrium expressions for its substitute. As a result, these expressions along with the related graphical representation, provide valuable insights on the mechanism through which a parameter affects the various interrelated markets. The rest of this section discusses the market and welfare impacts of a change in consumer preferences using the integrated heterogeneous agent framework presented in Section I.

System-Wide Market and Welfare Effects of Change in Consumer Preferences

The analysis in this part focuses on the impact of an increase in the consumer valuation for the reference product on the input and output markets for the reference product and its substitute, as well as its effects on the welfare of all interest groups involved (i.e., consumers, producers, middlemen and input suppliers in the markets for the two products). In addition to determining changes in the aggregate consumer and producer welfare, the heterogeneous agent framework enables us to determine the effects of the change in consumer preferences on different consumers and producers of the two products. Furthermore, by explicitly considering the interaction between the markets for the reference product and its substitute, the framework allows us to capture relevant indirect and feedback effects that are not accounted for when focusing solely on the market of the reference product.[10]

Beginning with the *direct consumer effects* of the change in consumer preferences, we see that an increase in the consumer valuation of the reference product, λ, (a) increases the utility associated with the consumption of this product (see equation (I.1)) and (b) attracts previous consumers of substitute products to the reference good. Graphically, the increase in λ causes an upward rotation of U_{rg} through the point $U - p_{rg}^c$

---

[10] While our analysis focuses on the case where the reference good and its substitute coexist after the increase in λ, the framework can be used to examine the case where the increase in λ is such that it drives the high quality substitute product out of the market (i.e., when $\lambda : U_{rg}' \geq U_{hs} \ \forall \alpha > \alpha_{ls}' \Rightarrow \lambda \geq \mu - (p_{hs}^c - p_{rg}^c)$).

in Figure II.1.1 and the switching of consumers with differentiating attributes $\alpha \in (\alpha'_{ls}, \alpha_{ls}]$ and $\alpha \in (\alpha_{rg}, \alpha'_{rg}]$ to the reference product.

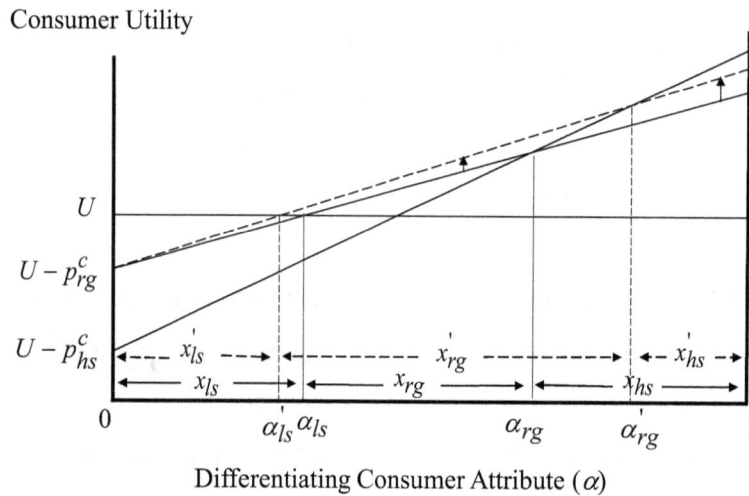

Figure II.1.1. Direct Effects of Increased λ on Consumption Decisions

The increased consumer valuation of the reference good and the subsequent attraction of previous consumers of substitute products increases the demand for the reference product and, through this, increases the consumer and producer prices of this product (see equations (I.24), (I.25) and (I.30)). Figure II.1.2 graphs the upward shift of D_{rg} and consequent increases in p^c_{rg}, p^f_{rg} and x_{rg} due to the increased λ.

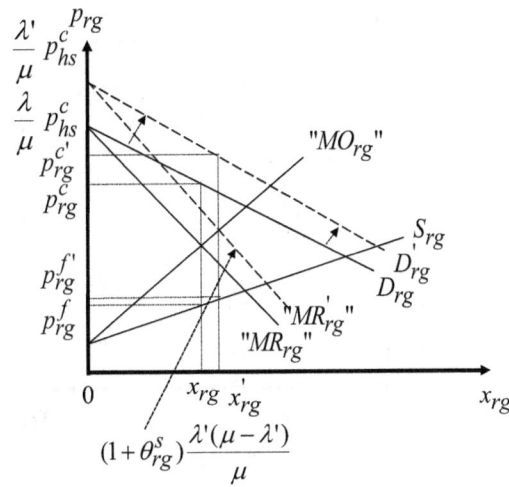

Figure II.1.2. Direct Effects of Increased λ on the Oligemporistic rg Market

In addition to affecting the market for the reference product, the increased consumer valuation of rg has a direct impact on the market for its substitute product. As shown earlier, the increased λ attracts to the reference good previous consumers of the substitute product, which reduces the demand for this product, and, through this, reduces the equilibrium quantity and (consumer and producer) prices of the substitute product (see equations (I.26), (I.27) and (I.31)). Formally, the increased λ causes a downward shift of the demand for the substitute product, D_{hs}, and a reduction in x_{hs}, p_{hs}^c and p_{hs}^f in Figure II.1.3.

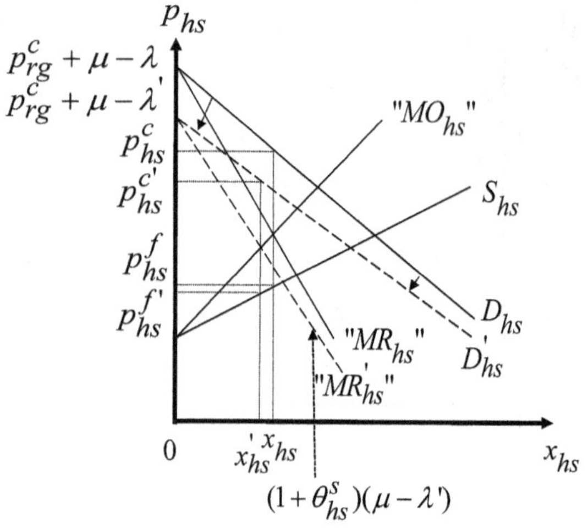

Figure II.1.3. Direct Effects of Increased λ on the Oligemporistic Market for the Substitute *hs* Product

Moving to the *direct producer effects* of the increased λ, we see that the increase in the producer price p_{rg}^f and decrease in p_{hs}^f (a) increase the net returns associated with the production of the reference product, (b) reduce the net returns associated with the production of its high quality substitute, and (c) drive previous producers of the substitute and alternative crops to the reference product. Graphically, the increase in p_{rg}^f causes an upward parallel shift of NR_{rg} while the reduction in p_{hs}^f causes a downward parallel shift of NR_{hs} and the switching of producers with differentiating attributes $A \in (A_{hs}', A_{hs}]$ and $A \in (A_{rg}, A_{rg}']$ in Figure II.1.4 to the reference product.

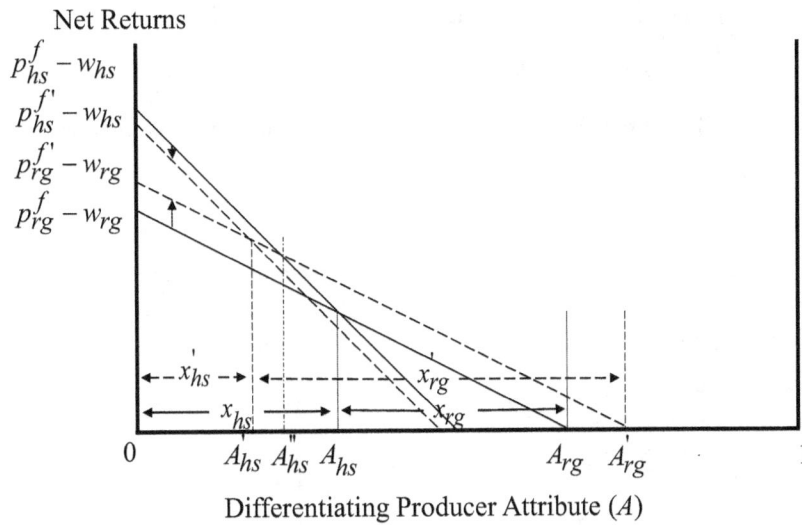

Net Returns

$p_{hs}^{f} - w_{hs}$

$p_{hs}^{f'} - w_{hs}$

$p_{rg}^{f'} - w_{rg}$

$p_{rg}^{f} - w_{rg}$

0 A_{hs}' A_{hs}'' A_{hs} A_{rg} A_{rg}' 1

Differentiating Producer Attribute (A)

Figure II.1.4. Direct Effects of Increased λ on Producer Decisions

The changes in the production decisions described above have a direct impact on the markets for the inputs used in the production of the reference product and its substitute. In particular, the increased consumer valuation of the reference product increases the demand for inputs used in the production of this product (as the equilibrium quantity of the reference product increases with λ) and decreases the demand for inputs used in the production of the substitute (so that the reduced production of this product under a stronger consumer preference for the reference good can be facilitated).

The increased equilibrium price and quantity of the inputs used in the production of the reference product result in increased profits for the suppliers of these inputs, while the reduced price and quantity of the inputs used in the production of the substitute decrease the profits of the suppliers of these inputs. The change in the profits of the rg input suppliers is given by $\Delta\Pi_{rg}^{I} = (w_{rg}' - c_{rg}^{I})x_{rg}' - (w_{rg} - c_{rg}^{I})x_{rg} > 0$, while the change in the profits of the hs input suppliers is $\Delta\Pi_{hs}^{I} = -\left[(w_{hs} - c_{hs}^{I})x_{hs} - (w_{hs}' - c_{hs}^{I})x_{hs}'\right] < 0$ (see Figure II.1.5).

It is important to note that the changes in w_{rg} and w_{hs} have a feedback effect on the markets of these inputs. Specifically, the increase in w_{rg} (decrease in w_{hs}) increases

D_{hs}^I (reduces D_{rg}^I) (see equations (I.20) and (I.21) and Figure I.6) which, in turn, lessens the impact of the increased λ on the prices and quantities of these inputs (see equations (I.28) and (I.29)). The total effects of the increased λ on the input markets are depicted in Figure II.1.5.

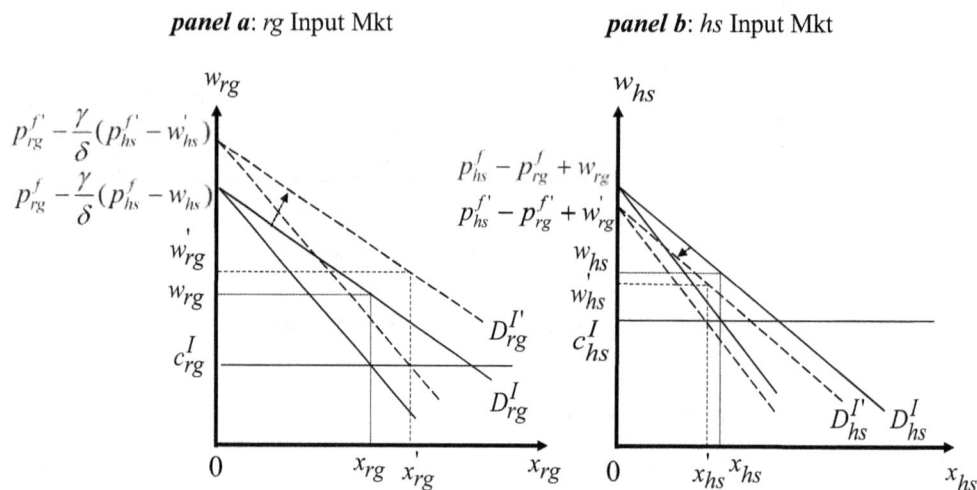

Figure II.1.5. Impact of Increased λ on Input Markets

In addition to affecting the market of the other input, the changes in the input prices affect the net returns associated with the production of the reference product and its substitute (with the increase in w_{rg} and decrease in w_{hs} moderating the changes depicted in Figure II.1.4). Figure II.1.6 graphs the total effects of the change in λ on the producers of the reference product and its substitute. In addition to depicting the total market effects of a change in λ, Figure II.1.6 shows that the producers gaining the most from the increased λ are those producing the reference product both before and after the increase in λ (i.e., producers with $A \in (A_{hs}, A_{rg}]$), followed by producers who switch from the alternative and substitute crops to the reference good (i.e., producers with $A \in (A_{rg}, A_{rg}']$ and $A \in (A_{hs}'', A_{hs}]$). Producers who continue to produce the substitute product after the increase in λ (i.e., producers with $A \in [0, A'_{hs}]$) lose, as do some of the high quality

substitute product producers who switch to the reference product (i.e., producers with

$A \in (A'_{hs}, A''_{hs})$), with the magnitude of this loss determined by the differentiating attribute

of these producers. Total producer gains and losses from the increased λ, are given by

$$G_p = \int_{A_{hs}}^{A_{hs}} (NR'_{rg} - NR_{hs})dA + \int_{A_{hs}}^{A_{rg}} (NR'_{rg} - NR_{rg})dA + \int_{A_{rg}}^{A'_{rg}} (NR'_{rg} - NR_a)dA \text{ and}$$

$$L_p = \int_{0}^{A_{hs}} (NR_{hs} - NR'_{hs})dA + \int_{A_{hs}}^{A''_{hs}} (NR_{hs} - NR'_{rg})dA \text{ , respectively.}$$

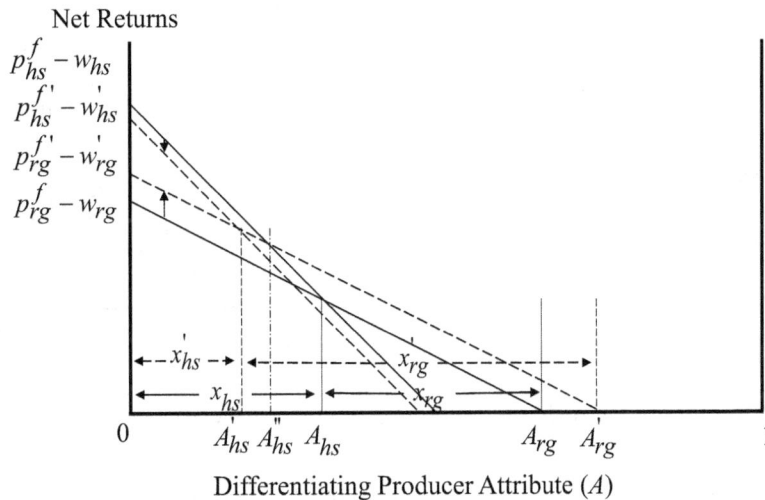

Figure II.1.6. Total Impact of Increased λ on Producer Decisions and Welfare

By affecting the producer net returns, the changes in the input prices also affect the

supply schedules of the two products graphed in Figures II.1.2 and II.1.3 (with the

changes in the input prices decreasing S_{rg} and increasing S_{hs}). The supply (and demand)

schedules for the two products are also affected by the producer (and consumer) prices of

their substitute (with the decrease in p^c_{hs} and p^f_{hs} shifting D_{rg} and S_{rg} downwards, and

the increase in p^c_{rg} and p^f_{rg} shifting D_{hs} and S_{hs} upwards, moderating the impact of the

higher λ in these markets; recall equations (I.8), (I.9), (I.18) and (I.19)). The total effects of these changes in the two markets are depicted in Figure II.1.7. Suppliers of the reference product realize an increase in their profits, with the change given by

$$\Delta\Pi_{rg} = (p_{rg}^{c'} - p_{rg}^{c})x_{rg}' + (p_{rg}^{c} - p_{rg}^{f'})(x_{rg}' - x_{rg}) - (p_{rg}^{f'} - p_{rg}^{f})x_{rg} > 0,$$

while the suppliers of the substitute see their profits fall with the change given by

$$\Delta\Pi_{hs} = -\left[(p_{hs}^{c} - p_{hs}^{c'})x_{hs} + (p_{hs}^{c'} - p_{hs}^{f})(x_{hs} - x_{hs}') - (p_{hs}^{f} - p_{hs}^{f'})x_{hs}'\right] < 0.$$

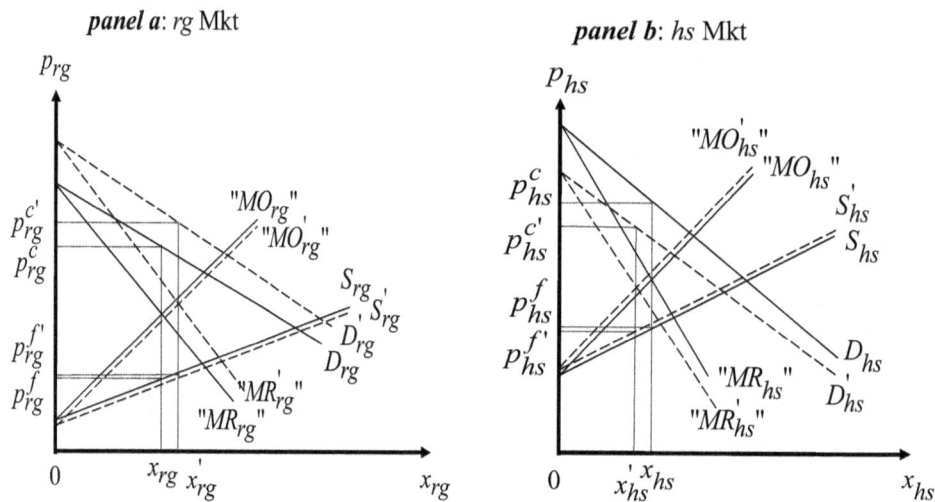

Figure II.1.7. Total Impact of Increased λ on the *rg* and *hs* Markets

Finally, the changes in the consumer prices p_{rg}^{c} and p_{hs}^{c} also affect the utility associated with the consumption of these products, moderating the direct impact of the increased λ depicted in Figure II.1.1. In particular, the increased p_{rg}^{c} reduces the utility associated with the consumption of the reference product, while the reduced p_{hs}^{c} increases the utility associated with the consumption of the substitute product (and reduce the number of consumers switching to the reference good). Figure II.1.8 depicts these market and welfare effects as well as the asymmetric impacts of the increased λ on consumer welfare in the consumer utility space. Consumers gaining the most from the increased λ are those consuming the reference product both before and after the increase in λ and have relatively stronger preference for quality (i.e., consumers located closer to α_{rg}), followed by consumers who find it optimal to switch from the high quality substitute to the reference product (i.e., consumers with $\alpha \in (\alpha_{rg}, \alpha'_{rg}]$). Consumers who prefer the substitute product before and after the increase in λ (i.e., consumers with $\alpha \in (\alpha'_{rg}, 1]$) also gain, as do consumers with $\alpha \in (\alpha'_{ls}, \alpha_{ls}]$ who enter the market for the reference product (the magnitude of this gain depends on the differentiating attribute α of these consumers). Consumer gains in this case are given by

$$G_c = \int_{\alpha'_{ls}}^{\alpha_{ls}} (U'_{rg} - U_{ls}) d\alpha + \int_{\alpha_{ls}}^{\alpha_{rg}} (U'_{rg} - U_{rg}) d\alpha + \int_{\alpha_{rg}}^{\alpha'_{rg}} (U'_{rg} - U_{hs}) d\alpha + \int_{\alpha'_{rg}}^{1} (U'_{hs} - U_{hs}) d\alpha.$$

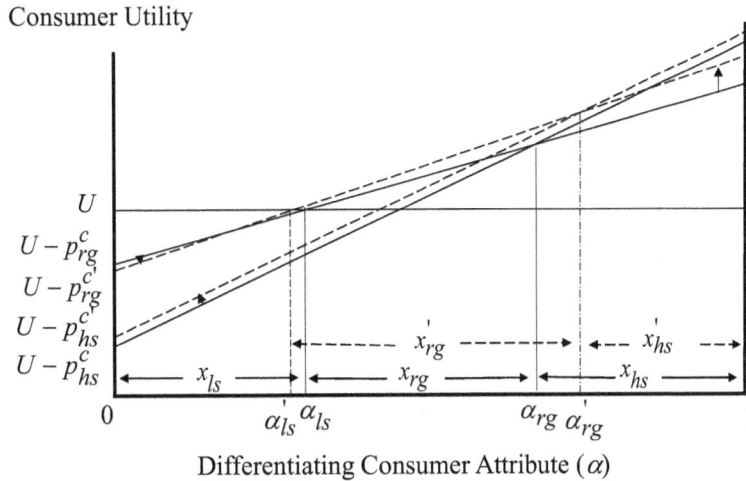

Figure II.1.8. Total Effects of Increased λ on Consumption Decisions and Welfare under Scenario I

Before concluding this section, it is important to note that the above analysis on the total effects of the increased λ on consumption decisions and welfare (and Figure II.1.8) are based on the assumption that the (positive) impact of the higher λ on the utility associated with the consumption of the reference product outweighs the (negative) effect of increased consumer price p_{rg}^c for all consumers of the reference product (i.e., $U'_{rg} > U_{rg}$ $\forall \alpha \in (\alpha_{ls}, \alpha_{rg}]$ which results in $\alpha'_{ls} < \alpha_{ls}$). A necessary condition for this to occur is $\Delta \lambda \alpha_{ls} > \Delta p_{rg}^c$. If the impact of the changing preferences on prices is such that

$\Delta\lambda\alpha_{ls} < \Delta p_{rg}^c$, $\alpha_{ls}' > \alpha_{ls}$ and consumers of the reference product with lower valuation of the good (i.e., consumers with lower values of α) realize a welfare loss and some of them exit the market for this product.

Figure II.1.9 graphs this case (termed as Scenario II) and shows that, when $\alpha_{ls}' > \alpha_{ls}$, consumers with $\alpha \in (\alpha_{ls}, \alpha_{ls}'')$ lose (with the welfare loss decreasing with the strength of their preference for quality) and those with $\alpha \in (\alpha_{ls}, \alpha_{ls}']$ find it optimal to exit the market for the reference product.

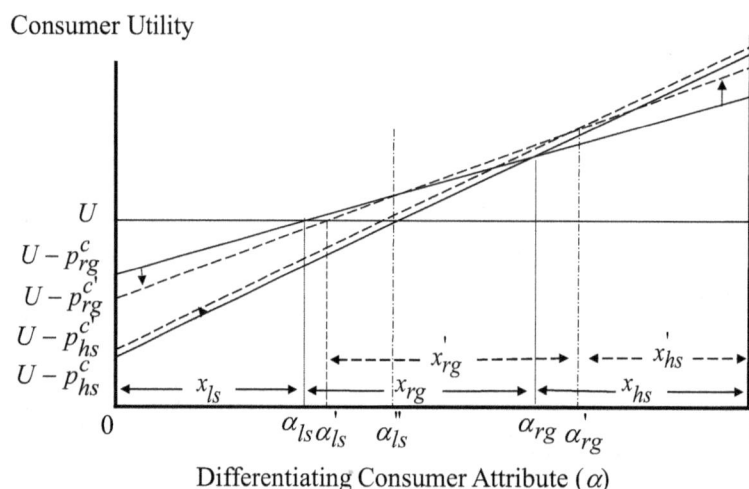

Figure II.1.9. Total Effects of Increased λ on Consumption Decisions and Welfare under Scenario II

While the relationship between $\Delta\lambda\alpha_{ls}$ and Δp_{rg}^c determines whether there will be consumers losing from the increased λ and consumers exiting the market for the reference good, the rest of the results are qualitatively the same with those examined earlier (i.e., those under Scenario I where $\Delta\lambda\alpha_{ls} > \Delta p_{rg}^c$).

Table II.1.1 summarizes the effects of increased λ on the welfare of all relevant interest groups, while Figures II.1.10 and II.1.11 summarize the system-wide market and welfare impacts of the increase in λ under the two scenarios considered here. For simplicity, the feedback effects on the *rg* and *hs* markets (depicted in Figure II.1.6) are not included in these Figures.

Table II.1.1. System-Wide Welfare Impacts of a Change in Consumer Preferences, λ

	Consumers of *ls* switching to *rg*	Consumers of *rg* switching to *ls*	Consumers of *rg*	Consumers of *hs* switching to *rg*	Consumers of *hs*	Producers of *rg*	Producers of *hs* switching to *rg*	Producers of *hs*	Suppliers of *rg*	Suppliers of *hs*	Input Suppliers *rg*	Input Suppliers *hs*
Scenario I	+	*NA*	+	+	+	+	some − some +	−	+	−	+	−
Scenario II	*NA*	−	some − some +	+	+	+	some − some +	−	+	−	+	−

+ denotes welfare gains
− denotes welfare losses
NA denotes non applicable

Condition for Scenario I: $\Delta\lambda\alpha_{ls} > \Delta p_{rg}^c$

Condition for Scenario II: $\Delta\lambda\alpha_{ls} < \Delta p_{rg}^c$

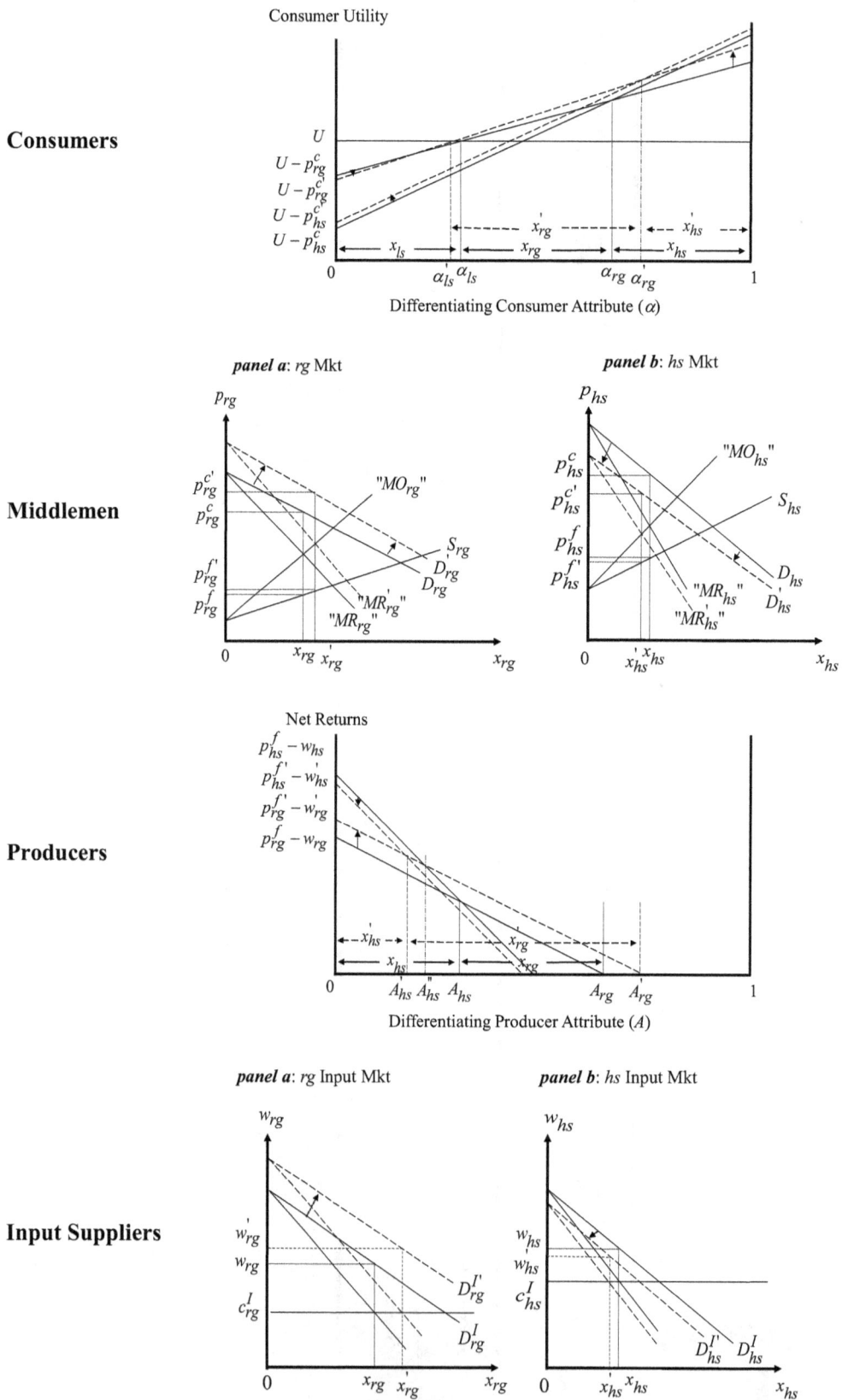

Figure II.1.10. System-Wide Market and Welfare Impacts of a Change in λ under Scenario I

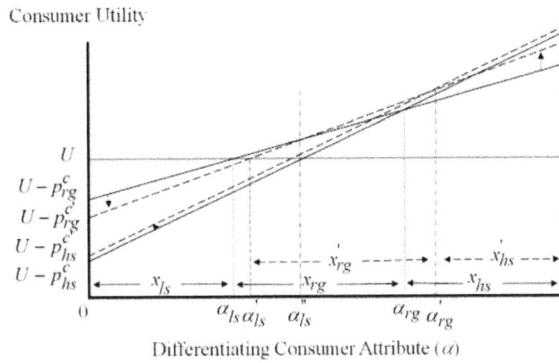

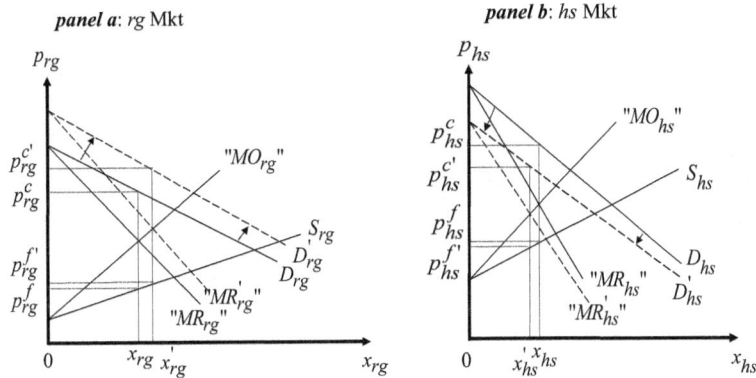

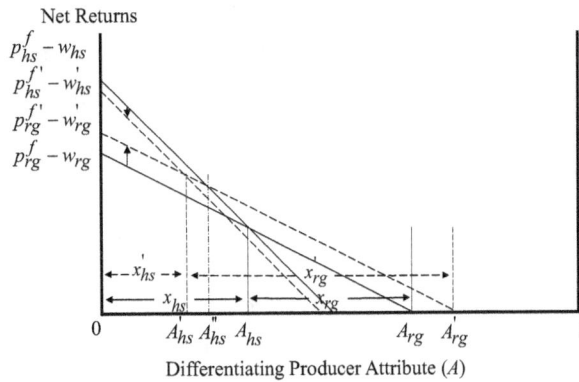

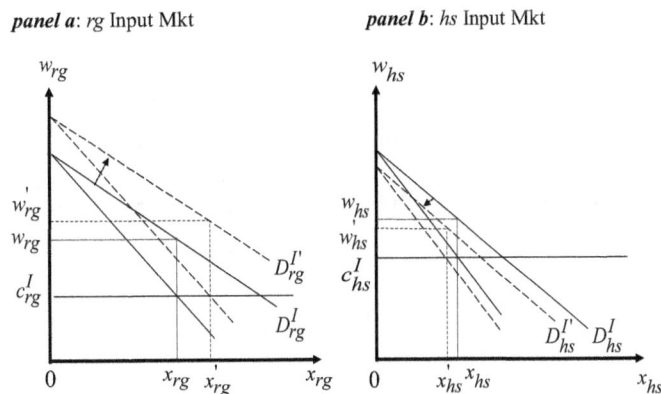

Figure II.1.11. System-Wide Market and Welfare Impacts of a Change in λ under Scenario II

II.2 Increased Market Power of Middlemen

The focus of this section is on the determination of the system-wide market and welfare impacts of increased market power of the middlemen in the supply channel of the reference product. Such an increase could be the outcome of things like increased concentration, collusive behavior among middlemen, stricter regulatory requirements that drive some firms out of the market, intellectual property rights, and merger and acquisition activity. Similar to the case of changing consumer preferences, to determine the system-wide market and welfare impacts of an increased middlemen market power, we compare and contrast the equilibrium prices, quantities, and welfare of the interest groups involved before and after the increase in market power. With the initial equilibrium conditions derived in Section I (and graphed in Figure I.9), our focus here is on the (system-wide) equilibrium conditions under the increased market power. Once we determine the effects of the increased market power on the market where it is exercised, we proceed in discussing its impacts on the vertically, horizontally and diagonally related markets and interest groups involved (i.e., consumers, producers, middlemen and input suppliers in the supply channels of the reference and substitute products).

Equilibrium Conditions under Increased θ_{rg}^s and/or θ_{rg}^b

The increase in the market power of middlemen in the supply channel of the reference product can refer to increased market power when selling the final product to consumers (i.e., increased oligopolistic power, captured by an increased market power parameter θ_{rg}^s) or/and increased market power when procuring the agricultural product from producers (i.e., increased oligopsonistic power, captured by an increased market power parameter θ_{rg}^b). In either case, the increased market power of middlemen translates into (a) increased consumer price p_{rg}^c; (b) reduced producer price p_{rg}^f; (c) reduced quantity x_{rg}; and (d) increased middlemen profits Π_{rg}. Graphically, the increased θ_{rg}^s can be depicted as creating a downward rotation of the marginal revenue curve facing the middlemen through its intercept at $\frac{\lambda}{\mu} p_{hs}^c$, while the increased θ_{rg}^b can be depicted as creating an upward rotation of the marginal outlay curve facing the middlemen through its intercept at $w_{rg} + \frac{\gamma}{\delta}(p_{hs}^f - w_{hs})$. These changes are illustrated in Figure II.2.1.

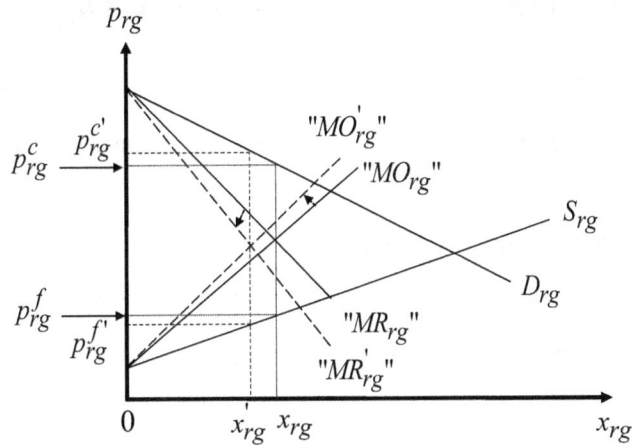

Figure II.2.1. Increased Market Power of Middlemen

Since the implications of increased θ_{rg}^s and θ_{rg}^b are the same, in what follows we refer to increased middlemen market power as increased θ_{rg} with the understanding that this increase can originate either from their oligopolistic or from their oligopsonistic position in the supply channel of the reference good.

In addition to affecting the market for the reference product, the increased θ_{rg} has an effect on the vertically, horizontally and diagonally related markets and our integrated framework of analysis can help identify the system-wide market and welfare impacts of this increase. Note that the equilibrium conditions/market reaction functions under the increased θ_{rg} can be derived by substituting $\theta_{rg}^{s'}$ and $\theta_{rg}^{b'}$ for θ_{rg}^s and θ_{rg}^b, respectively, in equations (I.24)-(I.31)). As mentioned earlier, the nature of the interdependence of markets captured by these expressions provides, along with the related graphical representation, valuable insights on the mechanism through which the increased θ_{rg} affects the different vertically, horizontally, and diagonally related markets. The section below discusses the market and welfare impacts of the increased θ_{rg} using the integrated heterogeneous agent framework presented in Section I.

System-Wide Market and Welfare Effects of Increased θ_{rg}

The analysis in this part focuses on the impact of the increased θ_{rg} on the input and output markets for the reference product and its substitute, as well as its effects on the welfare of all interest groups involved (i.e., consumers, producers, middlemen and input suppliers in the markets for the two products). In addition to determining changes in the aggregate consumer and producer welfare, our integrated heterogeneous agent framework enables us to (a) determine the effects of the increased θ_{rg} on different consumers and producers of the two products and (b) capture indirect and feedback effects that are not accounted for when focusing solely on the market of the reference product.

Beginning with the *direct consumer effects* of the increased θ_{rg}, we see that the increase in the consumer price of the reference product (a) reduces the utility associated with the consumption of this product and (b) drives consumers of the reference product to substitute products. Graphically, the increase in p_{rg}^{c} causes a downward parallel shift of U_{rg} and the exit of consumers with differentiating attributes $\alpha \in (\alpha_{ls}, \alpha_{ls}']$ and $\alpha \in (\alpha_{rg}', \alpha_{rg}]$ in Figure II.2.2 from the market for the reference product.

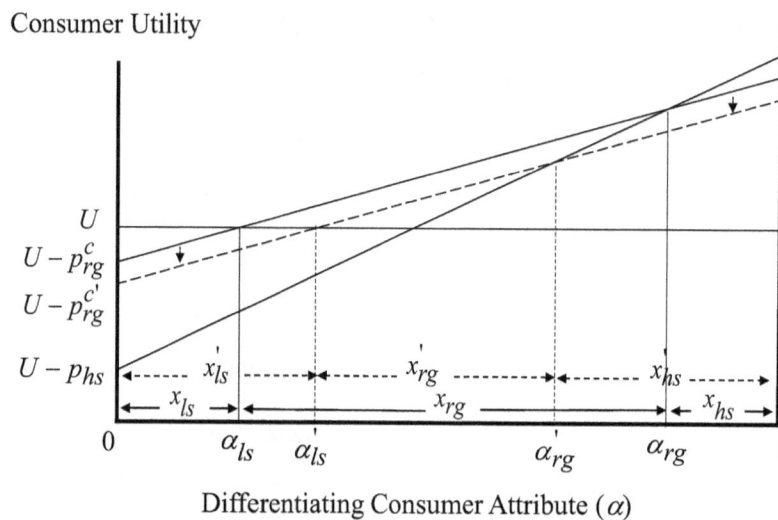

Figure II.2.2. Direct Effects of Increased θ_{rg} on Consumption Decisions

Similar to consumers, the increase in θ_{rg} hurts the producers of the reference product and

results in a number of them switching to alternative crops. Graphically, the reduced p_{rg}^f

causes an downward parallel shift of the net returns curve associated with the production

of the reference product and the switching of producers with $A \in (A_{hs}, A_{hs}']$ and

$A \in (A_{rg}', A_{rg}]$ in Figure II.2.3 to alternative products.

Net Returns

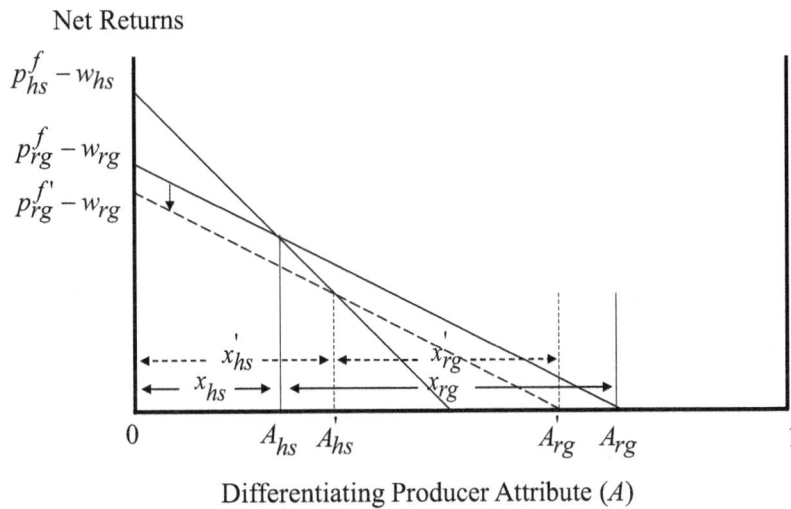

Differentiating Producer Attribute (A)

Figure II.2.3. Direct Effects of Increased θ_{rg} on Producer Decisions

In addition to affecting the market for the reference product, the changes in the consumer

and producer prices of the reference product caused by the increased θ_{rg} have a direct

impact on the market for the substitute product. In particular, the increased consumer

price and the reduced producer price of the reference product (due to the increased θ_{rg})

drive a number of consumers and producers out of the market for the reference product

affecting, this way, both the demand for and supply of the substitute product.

Formally, the increased p_{rg}^c causes an upward parallel shift of the demand for the

substitute product, D_{hs} (see equation (I.9) and Figure II.2.4), while the reduced p_{rg}^f causes

a downward parallel shift of the supply of the substitute product, S_{hs} (see equation (I.19) and Figure II.2.4). While the increased demand for, and supply of the substitute product always increase the equilibrium quantity and profits of the suppliers of this product, the effect on the equilibrium consumer and producer prices (p_{hs}^c and p_{hs}^f, respectively) is determined by the relative magnitude of the demand and supply effects of the increased θ_{rg} on the market for the substitute product. In particular, since a *ceteris paribus* increase in D_{hs} causes p_{hs}^c and p_{hs}^f to increase, while a similar increase in S_{hs} results in reduced p_{hs}^c and p_{hs}^f, when the demand effect dominates the supply effect so that

$$\Delta p_{rg}^c > \frac{(1+\theta_{hs}^s)(\mu-\lambda)+\theta_{hs}^b(\delta-\gamma)}{\delta-\gamma}\left[-\Delta p_{rg}^f + \Delta w_{rg} - \Delta w_{hs}\right] \text{ (where, as noted above,}$$

$\Delta p_{rg}^c > 0$ and $\Delta p_{rg}^f < 0$, while, as shown in Figure II.2.11 below, $\Delta w_{rg} < 0$ and $\Delta w_{hs} > 0$), the consumer and producer prices of the substitute product increase after the increase in θ_{rg} (Scenario I); when

$$\frac{\mu-\lambda}{\theta_{hs}^s(\mu-\lambda)+(1+\theta_{hs}^b)(\delta-\gamma)}\left[-\Delta p_{rg}^f + \Delta w_{rg} - \Delta w_{hs}\right] < \Delta p_{rg}^c <$$
$$< \frac{(1+\theta_{hs}^s)(\mu-\lambda)+\theta_{hs}^b(\delta-\gamma)}{\delta-\gamma}\left[-\Delta p_{rg}^f + \Delta w_{rg} - \Delta w_{hs}\right],$$

the consumer price of the substitute product increases while the producer price falls (Scenario II); while when the supply effect of the increased θ_{rg} dominates the demand effect so that $\Delta p_{rg}^c < \frac{\mu-\lambda}{\theta_{hs}^s(\mu-\lambda)+(1+\theta_{hs}^b)(\delta-\gamma)}\left[-\Delta p_{rg}^f + \Delta w_{rg} - \Delta w_{hs}\right]$, the increased θ_{rg} causes the consumer and producer prices of the substitute product to fall (Scenario III). Figure II.2.4 provides a graphical representation of the conditions leading to the three scenarios while panels 1, 2 and 3 of Figure II.2.5 graph the effects of the increased θ_{rg} on the market of the substitute product under these three scenarios.

Scenario III	Scenario II	Scenario I

$$\frac{\mu-\lambda}{\theta_{hs}^{s}(\mu-\lambda)+(1+\theta_{hs}^{b})(\delta-\gamma)}\left[-\Delta p_{rg}^{f}+\Delta w_{rg}-\Delta w_{hs}\right] \qquad \frac{(1+\theta_{hs}^{s})(\mu-\lambda)+\theta_{hs}^{b}(\delta-\gamma)}{\delta-\gamma}\left[-\Delta p_{rg}^{f}+\Delta w_{rg}-\Delta w_{hs}\right] \qquad \Delta p_{rg}^{c}$$

Figure II.2.4. Scenarios on the Effects of Increased θ_{rg} on the Prices of Substitute *hs* Product

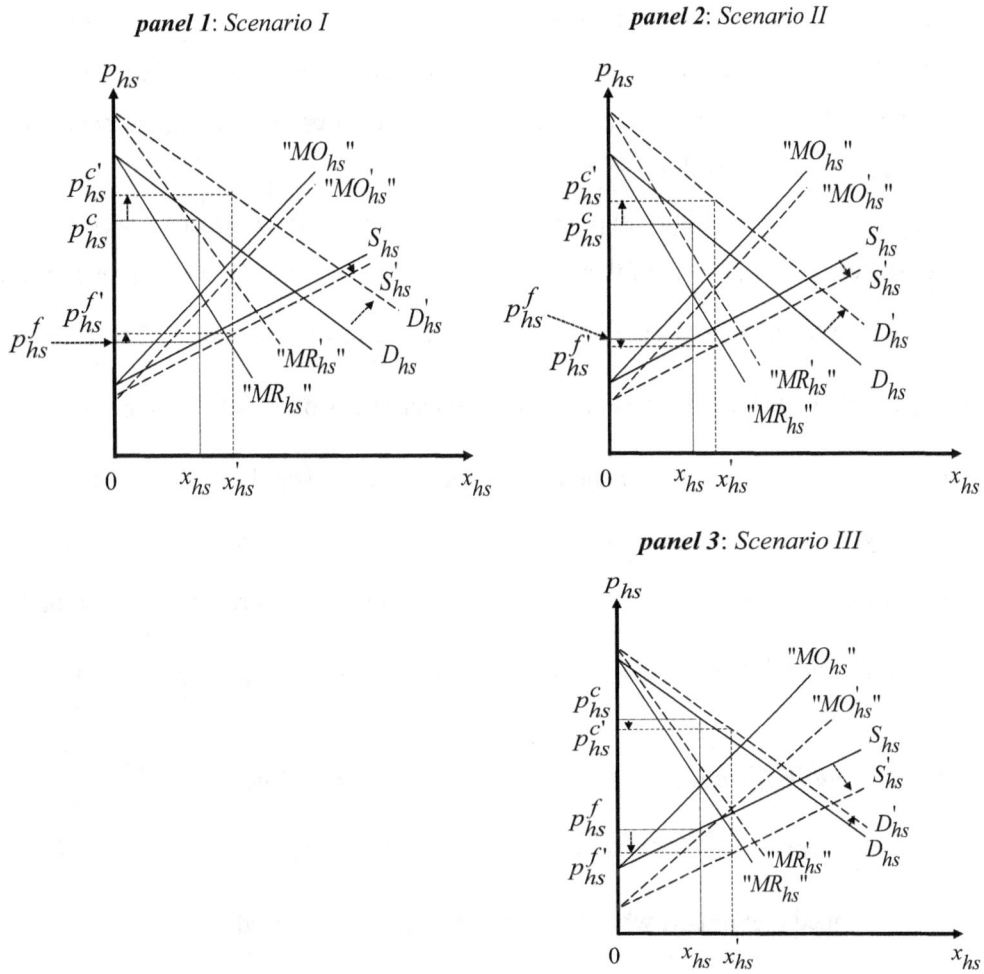

panel 1: Scenario I

panel 2: Scenario II

panel 3: Scenario III

Figure II.2.5. Effects of Increased θ_{rg} on the Market for the Substitute *hs* Product

It is important to note that for Scenario II to occur, the middlemen in the substitute product market should be able to exercise market power. If $\theta_{hs}^s = \theta_{hs}^b = 0$, the condition for Scenario I becomes $\Delta p_{rg}^c > \frac{\mu - \lambda}{\delta - \gamma}\left[-\Delta p_{rg}^f + \Delta w_{rg} - \Delta w_{hs}\right]$ and the condition for

Scenario III becomes $\Delta p_{rg}^c < \frac{\mu - \lambda}{\delta - \gamma}\left[-\Delta p_{rg}^f + \Delta w_{rg} - \Delta w_{hs}\right]$. Intuitively, under perfectly competitive middlemen in the substitute product market, the consumer and producer prices of this product will always move in the same direction. While the presence of middlemen market power is necessary for the consumer and producer prices of the substitute product to move in different directions, it is not sufficient for the emergence of Scenario II – as shown above, both Scenarios I and III can emerge in the presence of middlemen market power.

Since the equilibrium prices of the substitute product affect the welfare of the consumers and producers of this product, our analysis considers the market and welfare impacts of the increased θ_{rg} under the three scenarios outlined above. The case where the increased θ_{rg} causes the consumer and producer prices of its substitute product to increase (i.e., the case in which the demand effect dominates the supply effect of the increased θ_{rg}) is analyzed first followed by the other two scenarios considered here. In all cases, suppliers of the substitute product see their profits increase after the increase in θ_{rg}, with the change in profits given by $\Delta \Pi_{hs} = (p_{hs}^{c'} - p_{hs}^c)x_{hs} + (p_{hs}^{c'} - p_{hs}^{f'})(x_{hs}' - x_{hs}) - (p_{hs}^{f'} - p_{hs}^f)x_{hs} > 0.$

Market and Welfare Effects of the Increased θ_{rg} under Scenario I
(i.e., when $\Delta p_{rg}^c > \frac{(1+\theta_{hs}^s)(\mu - \lambda) + \theta_{hs}^b(\delta - \gamma)}{\delta - \gamma}\left[-\Delta p_{rg}^f + \Delta w_{rg} - \Delta w_{hs}\right]$)
As mentioned previously, when the demand effect of increased θ_{rg} dominates its supply effect, the increase in θ_{rg} increases the consumer and producer prices of its substitute product (recall panel 1 of Figure II.2.5 that depicts this scenario in the price-quantity space).

The increased consumer price of the substitute product, p_{hs}^c, reduces the utility associated with the consumption of this product and limits the number of consumers of the reference product switching to the substitute. Figure II.2.6 depicts these market and welfare effects in the consumer utility space. In addition, the figure shows that the consumers hurt the most from the increased θ_{rg} are those consuming the reference product both before and after the increase in θ_{rg} (i.e., consumers with $\alpha \in (\alpha_{ls}', \alpha_{rg}']$), followed by consumers who find it optimal to turn away from the reference product (i.e., consumers with $\alpha \in (\alpha_{rg}', \alpha_{rg}]$ and $\alpha \in (\alpha_{ls}, \alpha_{ls}']$), and consumers who consume the substitute before and after the increase in θ_{rg} (i.e., consumers with $\alpha \in (\alpha_{rg}, 1]$). Total consumer losses from the increased θ_{rg} are given by

$$L_c = \int_{\alpha_{ls}}^{\alpha_{ls}'} (U_{rg} - U_{ls}) d\alpha + \int_{\alpha_{ls}'}^{\alpha_{rg}'} (U_{rg} - U_{rg}') d\alpha + \int_{\alpha_{rg}'}^{\alpha_{rg}} (U_{rg} - U_{hs}') d\alpha + \int_{\alpha_{rg}}^{1} (U_{hs} - U_{hs}') d\alpha .$$

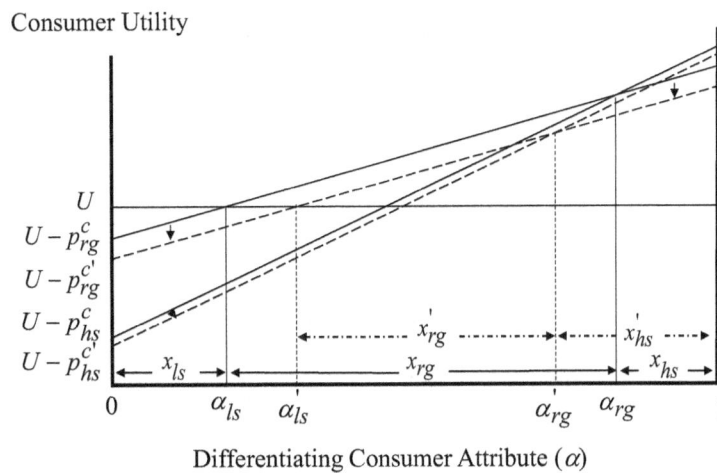

Figure II.2.6. Total Effects of Increased θ_{rg} on Consumption Decisions and Welfare under Scenarios I & II

While the increased p_{hs}^c reduces the desirability of the substitute product for consumers, the increased p_{hs}^f under Scenario I increases the net returns associated with the production of the substitute product and, thus, increases the incentives for switching to the production of this product. Figure II.2.7 depicts these market and welfare effects as well as the asymmetric impacts of the increased θ_{rg} in the producer net returns space. Producers losing the most from the increased θ_{rg} are those producing the reference product both before and after the increase in θ_{rg} (i.e., producers with $A \in (A_{hs}', A_{rg}']$), followed by producers who find it optimal to switch from the reference product to the alternative crop (i.e., producers with $A \in (A_{rg}', A_{rg})$), and the producers with $A \in (A_{hs}'', A_{hs}']$ who switch from the reference product to the substitute.

Producers who produce the substitute before and after the increase in θ_{rg} (i.e., producers with $A \in [0, A_{hs}]$) gain, as do some of the reference product producers who switch to the substitute (i.e., producers with $A \in (A_{hs}, A_{hs}'')$), with the magnitude of this gain determined by the efficiency parameter/differentiating attribute of these producers. Producer gains and losses in this case are given by

$$G_p = \int_0^{A_{hs}} (NR_{hs}' - NR_{hs})dA + \int_{A_{hs}}^{A_{hs}''} (NR_{hs}' - NR_{rg})dA \text{ and}$$

$$L_p = \int_{A_{hs}''}^{A_{hs}'} (NR_{rg} - NR_{hs}')dA + \int_{A_{hs}'}^{A_{rg}'} (NR_{rg} - NR_{rg}')dA + \int_{A_{rg}'}^{A_{rg}} (NR_{rg} - NR_{a})dA \text{ , respectively.}$$

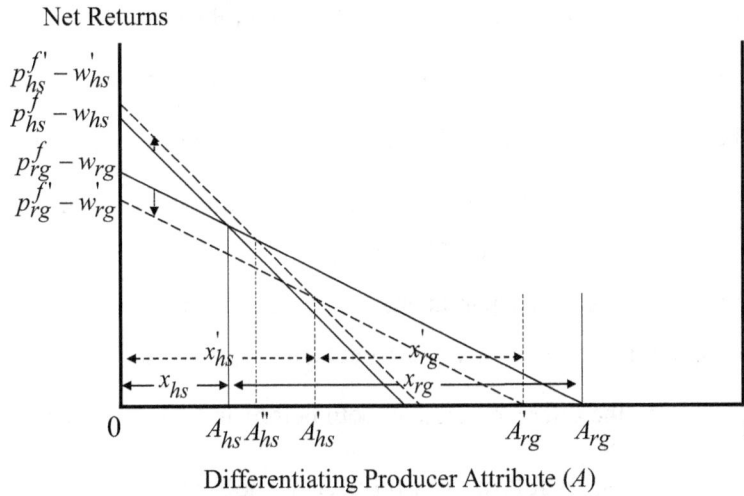

Figure II.2.7. Total Effects of Increased θ_{rg} on Producer Decisions and Welfare under Scenario I

Market and Welfare Effects of the Increased θ_{rg} under Scenario II (i.e., when

$$\frac{\mu - \lambda}{\theta_{hs}^s(\mu - \lambda) + (1 + \theta_{hs}^b)(\delta - \gamma)}\left[-\Delta p_{rg}^f + \Delta w_{rg} - \Delta w_{hs}\right] < \Delta p_{rg}^c <$$

$$< \frac{(1 + \theta_{hs}^s)(\mu - \lambda) + \theta_{hs}^b(\delta - \gamma)}{\delta - \gamma}\left[-\Delta p_{rg}^f + \Delta w_{rg} - \Delta w_{hs}\right]$$

As shown in panel 2 of Figure II.2.5, under Scenario II the consumer price of the substitute product increases while the producer price falls causing both consumers and producers of this product to lose.

Predictably, the ramifications of the increased θ_{rg} for the consumers of the different products are similar to those under Scenario I (described in the previous section and graphed in Figure II.2.6), as p_{hs}^c increases under both Scenarios I and II. Thus, the increased θ_{rg} under Scenario II hurts all reference and substitute product consumers with the greater losses incurred by those consumers who buy the reference product both before and after the increase in θ_{rg}.

Unlike Scenario I, producers of the substitute product lose under Scenario II as the increased θ_{rg} causes the producer price of the substitute product, p_{hs}^f, to fall. The reduced p_{hs}^f reduces the net returns associated with the production of this product and limits/reduces the number of producers who find it optimal to switch to the substitute product after the increase in θ_{rg} (recall that the reduction in the price received by the producers of the reference product creates incentives for a number of them to switch to the substitute and alternative crops; see Figure II.2.3).

Figure II.2.8 depicts these market and welfare effects in the producer net returns space. In addition, the figure shows that the producers losing the most from the increased θ_{rg} are those producing the reference product both before and after the increase in θ_{rg} (i.e., producers with $A \in (A_{hs}', A_{rg}')$), followed by producers who switch from the reference to the alternative and substitute crops (i.e., producers with $A \in (A_{rg}', A_{rg})$ and $A \in (A_{hs}, A_{hs}')$), and producers who continue to produce the substitute product after the increase in θ_{rg} (i.e., producers with $A \in [0, A_{hs}]$). Total producer losses from the increased θ_{rg} are

$$L_p = \int_0^{A_{hs}} (NR_{hs} - NR_{hs}')dA + \int_{A_{hs}}^{A_{hs}'} (NR_{rg} - NR_{hs}')dA + \int_{A_{hs}'}^{A_{rg}'} (NR_{rg} - NR_{rg}')dA + \int_{A_{rg}'}^{A_{rg}} (NR_{rg} - NR_a)dA$$

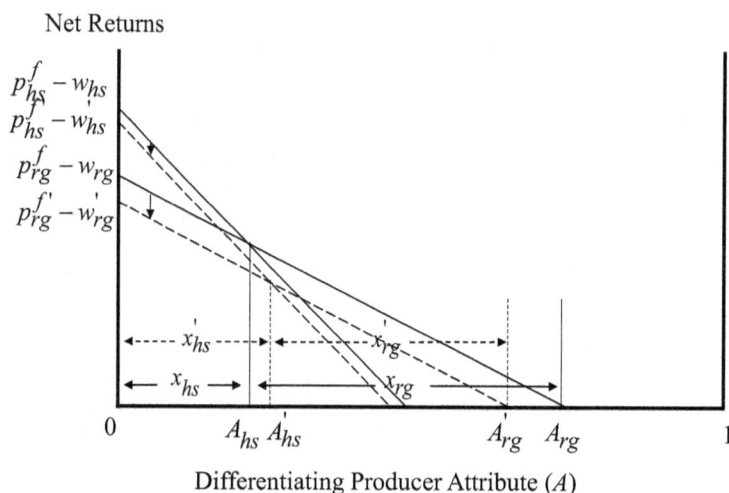

Figure II.2.8. Total Effects of Increased θ_{rg} on Producer Decisions and Welfare under Scenarios II & III

Market and Welfare Effects of the Increased θ_{rg} *under Scenario III*

(i.e., when $\Delta p_{rg}^c < \dfrac{\mu - \lambda}{\theta_{hs}^s(\mu - \lambda) + (1 + \theta_{hs}^b)(\delta - \gamma)}\left[-\Delta p_{rg}^f + \Delta w_{rg} - \Delta w_{hs}\right])$

When the supply effect of the increased θ_{rg} dominates the demand effect, the increase in

θ_{rg} causes the consumer and producer prices of the substitute good to fall. While the

effects of the reduced p_{hs}^f on producer decisions and welfare are similar to those under

Scenario II (described in the previous section and graphed in Figure II.2.8), the effects of

the increased θ_{rg} on consumers are different than those under Scenarios I and II.

Specifically, the reduced p_{hs}^c increases the utility associated with the

consumption of the substitute product and increases the number of consumers switching

from the reference product. Figure II.2.9 depicts these market and welfare effects as well

as the asymmetric impacts of the increased θ_{rg} on consumer welfare in the consumer

utility space. Similar to Scenarios I and II, consumers losing the most from the increased

θ_{rg} are those consuming the reference product both before and after the change in θ_{rg}

(i.e., consumers with $\alpha \in (\alpha_{ls}', \alpha_{rg}']$), followed by consumers who find it optimal to turn

away from the reference product (i.e., consumers with $\alpha \in (\alpha_{rg}', \alpha_{rg}'']$ and $\alpha \in (\alpha_{ls}, \alpha_{ls}']$).

Unlike Scenarios I and II, however, consumers who prefer the substitute product before

and after the increase in θ_{rg} (i.e., consumers with $\alpha \in (\alpha_{rg}, 1]$) gain, as do some of the

reference product consumers switching to the substitute (i.e., consumers with

$\alpha \in (\alpha_{rg}'', \alpha_{rg}]$), with the magnitude of this gain determined by the differentiating

attribute of these consumers. Consumer gains and losses in this case are given by

$$G_c = \int_{\alpha_{rg}''}^{\alpha_{rg}} (U_{hs}' - U_{rg})d\alpha + \int_{\alpha_{rg}}^{1} (U_{hs}' - U_{hs})d\alpha \text{ and}$$

$$L_c = \int_{\alpha_{ls}}^{\alpha_{ls}'} (U_{rg} - U_{ls})d\alpha + \int_{\alpha_{ls}'}^{\alpha_{rg}'} (U_{rg} - U_{rg}^t)d\alpha + \int_{\alpha_{rg}'}^{\alpha_{rg}''} (U_{rg} - U_{hs}')d\alpha, \text{ respectively.}$$

Consumer Utility

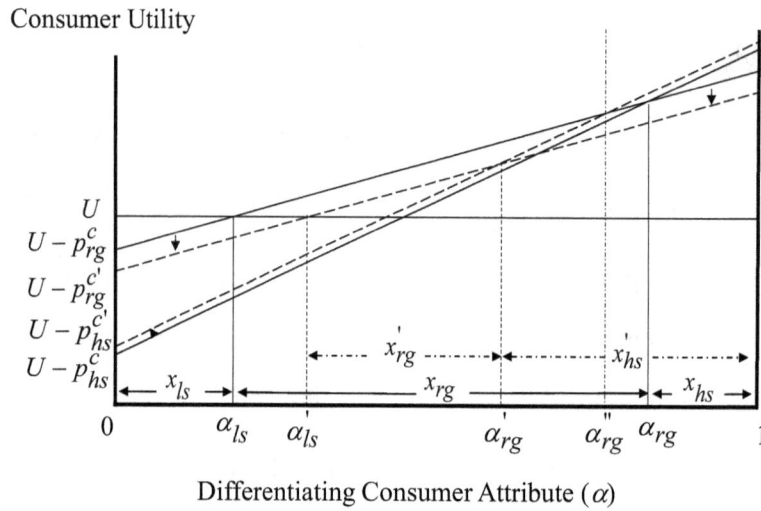

Differentiating Consumer Attribute (α)

Figure II.2.9. Total Effects of Increased θ_{rg} on Consumption Decisions and Welfare under Scenario III

In addition to affecting the decisions and welfare of consumers and producers of the substitute product, the changes in p_{hs}^{c} and p_{hs}^{f} have a feedback effect on the market for the reference product. In particular, an increase (decrease) in p_{hs}^{c} shifts the demand for the reference product D_{rg} upwards (downwards), while an increase (decrease) in p_{hs}^{f} causes an upward (downward) shift of the supply of the reference product S_{rg} (recall equations (I.8) and (I.18) and Figures I.3 and I.5). The total effects of the increased θ_{rg} under the three scenarios considered here are depicted in panels 1-3 of Figure II.2.10. In all cases, the increased θ_{rg} causes an increase in the reference product supplier profits given by $\Delta\Pi_{rg} = (p_{rg}^{c'} - p_{rg}^{c})x_{rg}' - (p_{rg}^{c} - p_{rg}^{f})(x_{rg} - x_{rg}') - (p_{rg}^{f} - p_{rg}^{f'})x_{rg}' > 0$.

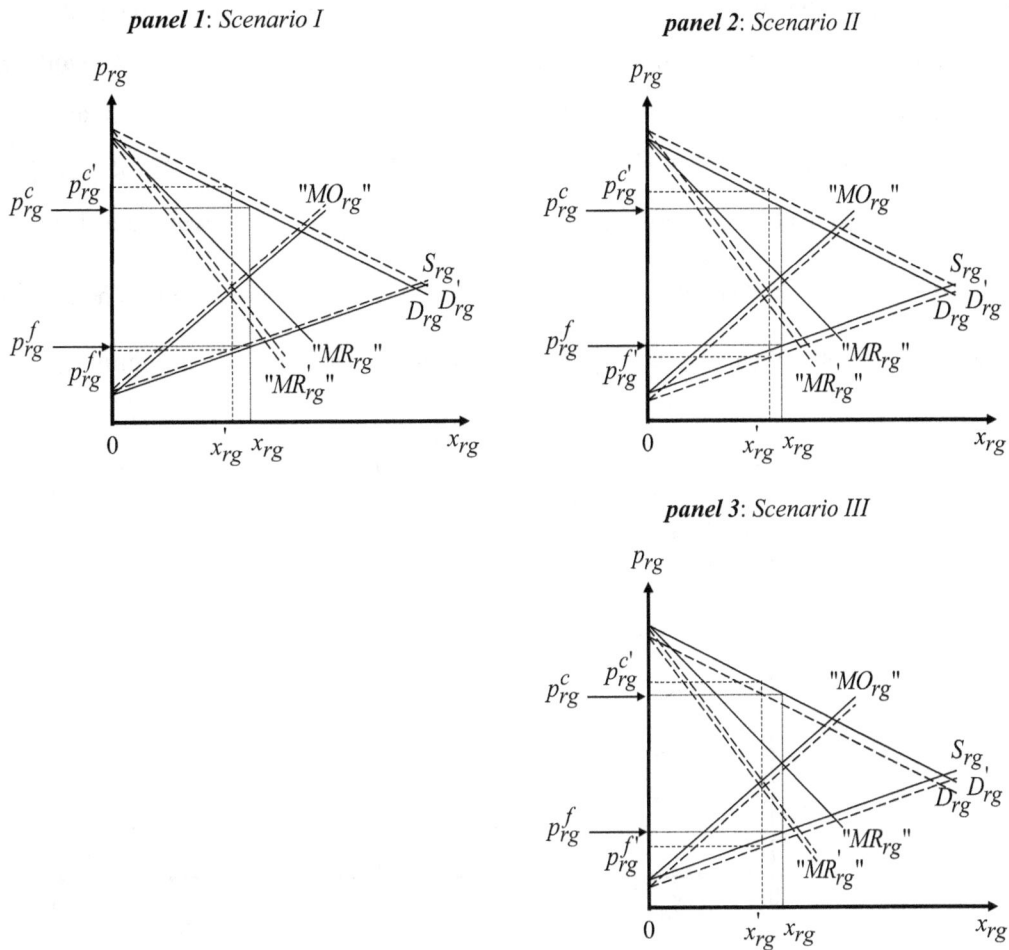

Figure II.2.10. Overall Impact of the Increased θ_{rg} on the rg Market

Finally, regarding the impact of the increased θ_{rg} on the markets for the inputs used in the production of the reference product and its substitute, no matter the effect of the change on p_{hs}^c and p_{hs}^f, the increased θ_{rg} reduces the demand for inputs used in the production of the reference product (as the equilibrium quantity of this product falls in the presence of increased market power; see equation (I.30)) and increases the demand for inputs used in the production of the substitute (so that the increased production of this product in the presence of increased θ_{rg} can be facilitated).

The reduced equilibrium price and quantity of the inputs used in the production of the reference product result in reduced profits for the suppliers of these inputs, while the increased price and quantity of the inputs used in the production of the substitute increase the profits of the suppliers of these inputs. The change in the profits of the rg input suppliers is given by $\Delta\Pi_{rg}^{I} = -\left[(w_{rg} - c_{rg}^{I})x_{rg} - (w_{rg}' - c_{rg}^{I})x_{rg}'\right] < 0$, while the change in the profits of the hs input suppliers is $\Delta\Pi_{hs}^{I} = (w_{hs}' - c_{hs}^{I})x_{hs}' - (w_{hs} - c_{hs}^{I})x_{hs} > 0$. The market and welfare effects of the increased θ_{rg} on the input markets are depicted in Figure II.2.11.

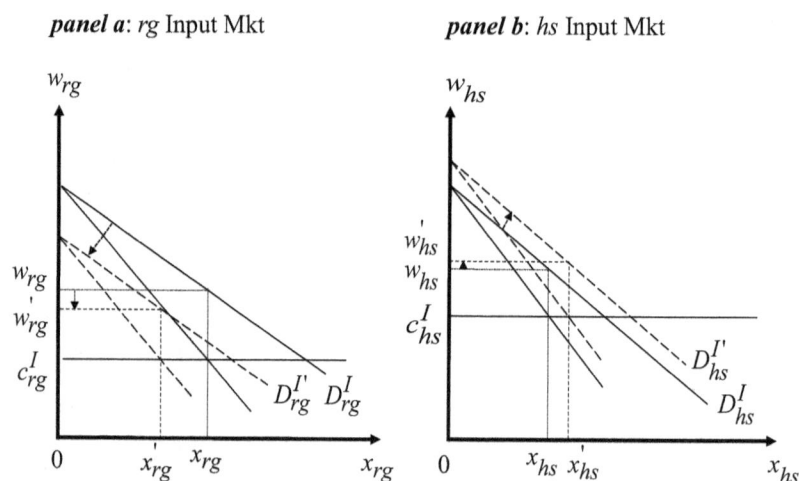

panel a: rg Input Mkt   *panel b*: hs Input Mkt

Figure II.2.11. Increased θ_{rg} Impact on the Input Markets

Overall, the analysis of the system-wide market and welfare impacts of an increased θ_{rg} indicates that: (a) the qualitative nature of the welfare effects on the consumers and producers of the substitute product is scenario-specific and depends on the conditions in the market for both the reference product and the substitute product; (b) the impacts of the increased market power of middlemen are asymmetric across the different consumers and producers affected by this increase; (c) determination of these asymmetric impacts requires a disaggregation of the benefits and costs to the level of the individual agent; and (d) in Scenarios I and III, some of the consumers (Scenario III) or some of the producers

(Scenario I) who find it optimal to switch from the reference product to its substitute after the increase in θ_{rg} realize welfare gains.

Table II.2.1 summarizes the asymmetric effects of increased θ_{rg} on the welfare of all relevant interest groups, while Figures II.2.12-II.2.14 summarize the system-wide market and welfare impacts of the increase in θ_{rg} under the different scenarios considered in this study. For simplicity, the feedback effect on the rg market (depicted in Figure II.2.10) is not included in Figures II.2.12- II.2.14.

Table II.2.1. System-Wide Welfare Impacts of Increased Market Power of Middlemen, θ_{rg}

	Consumers of rg switching to ls	Consumers of rg	Consumers of rg switching to hs	Consumers of hs	Producers of rg	Producers of rg switching to hs	Producers of hs	Suppliers of rg	Suppliers of hs	Input Suppliers rg	Input Suppliers hs
Scenario I	−	−	−	−	−	some + some −	+	−	+	−	+
Scenario II	−	−	−	−	−	−	−	−	+	−	+
Scenario III	−	−	some − some +	+	−	−	−	−	+	−	+

+ denotes welfare gains
− denotes welfare losses

Condition for Scenario I: $\Delta p_{rg}^c > \dfrac{(1+\theta_{hs}^s)(\mu-\lambda)+\theta_{hs}^b(\delta-\gamma)}{\delta-\gamma}\left[-\Delta p_{rg}^f + \Delta w_{rg} - \Delta w_{hs}\right]$

Condition for Scenario II: $\dfrac{\mu-\lambda}{\theta_{hs}^s(\mu-\lambda)+(1+\theta_{hs}^b)(\delta-\gamma)}\left[-\Delta p_{rg}^f + \Delta w_{rg} - \Delta w_{hs}\right] < \Delta p_{rg}^c < \dfrac{(1+\theta_{hs}^s)(\mu-\lambda)+\theta_{hs}^b(\delta-\gamma)}{\delta-\gamma}\left[-\Delta p_{rg}^f + \Delta w_{rg} - \Delta w_{hs}\right]$

Condition for Scenario III: $\Delta p_{rg}^c < \dfrac{\mu-\lambda}{\theta_{hs}^s(\mu-\lambda)+(1+\theta_{hs}^b)(\delta-\gamma)}\left[-\Delta p_{rg}^f + \Delta w_{rg} - \Delta w_{hs}\right]$

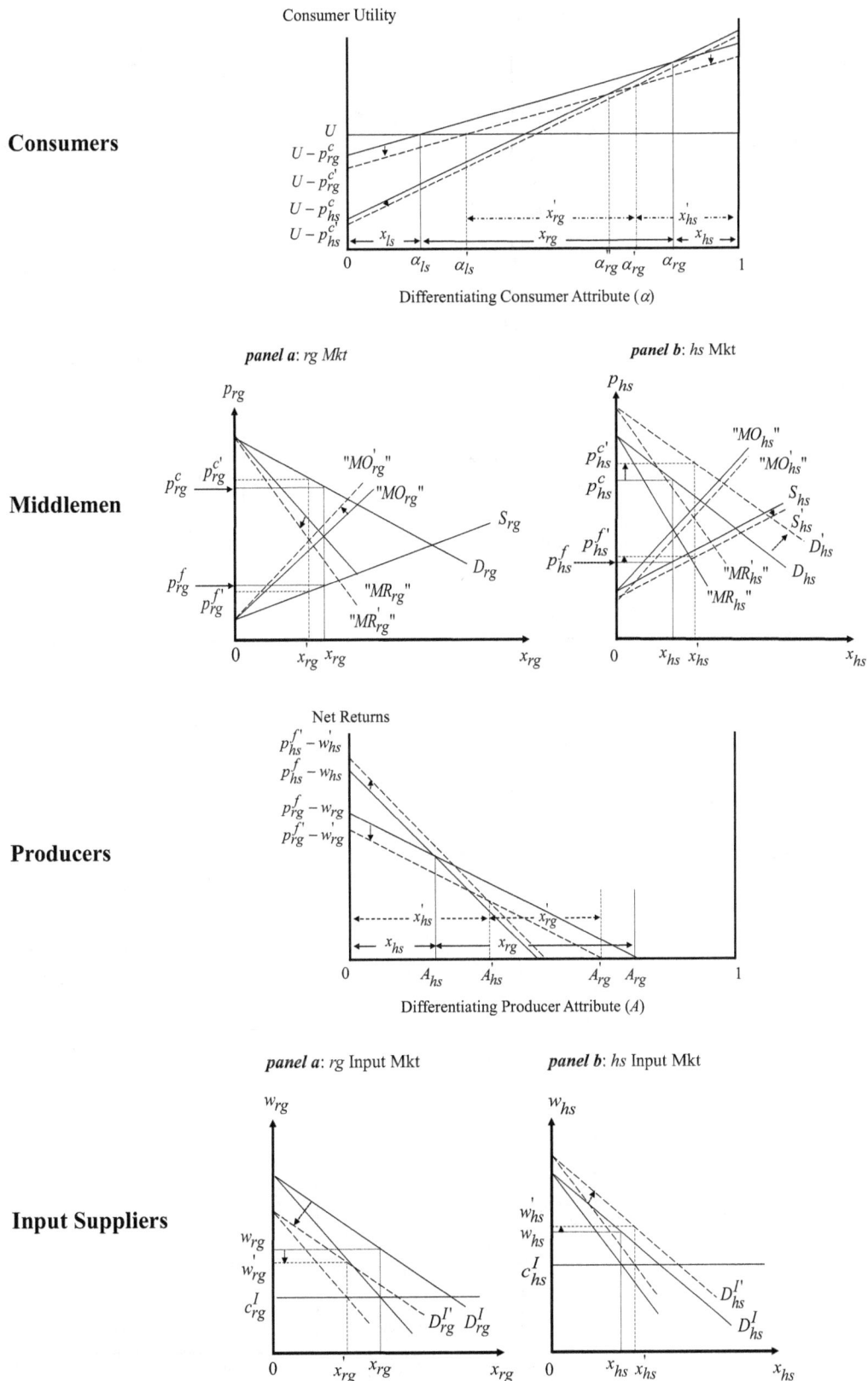

Figure II.2.12. System-Wide Market and Welfare Impacts of Increased θ_{rg} under Scenario I

Consumers

Consumer Utility

U
$U - p_{rg}^c$
$U - p_{rg}^{c'}$
$U - p_{hs}^c$
$U - p_{hs}^{c'}$

x_{ls} x_{rg} x_{rg}' x_{hs}'

0 α_{ls} α_{ls}' α_{rg}'' α_{rg} α_{rg}' 1

Differentiating Consumer Attribute (α)

Middlemen

panel a: *rg* Mkt

p_{rg}

p_{rg}^c $p_{rg}^{c'}$

"MO_{rg}'"
"MO_{rg}"

S_{rg}
D_{rg}

p_{rg}^f $p_{rg}^{f'}$

"MR_{rg}"
"MR_{rg}'"

0 x_{rg} x_{rg}' x_{rg}

panel b: *hs* Mkt

p_{hs}

$p_{hs}^{c'}$
p_{hs}^c

"MO_{hs}"
"MO_{hs}'"

S_{hs}
S_{hs}'

p_{hs}^f $p_{hs}^{f'}$

D_{hs}'
D_{hs}

"MR_{hs}'"
"MR_{hs}"

0 x_{hs} x_{hs}' x_{hs}

Producers

Net Returns

$p_{hs}^f - w_{hs}'$
$p_{hs}^f - w_{hs}$
$p_{rg}^f - w_{rg}$
$p_{rg}^{f'} - w_{rg}'$

x_{hs}' x_{rg}'
x_{hs} x_{rg}

0 A_{hs} A_{hs}' A_{rg}' A_{rg} 1

Differentiating Producer Attribute (A)

Input Suppliers

panel a: *rg* Input Mkt

w_{rg}

w_{rg}
w_{rg}'
c_{rg}^I

$D_{rg}^{I'}$ D_{rg}^I

0 x_{rg} x_{rg}' x_{rg}

panel b: *hs* Input Mkt

w_{hs}

w_{hs}'
w_{hs}
c_{hs}^I

$D_{hs}^{I'}$
D_{hs}^I

0 x_{hs} x_{hs}' x_{hs}

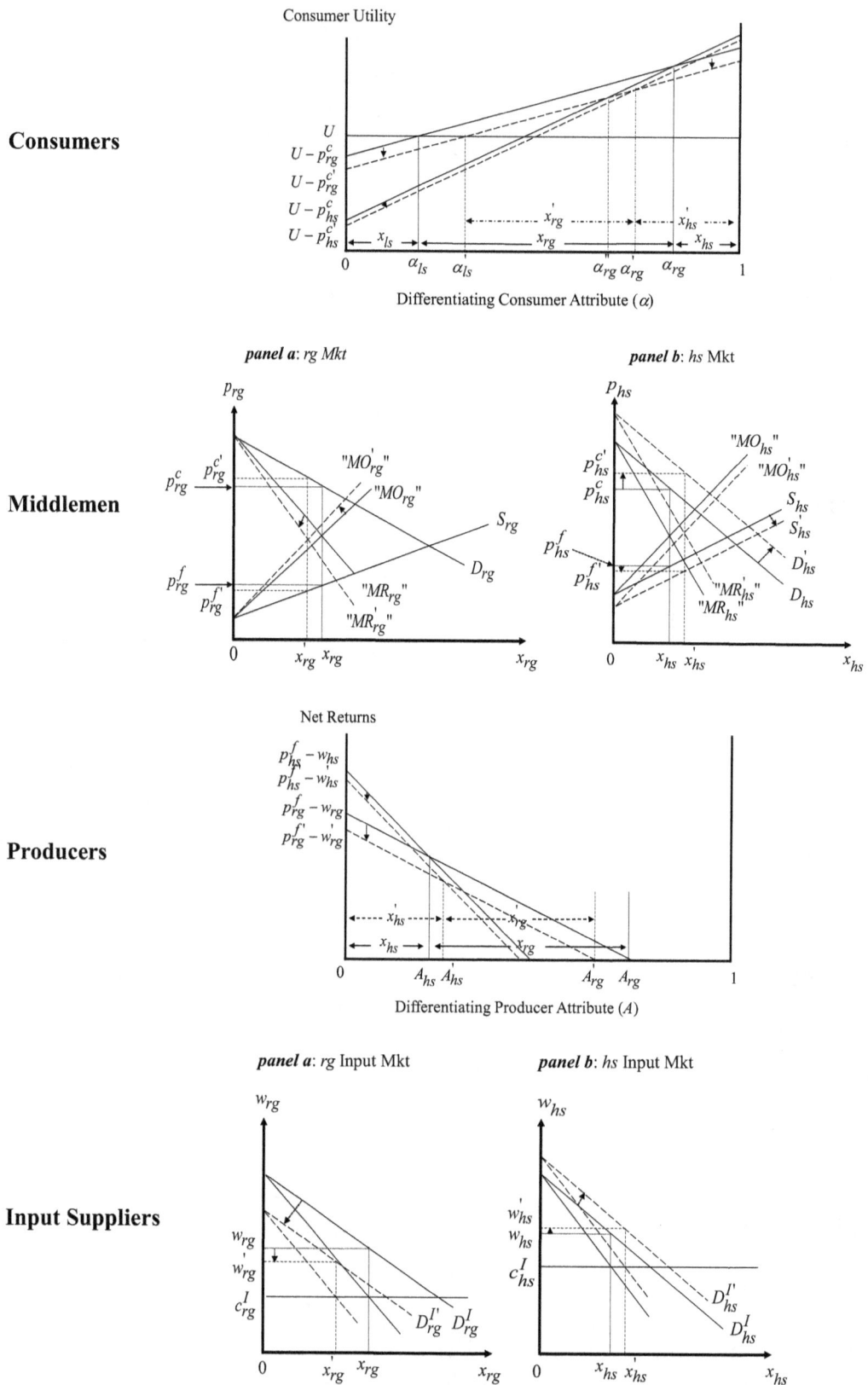

Figure II.2.13. System-Wide Market and Welfare Impacts of Increased θ_{rg} under Scenario II

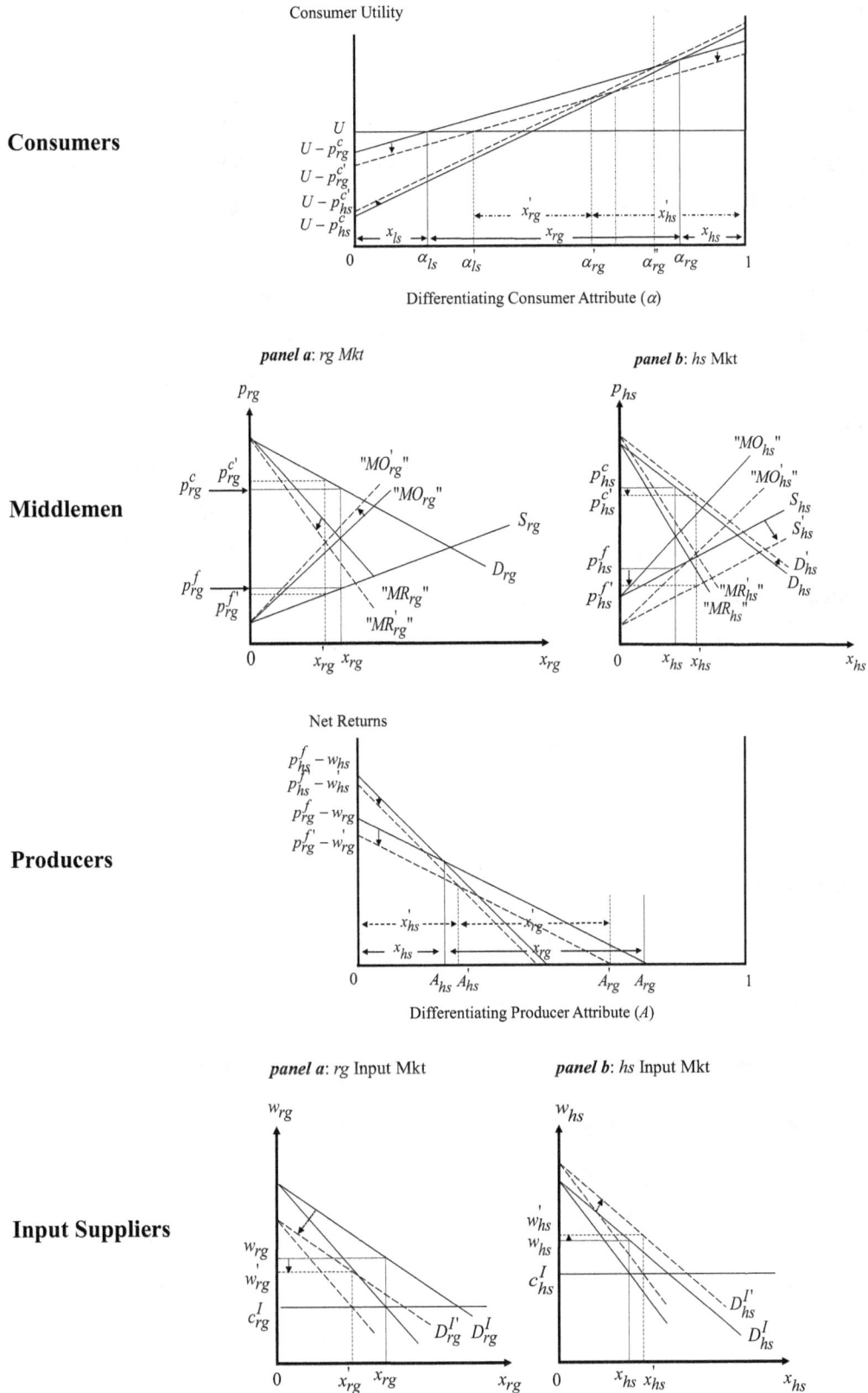

Figure II.2.14. System-Wide Market and Welfare Impacts of Increased θ_{rg} under Scenario III

Disaggregation of Welfare Changes and Comparison with Conventional Analysis

The conclusions outlined above are important because they indicate that a proper accounting of the differential welfare impacts of an increase in θ_{rg} requires a disaggregated analysis, particularly in Scenarios I and III where some of the consumers (Scenario III) or some of the producers (Scenario I) of the reference product realize welfare gains after they have optimally switched. As was pointed out earlier in the book, the aggregate welfare changes can be determined using the calculation of producer and consumer surplus from the supply and demand curves. As will be shown in this section, however, the proper allocation of these surplus changes to different consumers and producers requires an additional disaggregation.

To illustrate the issues involved in properly disaggregating the welfare changes, consider Scenario III where the consumer price of the reference good increases and the consumer price of the substitute good falls (a similar analysis could be undertaken for producers in Scenario I). Figure II.2.15 (which is the same as Figure II.2.9) shows the utility curves for the reference and substitute goods with the welfare changes disaggregated. The solid lines show the utility curves before the increase in θ_{rg}, while the dotted lines show the utility curves after the prices have taken their new equilibrium values as a result of the increase in middlemen market power.

Figure II.2.16 shows the demand curves derived from the utility curves (these demand curves were presented earlier in Figure I.3). Before θ_{rg} is increased, the consumer price of the reference good is p_{rg}^c, while the consumer price of the substitute good is p_{hs}^c. The corresponding quantities purchased are x_{rg} and x_{hs}. The increase in θ_{rg} raises the consumer price of the reference good to $p_{rg}^{c'}$. This increased price, in turn, shifts out the demand curve for the substitute product from $D_{hs}(p_{rg}^c)$ to $D_{hs}(p_{rg}^{c'})$. Recall that the price of the substitute product falls because of the shift out of the supply curve (not shown here; see Figure II.2.5, panel 3) – the resulting equilibrium price is $p_{hs}^{c'}$. At this price, consumption of the substitute good is x_{hs}'. The fall in the price of the substitute good causes the demand curve for the reference good to shift downward from

$D_{rg}(p_{hs}^c)$ to $D_{rg}(p_{hs}^{c'})$. Given price $p_{rg}^{c'}$, consumption of the reference good is x_{rg}'.

As shown in Figure II.2.15, the increase in θ_{rg} results in a loss of area a for the consumers located between α_{ls} and α_{ls}' that exit the market of the reference product, and a loss of area b to those that continue to purchase the reference good (those located between α_{ls}' and α_{rg}'). Of those that switch to the high quality substitute good, some lose (those located between α_{rg}' and α_{rg}''; the magnitude of the loss is area c plus area d) while some benefit (those located between α_{rg}'' and α_{rg}; the magnitude of the gain is area m). Finally, the consumers that originally purchased the high quality substitute gain (these consumers are located between α_{rg} and 1; the size of the gain is area n). At the aggregate level, the welfare change is thus $(m + n) - (a + b + c + d)$.

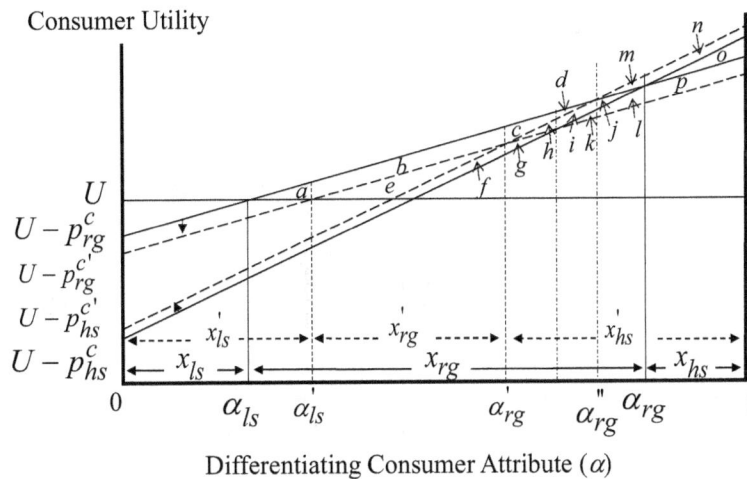

Total consumer welfare change: $(m + n) - (a + b + c + d)$

rg consumers that switch to hs: - some gain (area m)
                                             - some lose (area $c + d$)

rg consumers net gain $= m - (a + b + c + d)$
hs consumers net gain $= n$

Figure II.2.15. Consumer Welfare Impacts of Increased θ_{rg} under Scenario III: Consumer Utility Space

These aggregate welfare changes can also be obtained from the demand curves presented in Figure II.2.16 (the various welfare areas have been labeled so that they match the utility areas in Figure II.2.15). As noted earlier, there are two methods of calculating the welfare change. The first method is to calculate the overall change in consumer surplus (denote this as ΔCS_1) given by the change in consumer surplus in the reference market evaluated at the new equilibrium price of the substitute good, plus the change in consumer surplus in the substitute market evaluated at the original price of the reference good. The second method is to calculate the aggregate change in consumer surplus (denote this as ΔCS_2) as the change in consumer surplus in the reference market evaluated at the original price of the substitute good, plus the change in consumer surplus in the substitute market evaluated at the new equilibrium price of the reference good (see Thurman (1991)).

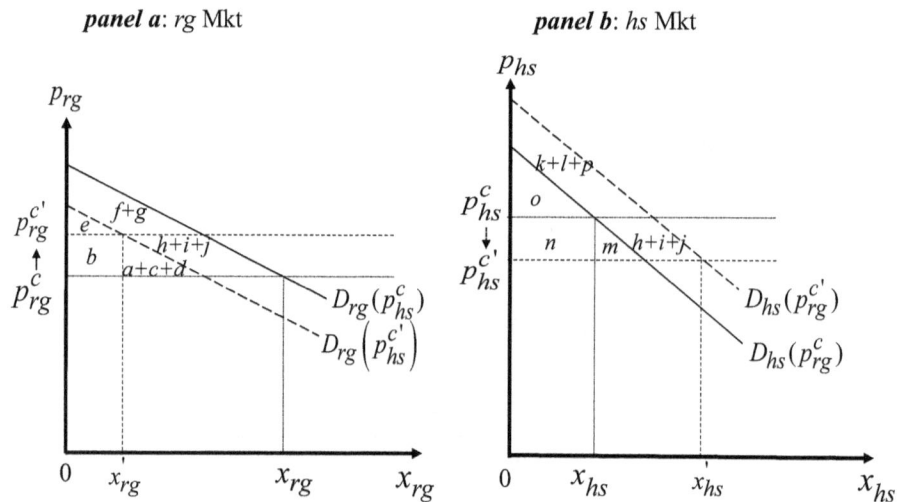

Figure II.2.16. Consumer Welfare Impacts of Increased θ_{rg} under Scenario III: Price-Quantity Space

Using the first method, the overall change in consumer surplus ΔCS_1 is given by:

$$\Delta CS_1 = -\int_{p_{rg}^c}^{p_{rg}^{c'}} x_{rg}(p_{rg}, p_{hs}^{c'})dp_{rg} + \int_{p_{hs}^{c'}}^{p_{hs}^c} x_{hs}(p_{hs}, p_{rg}^c)dp_{hs} = -(a+b+c+d)+(m+n)$$

The above expression allocates a loss of utility equal to $(a + b + c + d)$ to the reference market and a gain in utility equal to $(m + n)$ to the substitute market. However, while the aggregate change is correct, the allocation to the two markets is neither correct nor particularly insightful. While most of the original consumers of the reference good lose utility – this amount is equal to area $(a + b + c + d)$ – there are some of these consumers that gain; this gain is given by area m. As well, the original consumers of the substitute product gain an amount equal to area n. Allocating the cost and benefits according to the demand curves in each market overstates the benefits to those that originally consumed the substitute product and overstates the costs to those that originally consumed the reference product. In short, the calculation of consumer surplus from the demand curves does not provide a proper allocation of the costs and benefits to the various consumer groups.

A similar problem emerges if the second method is used. Using this method, the aggregate change in consumer surplus ΔCS_2 is:

$$
\begin{aligned}
\Delta CS_2 &= -\int_{p_{rg}^c}^{p_{rg}^{c'}} x_{rg}(p_{rg}, p_{hs}^c) dp_{rg} + \int_{p_{hs}^c}^{p_{hs}^{c}} x_{hs}(p_{hs}, p_{rg}^{c'}) dp_{hs} \\
&= -(a+b+c+d+h+i+j)+(m+n+h+i+j) \\
&= -(a+b+c+d)+(m+n)
\end{aligned}
$$

While calculation of the welfare change in this way also yields the correct measure of the aggregate welfare change, it also overstates both the loss in the reference market and the gain in the substitute market. While these overstated amounts cancel each other out at the aggregate level, they yield incorrect results if they are used to determine the distributional impacts of a middlemen market power increase.

The need to disaggregate the consumer surplus measures is clearly important in Scenario III, since in this scenario some consumers gain and others lose from the increase in θ_{rg}. However, if it is believed that the magnitude of the loss felt by consumers is also important (as would be the case if consumers exhibit loss aversion, for instance), then disaggregating the losses that occur in Scenarios I and II may also be required as the effects of the increased θ_{rg} were shown to vary among consumers.[11] The same

conclusions, of course, can be drawn regarding the need to disaggregate producer

welfare. In this case, there is a clear need to disaggregate producer welfare in Scenario I,

since in this case the producer price of the substitute good rises and some of the

producers that switch to producing the substitute good will be better off than they were

originally in producing the reference product. There may also be a need to disaggregate

the changes in producer welfare in Scenarios II and III, since, as was shown in the

previous sections, the welfare changes are not symmetric among producers.

---

[11] With loss aversion, consumers are risk averse in the domain of gain and risk loving in the domain of loss (Kahneman and Tversky, 1979). One of the implications of the risk loving behavior in the loss domain is that, to restore the loss they have incurred, consumers that have lost more will be more likely to engage in activities with an uncertain outcome. Thus, identifying those consumers that have lost the most may be important in determining who will be the most likely to undertake activities to oppose a middlemen market power increase.

II.3 Increased Market Power of Input Suppliers

The focus of this section is on the determination of the system-wide market and welfare impacts of increased market power of suppliers of the inputs used in the production of the reference product (increased θ_{rg}^I, hereafter). Once the effects of the increased θ_{rg}^I on the market where it occurs have been determined (i.e., the input market for the reference product), we proceed in discussing its impacts on the vertically, horizontally and diagonally related markets and interest groups involved (i.e., consumers, producers, middlemen and input suppliers in the supply channels of the reference good and its substitute products).

Equilibrium Conditions under an Increased θ_{rg}^I

An increase in the market power of the suppliers of the inputs used in the production of the reference product, θ_{rg}^I, results in an increased price of these inputs. Graphically, the increased θ_{rg}^I can be depicted as increasing the slope of the effective marginal revenue curve faced by the input suppliers in the reference product supply channel, and, subsequently, the price of this input from w_{rg} to w_{rg}' in Figure II.3.1

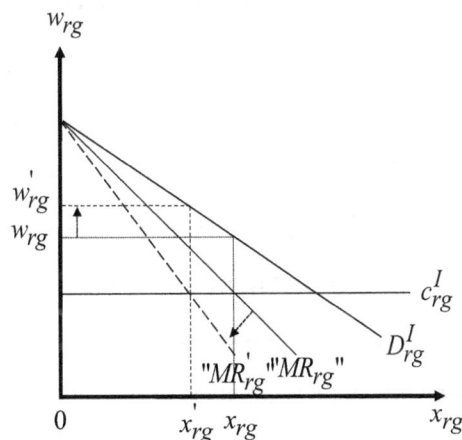

Figure II.3.1. Increased Market Power of Input Suppliers

In addition to increasing the price of the reference input, the increased θ_{rg}^{I} results in reduced equilibrium quantity (compare x_{rg} and $x_{rg}^{'}$ in Figure II.3.1) and greater profits for the suppliers of this input.

Besides affecting the market for the reference input, the increased θ_{rg}^{I} has an effect on (vertically, horizontally and diagonally) related markets and our integrated framework of analysis can help identify the system-wide market and welfare impacts of this change. The equilibrium conditions/market reaction functions under the increased θ_{rg}^{I} can be derived by substituting $\theta_{rg}^{I'}$ for θ_{rg}^{I} in equations (I.24)-(I.31). As mentioned earlier, the nature of the interdependence of markets captured by these expressions provide, along with the related graphical representation, valuable insights on the mechanism through which the increased θ_{rg}^{I} affects the different markets. The rest of this section discusses the market and welfare impacts of the increased θ_{rg}^{I} using the integrated heterogeneous agent framework presented in Section I.

System-Wide Market and Welfare Effects of an Increased θ_{rg}^{I}

The analysis in this part focuses on the impact of the increased θ_{rg}^{I} on the input and output markets for the reference product and its substitute, as well as its effects on the welfare of all interest groups involved (i.e., consumers, producers, middlemen and input suppliers in the markets for the two products). In addition to determining changes in the aggregate consumer and producer welfare, our integrated heterogeneous agent framework enables us to (a) determine the effects of the increased θ_{rg}^{I} on different consumers and producers of the two products and (b) capture indirect and feedback effects that are not accounted for when focusing solely on the market of the reference input.

Beginning with the *direct producer effects* of the increased θ_{rg}^{I}, we see that the increase in the price of the reference input, w_{rg}, (a) reduces the net returns associated with the production of the product utilizing this input in its production process (i.e., the reference product), and (b) drives previous producers of the reference product to the substitute and alternative crops. Graphically, the increase in w_{rg} causes a downward parallel shift of NR_{rg} and the switching of producers with differentiating attributes $A \in (A_{hs}, A'_{hs}]$ and $A \in (A'_{rg}, A_{rg}]$ in Figure II.3.2 to the substitute and alternative crops, respectively.

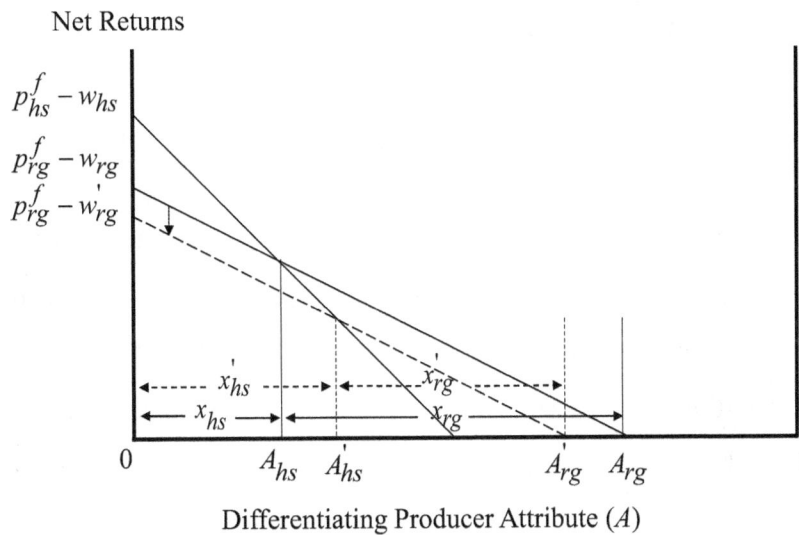

Figure II.3.2. Direct Effects of an Increased θ^I_{rg} on Producer Decisions

The reduced appeal of the reference product due to its increased input costs reduces the supply of the reference product and, through this, increases the consumer and producer prices of this product (see equations (I.24) and (I.25)). Figure II.3.3 graphs the upward parallel shift of S_{rg} and consequent decrease in x_{rg} and increases in p^c_{rg} and p^f_{rg} due to the increased θ^I_{rg}.

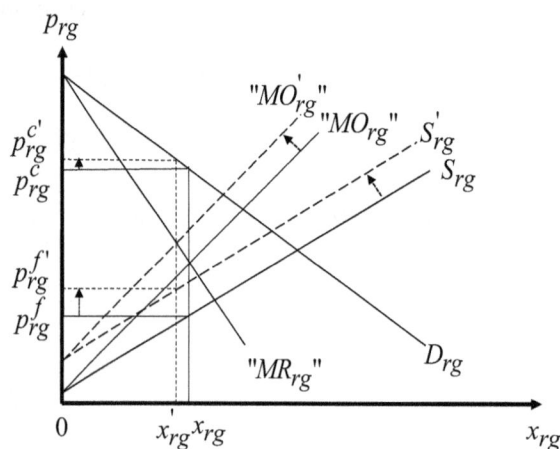

Figure II.3.3. Direct Effects of an Increased θ_{rg}^I on the Oligemporistic *rg* Market

Moving to the *direct consumer effects* of the increased θ_{rg}^I, we see that the increase in the consumer price of the reference product (a) reduces the utility associated with the consumption of this product and (b) drives some of the consumers of the reference product to its substitutes. Graphically, the increase in p_{rg}^c causes an downward parallel shift of U_{rg} and the switching of consumers with differentiating attributes $\alpha \in (\alpha_{ls}, \alpha_{ls}']$ and $\alpha \in (\alpha_{rg}', \alpha_{rg}]$ in Figure II.3.4 to *ls* and *hs* substitute products, respectively.

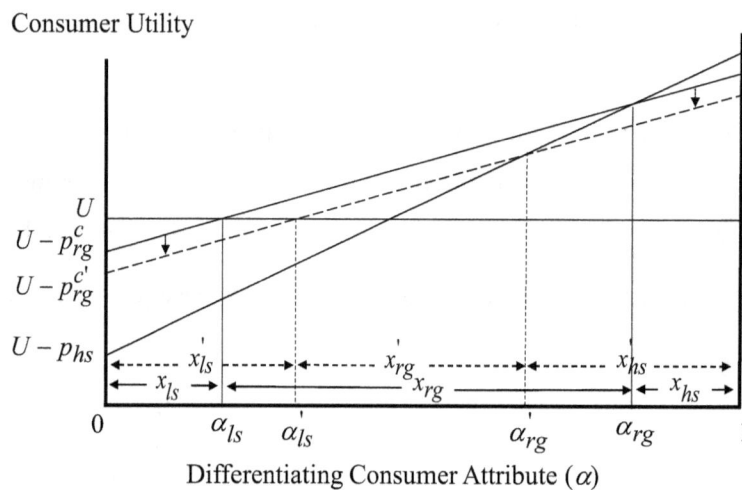

Figure II.3.4. Direct Effects of an Increased θ_{rg}^I on Consumption Decisions

In addition to affecting the market for the reference product, the changes in this market caused by the increased θ_{rg}^I have a direct impact on the market for the substitute product. In particular, the increased consumer and input prices of the reference product due to the higher θ_{rg}^I drive a number of consumers and producers out of the market for the reference product affecting, this way, both the demand for and supply of the substitute product.

Formally, the increased p_{rg}^c causes an upward parallel shift of the demand for the substitute product, D_{hs} (see equation (I.9) and Figure II.3.6), while the increased w_{rg} and p_{rg}^f cause a downward parallel shift of the supply of the substitute product, S_{hs} (see equation (I.19) and Figure II.3.6). While the increased demand for, and supply of the substitute product always increase the equilibrium quantity and profits of the suppliers of this product, the effect on the equilibrium consumer and producer prices (p_{hs}^c and p_{hs}^f, respectively) is determined by the relative magnitude of the demand and supply effects of the increased θ_{rg}^I on the market for the substitute product. In particular, since a *ceteris paribus* increase in D_{hs} causes p_{hs}^c and p_{hs}^f to increase, while a similar increase in S_{hs} results in reduced p_{hs}^c and p_{hs}^f, when the demand effect dominates the supply effect so that $\Delta p_{rg}^c > \frac{(1+\theta_{hs}^s)(\mu-\lambda)+\theta_{hs}^b(\delta-\gamma)}{\delta-\gamma}\left[\Delta w_{rg} - \Delta p_{rg}^f - \Delta w_{hs}\right]$ (where, as noted above, $\Delta p_{rg}^c > 0$, $\Delta p_{rg}^f > 0$ and $\Delta w_{rg} > 0$, while, as shown in Figure II.3.12 below, $\Delta w_{hs} > 0$), the consumer and producer prices of the substitute product increase after the increase in θ_{rg}^I (Scenario I); when

$$\frac{\mu-\lambda}{\theta_{hs}^s(\mu-\lambda)+(1+\theta_{hs}^b)(\delta-\gamma)}\left[\Delta w_{rg} - \Delta p_{rg}^f - \Delta w_{hs}\right] < \Delta p_{rg}^c <$$
$$< \frac{(1+\theta_{hs}^s)(\mu-\lambda)+\theta_{hs}^b(\delta-\gamma)}{\delta-\gamma}\left[\Delta w_{rg} - \Delta p_{rg}^f - \Delta w_{hs}\right],$$

the consumer price of the substitute product increases while the producer price falls

(Scenario II); while when the supply effect of the increased θ_{rg}^I dominates the demand

effect so that $\Delta p_{rg}^c < \dfrac{\mu - \lambda}{\theta_{hs}^s(\mu - \lambda) + (1 + \theta_{hs}^b)(\delta - \gamma)}\left[\Delta w_{rg} - \Delta p_{rg}^f - \Delta w_{hs}\right]$, the increase of

θ_{rg}^I causes the consumer and producer prices of the substitute product to fall (Scenario

III). Figure II.3.5 provides a graphical representation of the conditions leading to the

three scenarios while panels 1, 2 and 3 of Figure II.3.6 graph the effects of the increased

θ_{rg}^I on the market of the substitute product under these three scenarios.

It is important to note that for Scenario II to occur, the middlemen in the

substitute product market should be able to exercise market power. If $\theta_{hs}^s = \theta_{hs}^b = 0$, the

condition for Scenario I becomes $\Delta p_{rg}^c > \dfrac{\mu - \lambda}{\delta - \gamma}\left[\Delta w_{rg} - \Delta p_{rg}^f - \Delta w_{hs}\right]$ and the condition

for Scenario III becomes $\Delta p_{rg}^c < \dfrac{\mu - \lambda}{\delta - \gamma}\left[\Delta w_{rg} - \Delta p_{rg}^f - \Delta w_{hs}\right]$. Intuitively, under perfectly

competitive middlemen in the substitute product market, the consumer and producer

prices of this product will always move in the same direction. While the presence of

middlemen market power is necessary for the consumer and producer prices of the

substitute product to move in different directions, it is not sufficient for the emergence of

Scenario II – as shown above, both Scenarios I and III can emerge in the presence of

middlemen market power.

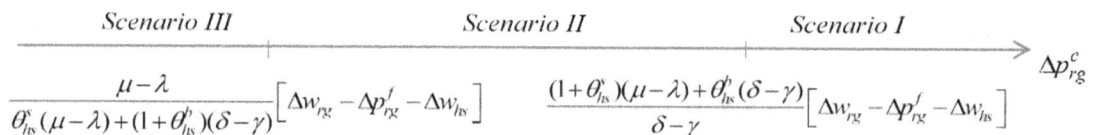

Figure II.3.5. Scenarios on the Effects of Increased θ_{rg}^I on the Prices of Substitute *hs* Product

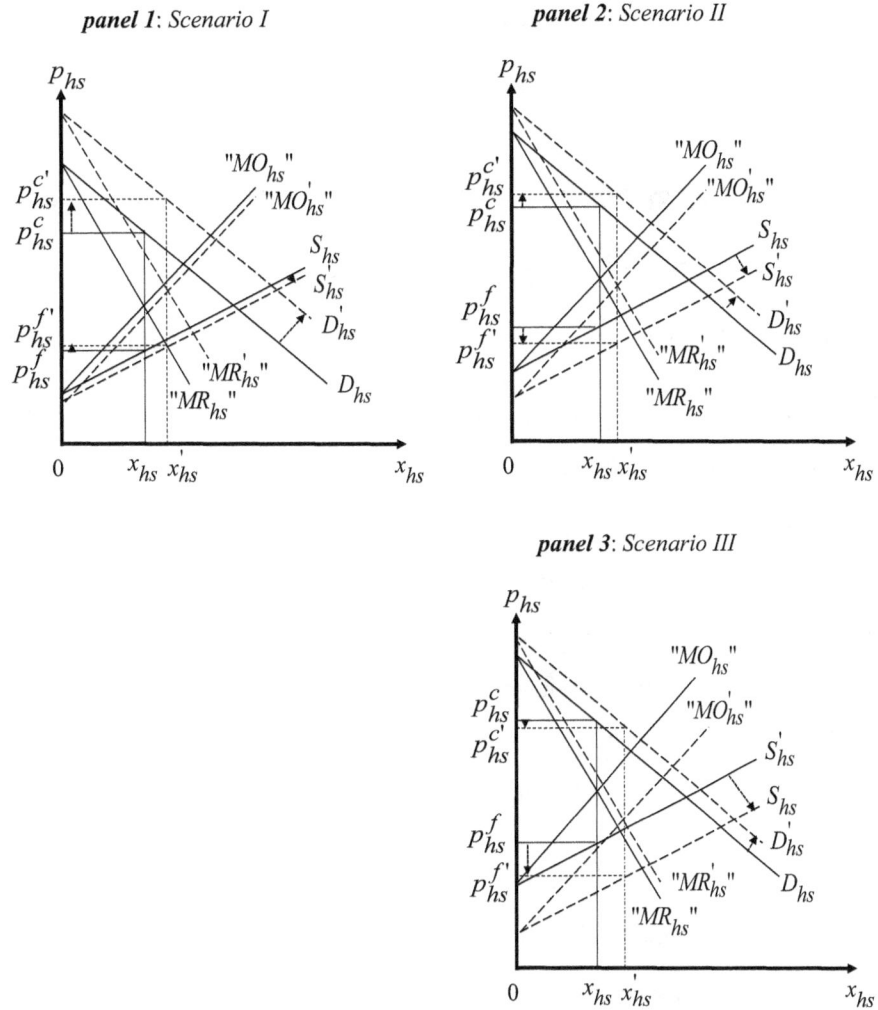

panel 1: Scenario I *panel 2*: Scenario II

panel 3: Scenario III

Figure II.3.6. Effects of Increased θ_{rg}^I on the Market for the Substitute *hs* Product

Since the equilibrium prices of the substitute product affect the welfare of the consumers and producers of this product, our analysis considers the market and welfare impacts of the increased θ_{rg}^I under the three scenarios outlined above. The case where the increase in θ_{rg}^I causes the consumer and producer prices of its substitute product to increase (i.e., the case in which the demand effect dominates the supply effect of the increased θ_{rg}^I) is analyzed first followed by the other two scenarios considered here. In all cases, suppliers of the substitute product see their profits increase after the increase in θ_{rg}^I by

$$\Delta\Pi_{hs} = (p_{hs}^{c'} - p_{hs}^{c})x_{hs} + (p_{hs}^{c'} - p_{hs}^{f'})(x_{hs}' - x_{hs}) - (p_{hs}^{f'} - p_{hs}^{f})x_{hs} > 0.$$

Market and Welfare Effects of the Increase in θ_{rg}^I θ_{rg}^I under Scenario I

(i.e., when $\Delta p_{rg}^c > \dfrac{(1+\theta_{hs}^s)(\mu-\lambda)+\theta_{hs}^b(\delta-\gamma)}{\delta-\gamma}\left[\Delta w_{rg} - \Delta p_{rg}^f - \Delta w_{hs}\right]$)

As mentioned previously, when the demand effect of the increased θ_{rg}^I dominates its

supply effect, the increase in θ_{rg}^I increases the consumer and producer prices of its

substitute product (recall panel 1 of Figure II.3.6 that depicts this scenario in the price-

quantity space).

The increased consumer price of the substitute product, p_{hs}^c, reduces the utility

associated with the consumption of this product and limits the number of consumers of

the reference product switching to the substitute. Figure II.3.7 depicts these market and

welfare effects in the consumer utility space. In addition, the figure shows that the

consumers hurt the most from the increased θ_{rg}^I are those consuming the reference

product both before and after the increase in θ_{rg}^I (i.e., consumers with $\alpha \in (\alpha_{ls}', \alpha_{rg}']$),

followed by consumers who find it optimal to turn away from the reference product (i.e.,

consumers with $\alpha \in (\alpha_{rg}', \alpha_{rg}]$ and $\alpha \in (\alpha_{ls}, \alpha_{ls}']$), and consumers who consume the

substitute before and after the increase in θ_{rg}^I (i.e., consumers with $\alpha \in (\alpha_{rg}, 1]$). Total

consumer losses from the increased θ_{rg}^I are given by

$$L_c = \int_{\alpha_{ls}}^{\alpha_{ls}'} (U_{rg} - U_{ls})d\alpha + \int_{\alpha_{ls}'}^{\alpha_{rg}'} (U_{rg} - U_{rg}')d\alpha + \int_{\alpha_{rg}'}^{\alpha_{rg}} (U_{rg} - U_{hs}')d\alpha + \int_{\alpha_{rg}}^{1} (U_{hs} - U_{hs}')d\alpha.$$

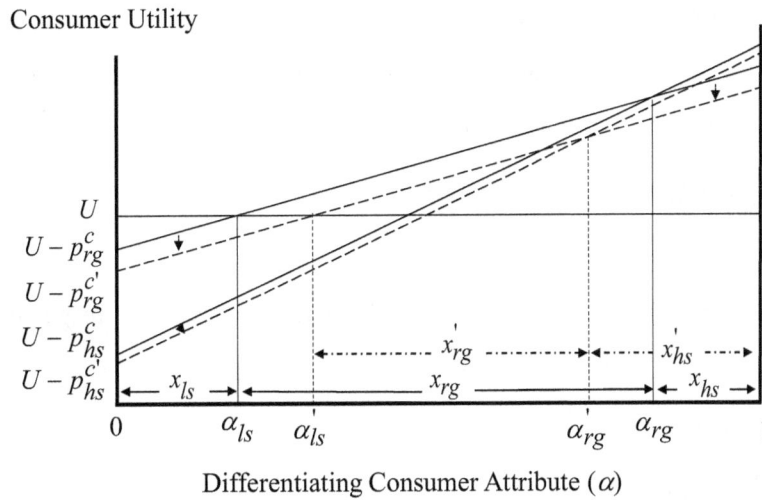

Consumer Utility

U
$U - p_{rg}^c$
$U - p_{rg}^{c'}$
$U - p_{hs}^c$
$U - p_{hs}^{c'}$

x_{ls} x_{rg}' x_{hs}'
x_{ls} x_{rg} x_{hs}

0 α_{ls} α_{ls}' α_{rg}' α_{rg} 1

Differentiating Consumer Attribute (α)

Figure II.3.7. Total Effects of Increased θ_{rg}^I on Consumption Decisions and Welfare under Scenarios I & II

While the increased p_{hs}^c reduces the desirability of the substitute product for consumers, the increased p_{hs}^f under Scenario I increases the net returns associated with the production of the substitute product and, thus, increases the incentives for switching to the production of this product. Figure II.3.8 depicts these market and welfare effects as well as the asymmetric impacts of the increased θ_{rg}^I in the producer net returns space. Producers losing the most from the increased θ_{rg}^I are those producing the reference product both before and after the increase in θ_{rg}^I (i.e., producers with $A \in (A_{hs}', A_{rg}']$), followed by producers who find it optimal to switch from the reference product to the alternative crop (i.e., producers with $A \in (A_{rg}', A_{rg}]$), and the producers with $A \in (A_{hs}'', A_{hs}']$ who switch from the reference product to the substitute.

Producers who produce the substitute before and after the increase in θ_{rg}^I (i.e., producers with $A \in [0, A_{hs}'')$) gain, as do some of the reference product producers who switch to the substitute (i.e., producers with $A \in (A_{hs}^{'}, A_{hs}^{"})$), with the magnitude of this gain determined by the efficiency parameter/differentiating attribute of these producers. Producer gains and losses in this case are given by

$$G_p = \int_0^{A_{hs}^{'}} (NR_{hs}^{'} - NR_{hs})dA + \int_{A_{hs}^{'}}^{A_{hs}^{"}} (NR_{hs}^{'} - NR_{rg})dA \text{ and}$$

$$L_p = \int_{A_{hs}^{'}}^{A_{hs}^{"}} (NR_{rg} - NR_{hs}^{'})dA + \int_{A_{hs}^{"}}^{A_{rg}^{'}} (NR_{rg} - NR_{rg}^{'})dA + \int_{A_{rg}^{'}}^{A_{rg}} (NR_{rg} - NR_a)dA , \text{ respectively.}$$

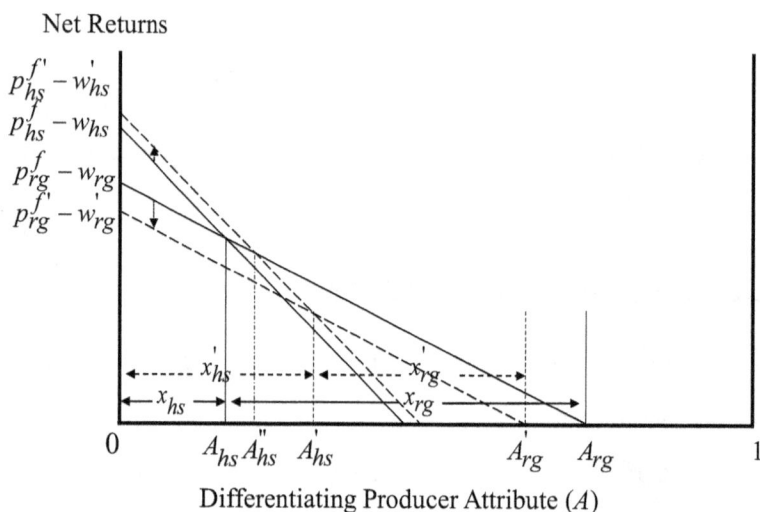

Figure II.3.8. Total Effects of Increased θ_{rg}^{I} on Producer Decisions and Welfare under Scenario I

Market and Welfare Effects of the Increase in θ_{rg}^{I} ***under Scenario II (i.e., when***

$$\frac{\mu - \lambda}{\theta_{hs}^s(\mu - \lambda) + (1 + \theta_{hs}^b)(\delta - \gamma)}\left[\Delta w_{rg} - \Delta p_{rg}^f - \Delta w_{hs}\right] < \Delta p_{rg}^c <$$

$$< \frac{(1 + \theta_{hs}^s)(\mu - \lambda) + \theta_{hs}^b(\delta - \gamma)}{\delta - \gamma}\left[\Delta w_{rg} - \Delta p_{rg}^f - \Delta w_{hs}\right])$$

As shown in panel 2 of Figure II.3.6, under Scenario II the consumer price of the substitute product increases while the producer price falls causing both consumers and producers of this product to lose.

Predictably, the ramifications of the increased θ_{rg}^I for the consumers of the different products are similar to those under Scenario I (described in the previous section and graphed in Figure II.3.7), as p_{hs}^c increases under both Scenarios I and II. Thus, the increased θ_{rg}^I under Scenario II hurts all reference and substitute product consumers with the greater losses incurred by those consumers who buy the reference product both before and after the increase in θ_{rg}^I.

Unlike Scenario I, producers of the substitute product lose under Scenario II as the increased θ_{rg}^I causes the producer price of the substitute product, p_{hs}^f, to fall. The reduced p_{hs}^f reduces the net returns associated with the production of this product and limits the number of producers who find it optimal to switch to the substitute product after the increase in θ_{rg}^I (recall that the increased w_{rg} creates incentives for a number of producers of the reference product to switch to the production of the substitute and alternative crops; see Figure II.3.2).

Figure II.3.9 depicts these market and welfare effects in the producer net returns space. In addition, the figure shows that the producers losing the most from the increased θ_{rg}^I are those producing the reference product both before and after the increase in θ_{rg}^I (i.e., producers with $A \in (A_{hs}', A_{rg}')$), followed by producers who switch from the reference to the alternative and substitute crops (i.e., producers with $A \in (A_{rg}', A_{rg}]$ and $A \in (A_{hs}, A_{hs}')$), and producers who continue to produce the substitute product after the increase in θ_{rg}^I (i.e., producers with $A \in [0, A_{hs})$). Total producer losses from the increased θ_{rg}^I are

$$L_p = \int_0^{A_{hs}} (NR_{hs} - NR_{hs}')dA + \int_{A_{hs}}^{A_{hs}'} (NR_{rg} - NR_{hs}')dA + \int_{A_{hs}'}^{A_{rg}'} (NR_{rg} - NR_{rg}')dA + \int_{A_{rg}'}^{A_{rg}} (NR_{rg} - NR_a)dA$$

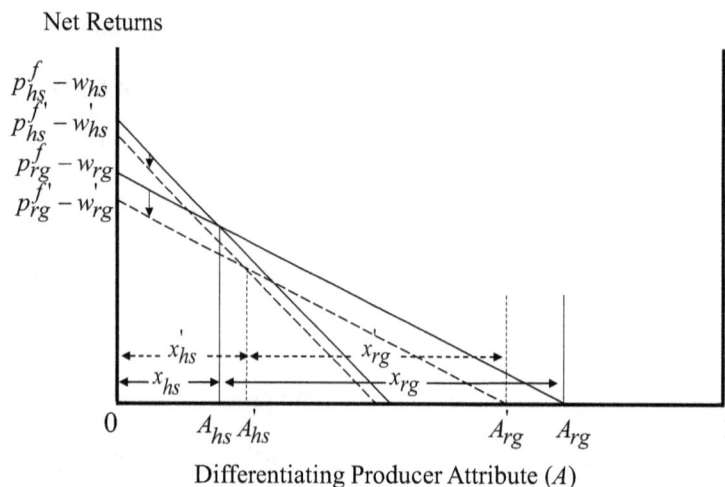

Figure II.3.9. Total Effects of Increased θ_{rg}^I on Producer Decisions and Welfare under Scenarios II & III

Market and Welfare Effects of the Increase in θ_{rg}^I under Scenario III

(i.e., when $\Delta p_{rg}^c < \dfrac{\mu - \lambda}{\theta_{hs}^s (\mu - \lambda) + (1 + \theta_{hs}^b)(\delta - \gamma)} \left[\Delta w_{rg} - \Delta p_{rg}^f - \Delta w_{hs} \right]$)

When the supply effect of the increased θ_{rg}^I dominates the demand effect, the increased

θ_{rg}^I causes the consumer and producer prices of the substitute good to fall. While the

effects of the reduced p_{hs}^f on producer decisions and welfare are similar to those under

Scenario II (described in the previous section and graphed in Figure II.3.9), the effects of

the increased θ_{rg}^I on consumers are different than those under Scenarios I and II.

Specifically, the reduced p_{hs}^c increases the utility associated with the

consumption of the substitute product and increases the number of consumers switching

from the reference product. Figure II.3.10 depicts these market and welfare effects as

well as the asymmetric impacts of the increased θ_{rg}^I on consumer welfare in the

consumer utility space. Similar to Scenarios I and II, consumers losing the most from the

increased θ_{rg}^I are those consuming the reference product both before and after the increase in θ^I_{rg} (i.e., consumers with $\alpha \in (\alpha'_{ls}, \alpha'_{rg}]$), followed by consumers who find

it optimal to turn away from the reference product (i.e., consumers with $\alpha \in (\alpha'_{rg}, \alpha''_{rg}]$

and $\alpha \in (\alpha_{ls}, \alpha'_{ls}]$). Unlike Scenarios I and II, however, consumers who prefer the

substitute product before and after the increase in θ^I_{rg} (i.e., consumers with

$\alpha \in (\alpha_{rg}, 1]$) gain, as do some of the reference product consumers who switch to the

substitute (i.e., consumers with $\alpha \in (\alpha''_{rg}, \alpha_{rg}]$), with the magnitude of this gain

determined by the differentiating attribute of these consumers. Consumer gains and

losses in this case are given by $G_c = \int\limits_{\alpha''_{rg}}^{\alpha_{rg}} (U'_{hs} - U_{rg})d\alpha + \int\limits_{\alpha_{rg}}^{1} (U'_{hs} - U_{hs})d\alpha$ and

$$L_c = \int\limits_{\alpha_{ls}}^{\alpha'_{ls}} (U_{rg} - U_{ls})d\alpha + \int\limits_{\alpha'_{ls}}^{\alpha'_{rg}} (U_{rg} - U'_{rg})d\alpha + \int\limits_{\alpha'_{rg}}^{\alpha''_{rg}} (U_{rg} - U'_{hs})d\alpha \text{, respectively.}$$

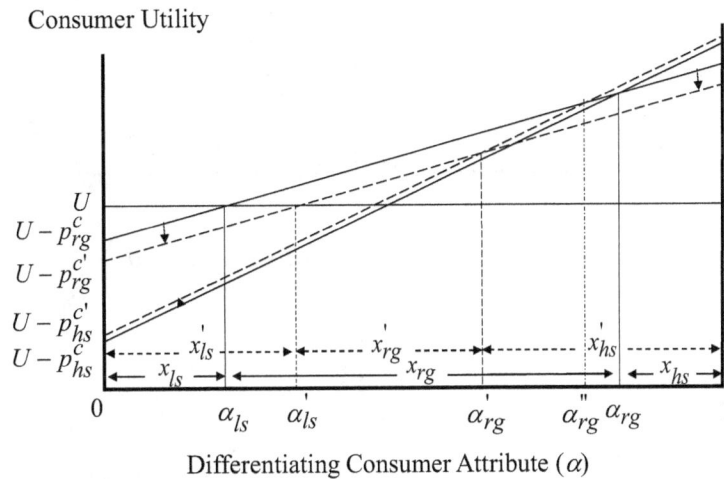

Figure II.3.10. Total Effects of Increased θ^I_{rg} on Consumption Decisions and Welfare under Scenario III

In addition to affecting the decisions and welfare of consumers and producers of the

substitute product, the changes in p^c_{hs} and p^f_{hs} have a feedback effect on the market for the reference product. In particular, an increase (decrease) in p_{hs}^c shifts the demand for the reference product D_{rg} upwards (downwards), while an increase (decrease) in p_{hs}^f causes an upward (downward) shift of the supply of the reference product S_{rg} (recall equations (I.8) and (I.18) and Figures I.3 and I.5). The total effects of the increased θ_{rg}^I under the three scenarios considered here are depicted in panels 1-3 of Figure II.3.11. In all cases, the increased θ_{rg}^I causes a reduction in the reference product supplier profits with the change in profits given by $\Delta\Pi_{rg} = -\left[(p_{rg}^{c'} - p_{rg}^c)x_{rg}' - (p_{rg}^c - p_{rg}^f)(x_{rg} - x_{rg}') - (p_{rg}^{f'} - p_{rg}^f)x_{rg}' \right] < 0$.

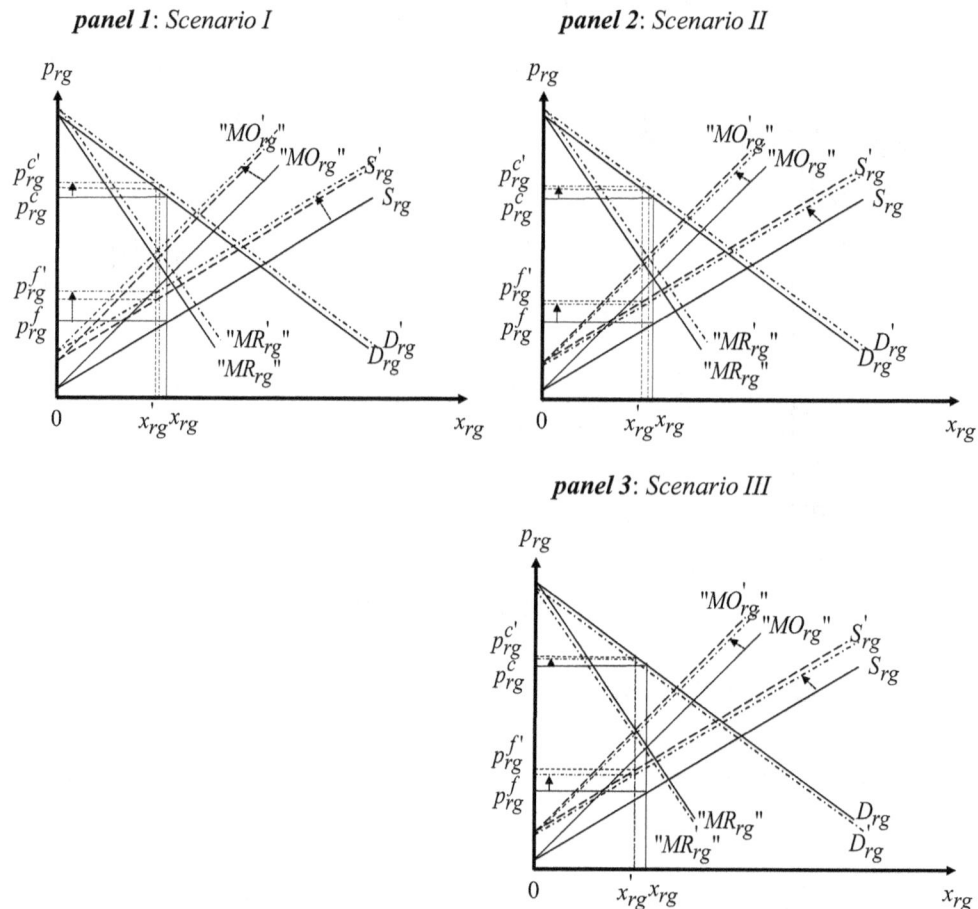

panel 1: Scenario I   *panel 2*: Scenario II

panel 3: Scenario III

Figure II.3.11. Overall Impact of the Increased θ_{rg}^I on the rg Market

Regarding the impact of the increased θ_{rg}^I on the market for the inputs used in the production of the substitute product, no matter the effect of the change on p_{hs}^c and p_{hs}^f, the increase in θ_{rg}^I increases the demand for inputs used in the production of its substitute (as the equilibrium quantity of the substitute product increases as a result of the increase in θ_{rg}^I). The increased demand for hs inputs results, then, in higher equilibrium input price and quantity (see equations (I.29) and (I.31)), and an increase in the profits of the suppliers of these inputs given by $\Delta\Pi_{hs}^I = (w_{hs}' - c_{hs}^I)x_{hs}' - (w_{hs} - c_{hs}^I)x_{hs} > 0$. Figure II.3.12, panel b graphs the changes in the market for the input used in the production of the substitute product due to the increased θ_{rg}^I.

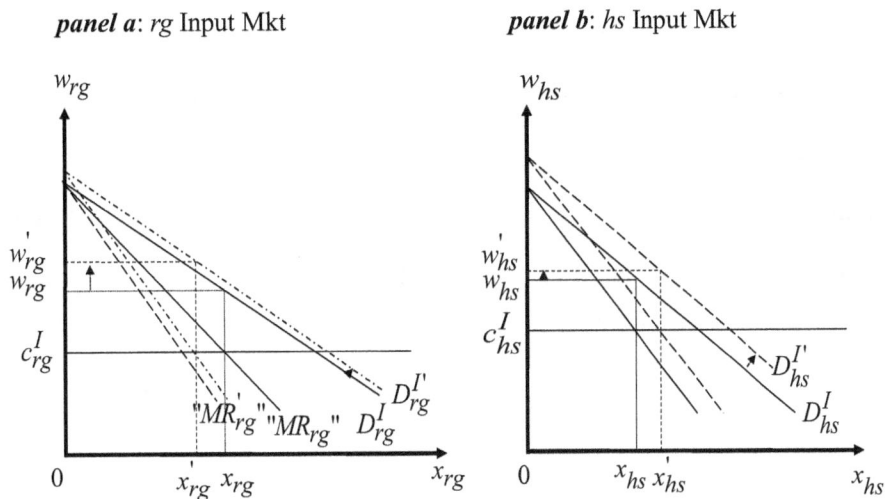

Figure II.3.12. Total Effect of an Increase in θ_{rg}^I on the Input Markets

Finally, the change in w_{hs} has a feedback effect on the market of the reference input. Specifically, the increase in w_{hs} increases the demand for the reference input D_{rg}^I (see equation (I.20) and Figure I.6) which, in turn, (a) bolsters the impact of the increased θ_{rg}^I on the price of this input, and (b) lessens its impact on the quantity of the subsidized input (see equations (I.28) and (I.30)). The total effects of the increased θ_{rg}^{I} on the input markets are depicted in Figure II.3.12.

Overall, the analysis of the system-wide market and welfare impacts of increased θ_{rg}^{I} indicates that: (a) the qualitative nature of the welfare effects on the consumers and producers of the substitute product is scenario-specific and depends on the conditions in the market for both the reference product and the substitute product; (b) the impacts of the increased market power of input suppliers are asymmetric across the different consumers and producers affected by this increase; (c) determination of these asymmetric impacts requires a disaggregation of the benefits and costs to the level of the individual agent; and (d) in Scenarios I and III, some of the consumers (Scenario III) or some of the producers (Scenario I) who find it optimal to switch from the reference product to its substitute after the increase in θ_{rg}^{I} realize welfare gains.

The asymmetric impact of the increase in θ_{rg}^{I} on the welfare of all relevant interest groups is summarized in Table II.3.1, while Figures II.3.13-II.3.15 summarize the system-wide market and welfare impacts of the increased θ_{rg}^{I} under the different scenarios considered in this study. For simplicity, the feedback effects described above (Figures II.3.11 and II.3.12) are not included in Figures II.3.13-II.3.15.

Table II.3.1. System-Wide Welfare Impacts of an Increase in Input Supplier Market Power, θ_{rg}^{I}

	Consumers of rg switching to ls	Consumers of rg	Consumers of rg switching to hs	Consumers of hs	Producers of rg	Producers of rg switching to hs	Producers of hs	Suppliers of rg	Suppliers of hs	Input Suppliers rg	Input Suppliers hs
Scenario I	−	−	−	−	−	some + some −	+	−	+	+	+
Scenario II	−	−	−	−	−	−	−	−	+	+	+
Scenario III	−	−	some − some +	+	−	−	−	−	+	+	+

+ denotes welfare gains
− denotes welfare losses

Condition for Scenario I: $\Delta p_{rg}^{c} > \dfrac{(1+\theta_{hs}^{s})(\mu-\lambda)+\theta_{hs}^{b}(\delta-\gamma)}{\delta-\gamma}\left[\Delta w_{rg}-\Delta p_{rg}^{f}-\Delta w_{hs}\right]$

Condition for Scenario II: $\dfrac{\mu-\lambda}{\theta_{hs}^{s}(\mu-\lambda)+(1+\theta_{hs}^{b})(\delta-\gamma)}\left[\Delta w_{rg}-\Delta p_{rg}^{f}-\Delta w_{hs}\right] < \Delta p_{rg}^{c} < \dfrac{(1+\theta_{hs}^{s})(\mu-\lambda)+\theta_{hs}^{b}(\delta-\gamma)}{\delta-\gamma}\left[\Delta w_{rg}-\Delta p_{rg}^{f}-\Delta w_{hs}\right]$

Condition for Scenario III: $\Delta p_{rg}^{c} < \dfrac{\mu-\lambda}{\theta_{hs}^{s}(\mu-\lambda)+(1+\theta_{hs}^{b})(\delta-\gamma)}\left[\Delta w_{rg}-\Delta p_{rg}^{f}-\Delta w_{hs}\right]$

- 88 -

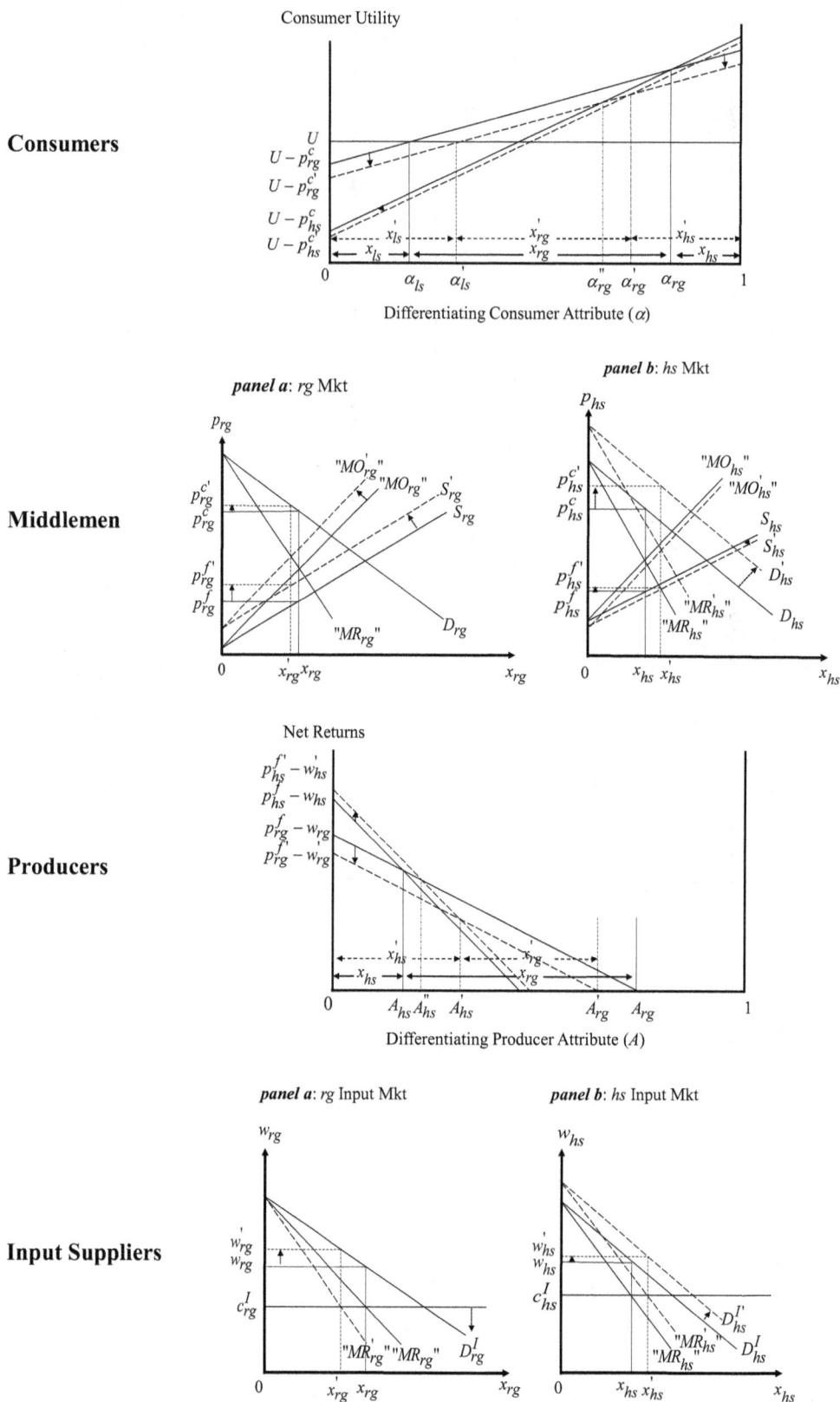

Figure II.3.13. System-Wide Market and Welfare Impacts of Increased θ_{rg}^I under Scenario I

Consumers

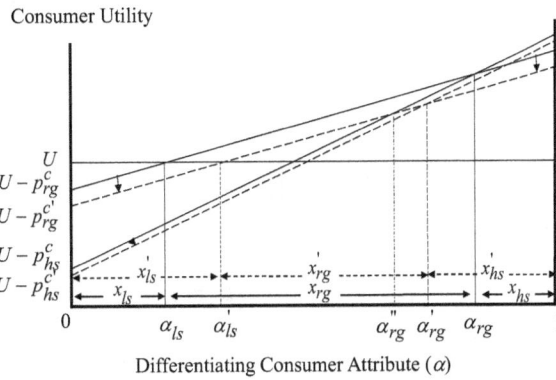

Middlemen

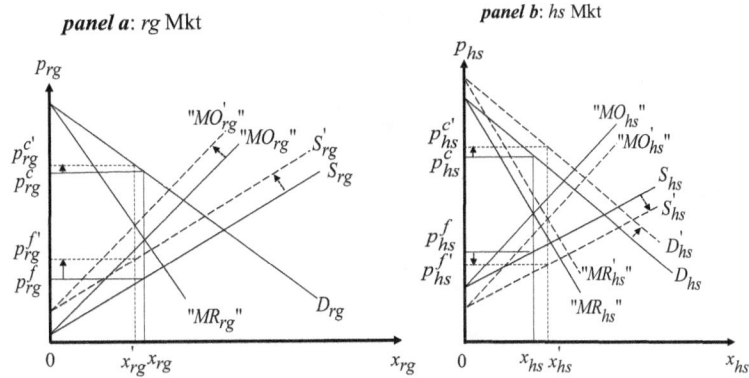

Producers

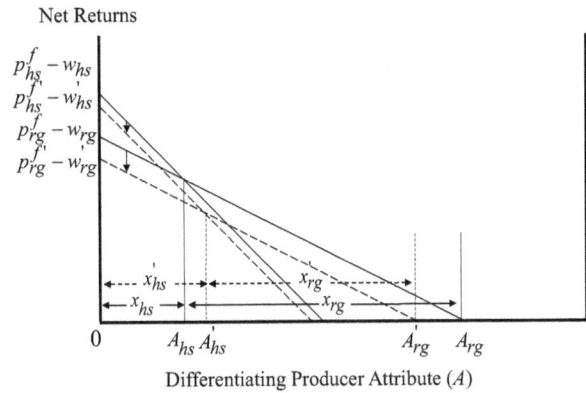

Input Suppliers

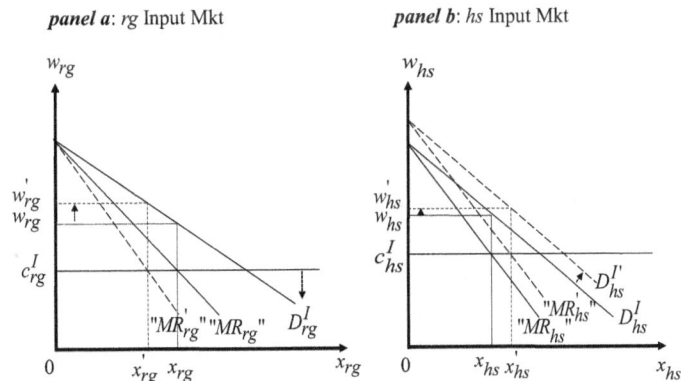

Figure II.3.14. System-Wide Market and Welfare Impacts of Increased θ_{rg}^{I} under Scenario II

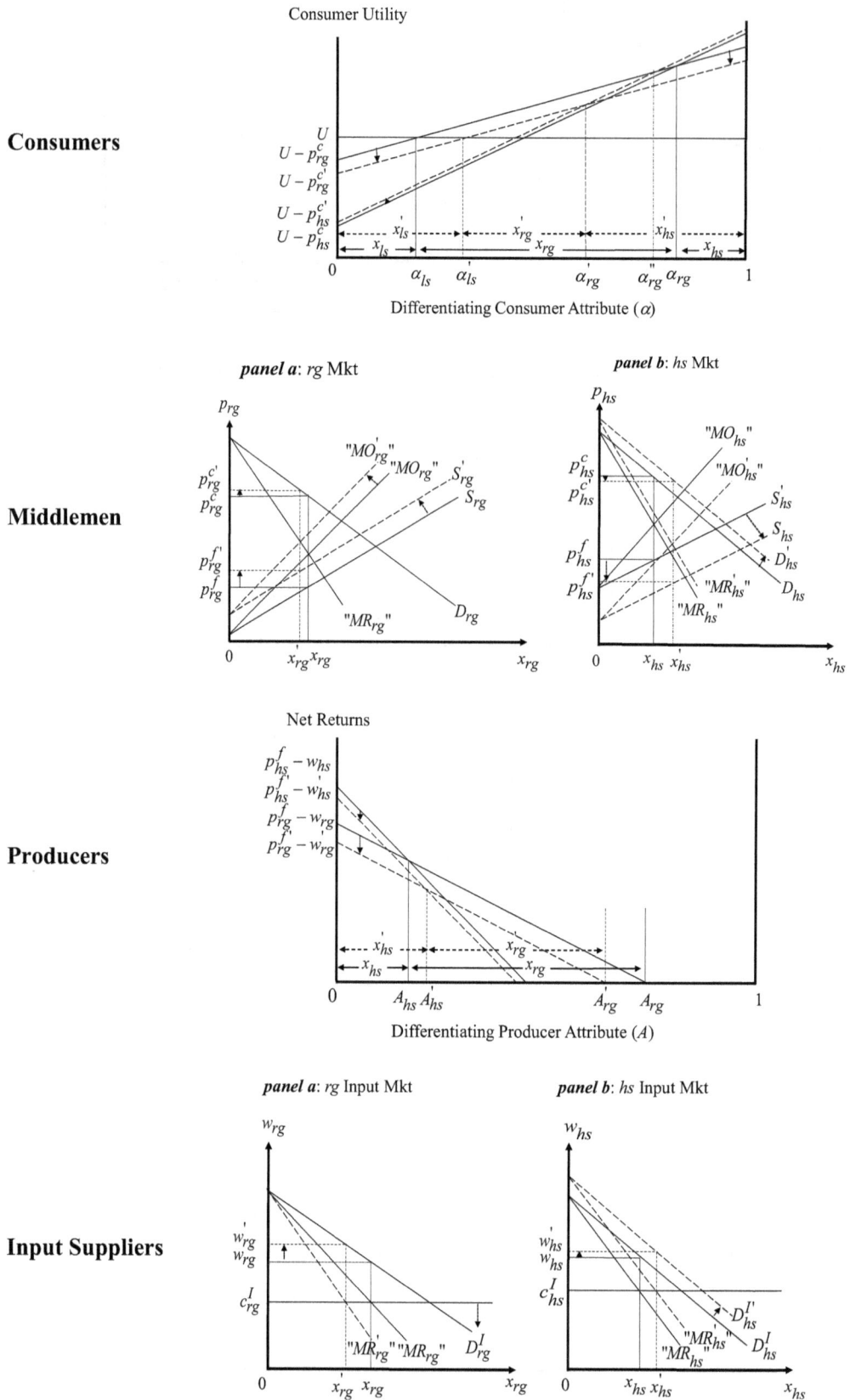

Figure II.3.15. System-Wide Market and Welfare Impacts of Increased θ_{rg}^I under Scenario III

Disaggregation of Welfare Changes and Comparison with Conventional Analysis
Before concluding this section, it is important to note that the key findings of the analysis outlined above are important because they indicate that a proper accounting of the differential welfare impacts of an increase in θ_{rg}^{I} requires a disaggregated analysis, particularly in Scenarios I and III where some of the consumers (Scenario III) or some of the producers (Scenario I) of the reference product realize welfare gains after they have optimally switched. While, as was pointed out earlier in the book, the aggregate welfare changes can be determined using the calculation of producer and consumer surplus from the supply and demand curves, the allocation of the welfare changes to the two markets is incorrect.

Following the same approach developed in the case of the increased θ_{rg} in Section II.2 (as in both cases the changes in the consumer prices of the different products are qualitatively the same), it can be shown that, similar to the case of increased θ_{rg} Scenario III, allocating the costs and benefits according to the demand curves in each market overstates the benefits to those that originally consumed the substitute product and overstates the costs to those that originally consumed the reference product (i.e., overstates both the loss in the reference market and the gain in the substitute market). In short, the calculation of consumer surplus from the demand curves does not provide a proper allocation of the costs and benefits to the various consumer groups. While these overstated amounts cancel each other out at the aggregate level, they yield incorrect results if they are used to determine the distributional impacts of an increase in input supplier market power.

The need to disaggregate the consumer surplus measures is clearly important in Scenario III, since in this scenario some consumers gain and others lose from the increase in θ_{rg}^{I}. However, if it is believed that the magnitude of the loss felt by consumers is also important (as would be the case if consumers exhibit loss aversion, for instance), then disaggregating the losses that occur in Scenarios I and II may also be required as the effects of the increased θ_{rg}^{I} were shown to vary among consumers. The same conclusions, of course, can be drawn regarding the need to disaggregate producer welfare. In this case, there is a clear need to disaggregate producer welfare in Scenario I, since in this case the producer price of the substitute good rises and some of the producers that switch to producing the substitute good will be better off than they were originally in producing the reference product. There may also be a need to disaggregate the changes in producer welfare in Scenarios II and III, since, as was shown in the previous sections, the welfare changes are not symmetric among producers.

II.4. Changes in Cost Structure

Consider now the market and welfare impacts of a reduction in the costs faced by the suppliers of the inputs used in the production of the reference product. Such cost reduction can be the outcome of firm strategies (like adoption of cost-reducing technologies and process innovation activities and synergies from mergers and acquisitions), government policies (like input and R&D subsidies), or/and changes in the market conditions affecting the cost structure of the input suppliers.

To determine the system-wide market and welfare impacts of a reduction in the costs faced by the input suppliers in the supply channel of interest, we compare and contrast the equilibrium prices, quantities, and welfare of the interest groups involved before and after the cost reduction. With the initial equilibrium conditions derived in Section I (and graphed in Figure I.9), our focus here is on the (system-wide) equilibrium conditions under the cost reduction. Once the effects of the cost reduction on the market where it is introduced have been determined (i.e., the input market for the reference product), we proceed in discussing its impacts on the vertically, horizontally and diagonally related markets and interest groups involved (i.e., consumers, producers, middlemen and input suppliers in the supply channels of the reference good and its substitute products).

Equilibrium Conditions under Reduced Input Supplier Costs

The reduction in the costs faced by the input suppliers results in a reduction in the price of the input that is dependent on the degree of market power possessed/exercised by the suppliers of this input. Graphically, the cost reduction can be depicted as creating a downward parallel shift of the marginal cost schedule faced by the (imperfectly competitive) suppliers of the reference input, and a subsequent reduction in the price of this input from w_{rg} to w_{rg}' in Figure II.4.1.

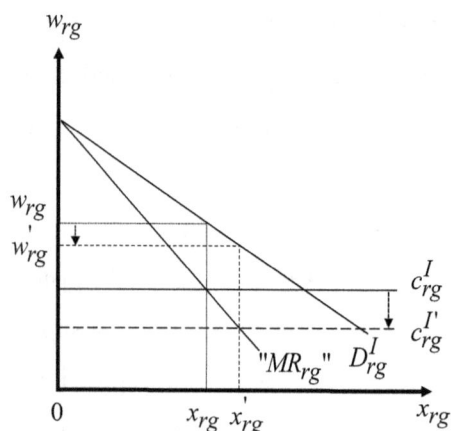

Figure II.4.1. Cost-Reduction in an (Imperfectly Competitive) Input Market

In addition to reducing the price of the reference input, the cost reduction results in increased equilibrium quantity (compare x_{rg} and x'_{rg} in Figure II.4.1) and greater profits for the suppliers of this input (as the cost reduction exceeds the reduction in w_{rg}).

Besides affecting the market for the reference input, this cost reduction has an effect on the vertically, horizontally and diagonally related markets and our integrated framework of analysis can help identify the system-wide market and welfare impacts of this change. The equilibrium conditions/market reaction functions in the presence of the cost reduction can be derived by substituting $c_{rg}^{I'}$ for c_{rg}^{I} in equations (I.24)-(I.31). As mentioned earlier, the nature of the interdependence of markets captured by these expressions provide, along with the related graphical representation, valuable insights on the mechanism through which the reduced c_{rg}^{I} affects the different markets. The section below discusses the market and welfare impacts of the reduced c_{rg}^{I} using the integrated heterogeneous agent framework presented in Section I.

System-Wide Market and Welfare Effects of a Cost Reduction

The analysis in this part focuses on the impact of the cost reduction on the input and output markets for the reference product and its substitute, as well as its effects on the welfare of all interest groups involved (i.e., consumers, producers, middlemen and input suppliers in the markets for the two products). In addition to determining changes in the aggregate consumer and producer welfare, our integrated heterogeneous agent framework enables us to (a) determine the effects of the cost reduction on different consumers and producers of the two products and (b) capture indirect and feedback effects that are not accounted for when focusing solely on the market of the reference input.

Beginning with the *direct producer effects* of the cost reduction, we see that the reduction in the price of the reference input, w_{rg}, (a) increases the net returns associated with the production of the reference product and (b) attracts to the reference product previous producers of substitute and alternative crops. Graphically, the reduction in w_{rg} causes an upward parallel shift of NR_{rg} and the switching of producers with differentiating attributes $A \in (A'_{hs}, A_{hs}]$ and $A \in (A_{rg}, A'_{rg}]$ in Figure II.4.2 to the reference product.

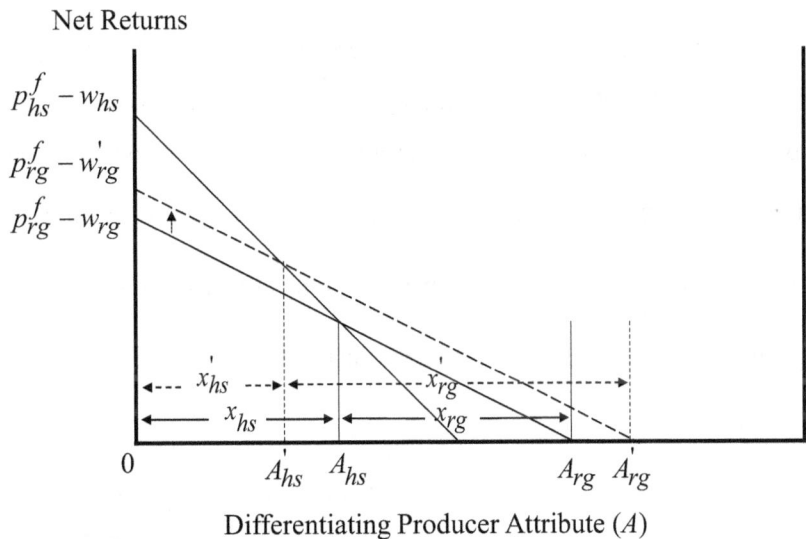

Figure II.4.2. Direct Effects of a Cost Reduction on Producer Decisions

The increased appeal of the reference product due to its reduced input costs increases the supply of the reference product and, through this, reduces the consumer and producer prices of this product (see equations (I.24), (I.25) and (I.30)). Figure II.4.3 graphs the downward parallel shift of S_{rg} and consequent increase in x_{rg} and reductions in p_{rg}^c and p_{rg}^f due to the cost reduction.

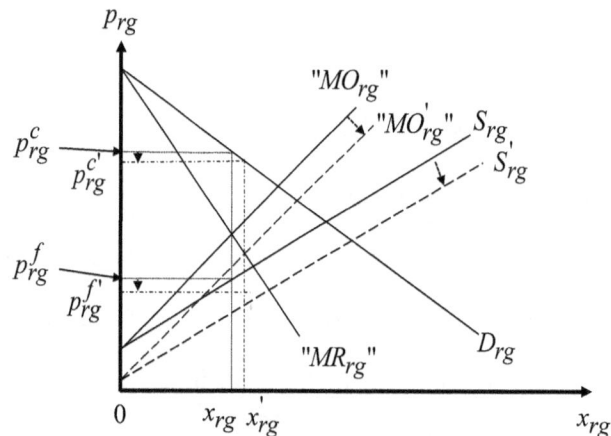

Figure II.4.3. Direct Effects of a Cost Reduction on the Oligemporistic rg Market

Moving to the *direct consumer effects* of the cost reduction, we see that the reduction in the consumer price of the reference product (a) increases the utility associated with the consumption of this product and (b) attracts previous consumers of substitute products to the reference good. Graphically, the reduction in p_{rg}^c causes an upward parallel shift of U_{rg} and the switching of consumers with differentiating attributes $\alpha \in (\alpha_{ls}', \alpha_{ls}]$ and $\alpha \in (\alpha_{rg}, \alpha_{rg}']$ in Figure II.4.4 to the reference product.

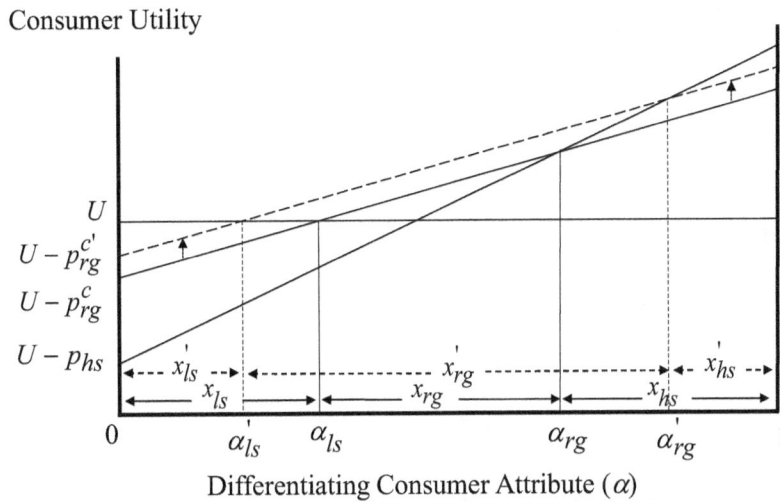

Figure II.4.4. Direct Effects of a Cost Reduction on Consumption Decisions

In addition to affecting the market for the reference product, the changes in this market caused by the cost reduction have a direct impact on the market for the substitute product. The reduced consumer price and the increased returns to the production of the reference product in the presence of the cost reduction attract to the reference product previous consumers and producers of the substitute, affecting, this way, both the demand for and supply of the substitute product.

Formally, the reduced p_{rg}^c causes a downward parallel shift of the demand for the substitute product, D_{hs} (see equation (I.9) and Figure II.4.6), while the reduced w_{rg} and p_{rg}^f cause an upward parallel shift of the supply of the substitute product, S_{hs} (as the reduction in w_{rg} exceeds that in p_{rg}^f; see equation (I.19) and Figure II.4.6). While the reduced demand for, and supply of the substitute product always reduce the equilibrium quantity and profits of the suppliers of this product, the effect on the equilibrium consumer and producer prices (p_{hs}^c and p_{hs}^f, respectively) is determined by the relative magnitude of the demand and supply effects of the cost reduction on the market for the substitute product. In particular, since a *ceteris paribus* decrease in D_{hs} causes p_{hs}^c and

p_{hs}^f to fall, while a similar decrease in S_{hs} results in increased p_{hs}^c and p_{hs}^f, when the supply effect dominates the demand effect so that

$$\left|\Delta p_{rg}^c\right| < \frac{\mu - \lambda}{\theta_{hs}^s(\mu - \lambda) + (1+\theta_{hs}^b)(\delta - \gamma)}\left[\Delta p_{rg}^f - \Delta w_{rg} + \Delta w_{hs}\right] \text{ (where, as noted above,}$$

$\Delta p_{rg}^c < 0$, $\Delta p_{rg}^f < 0$ and $\Delta w_{rg} < 0$, while, as shown in Figure II.4.12 below, $\Delta w_{hs} < 0$), the consumer and producer prices of the substitute product increase after the cost reduction (Scenario I); when

$$\frac{\mu - \lambda}{\theta_{hs}^s(\mu - \lambda) + (1+\theta_{hs}^b)(\delta - \gamma)}\left[\Delta p_{rg}^f - \Delta w_{rg} + \Delta w_{hs}\right] < \left|\Delta p_{rg}^c\right| < \frac{(1+\theta_{hs}^s)(\mu - \lambda) + \theta_{hs}^b(\delta - \gamma)}{\delta - \gamma}\left[\Delta p_{rg}^f - \Delta w_{rg} + \Delta w_{hs}\right],$$

the producer price of the substitute product increases while the consumer price falls (Scenario II); while when the demand effect of the cost reduction dominates the supply effect so that $\left|\Delta p_{rg}^c\right| > \frac{(1+\theta_{hs}^s)(\mu - \lambda) + \theta_{hs}^b(\delta - \gamma)}{\delta - \gamma}\left[\Delta p_{rg}^f - \Delta w_{rg} + \Delta w_{hs}\right]$, the cost reduction

causes both the consumer and producer prices of the substitute product to fall (Scenario III). Figure II.4.5 provides a graphical representation of the conditions leading to the three scenarios while panels 1, 2 and 3 of Figure II.4.6 graph the effects of the cost reduction on the market of the substitute product under these three scenarios.

It is important to note that for Scenario II to occur, the middlemen in the substitute product market should be able to exercise market power. If $\theta_{hs}^s = \theta_{hs}^b = 0$, the condition for Scenario I becomes $\left|\Delta p_{rg}^c\right| < \frac{\mu - \lambda}{\delta - \gamma}\left[\Delta p_{rg}^f - \Delta w_{rg} + \Delta w_{hs}\right]$ and the condition for

Scenario III becomes $\left|\Delta p_{rg}^c\right| > \frac{\mu - \lambda}{\delta - \gamma}\left[\Delta p_{rg}^f - \Delta w_{rg} + \Delta w_{hs}\right]$. Intuitively, under perfectly

competitive middlemen in the substitute product market, the consumer and producer prices of this product will always move in the same direction. While the presence of middlemen market power is necessary for the consumer and producer prices of the substitute product to move in different directions, it is not sufficient for the emergence of Scenario II – as shown above, both Scenarios I and III can emerge in the presence of middlemen market power.

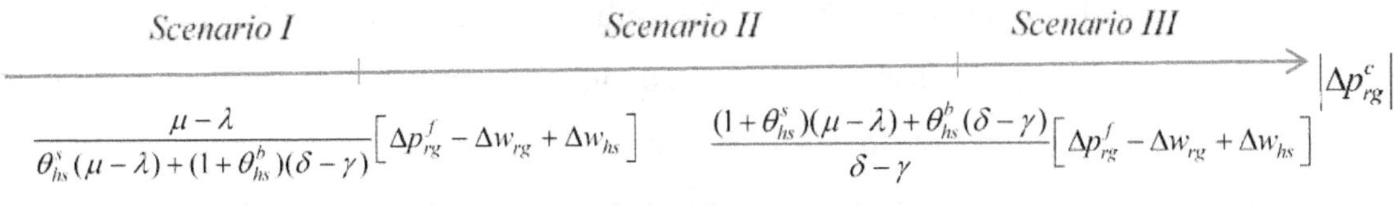

Figure II.4.5. Scenarios on the Effects of a Cost Reduction on Prices of Substitute *hs* Product

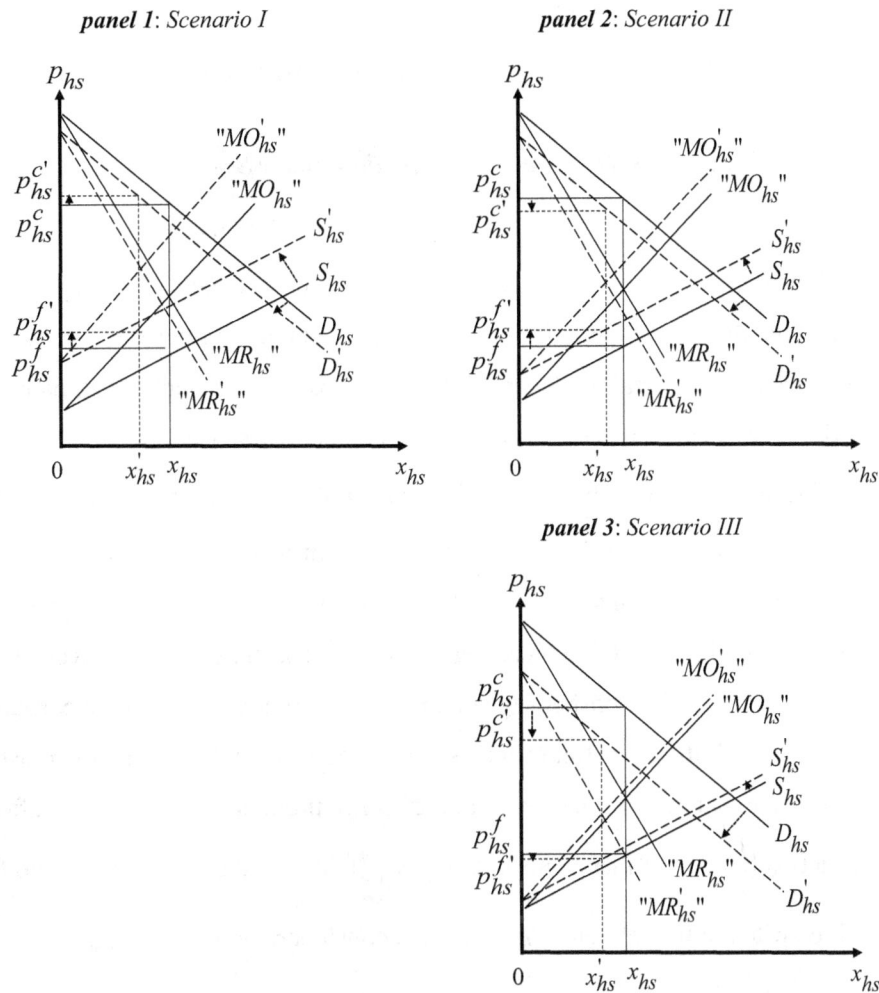

Figure II.4.6. Effects of a Cost Reduction on the Market for the Substitute *hs* Product

Since the equilibrium prices of the substitute product affect the welfare of the consumers and producers of this product, our analysis considers the market and welfare impacts of the cost reduction under the three scenarios outlined above. The case where the cost reduction in the market of the reference product causes the consumer and producer prices of its substitute product to increase (i.e., the case in which the supply effect dominates the demand effect of the cost reduction) is analyzed first followed by the two other scenarios considered here. In all cases, suppliers of the substitute product realize a reduction in profits, with the change given by:

$$\Delta\Pi_{hs} = -\left[(p_{hs}^{c'} - p_{hs}^c)x_{hs}' - (p_{hs}^{f'} - p_{hs}^f)x_{hs}' - (p_{hs}^c - p_{hs}^f)(x_{hs} - x_{hs}')\right] < 0.$$

Market and Welfare Effects of the Cost Reduction under Scenario I
(i.e., when $\left|\Delta p_{rg}^c\right| < \dfrac{\mu - \lambda}{\theta_{hs}^s(\mu - \lambda) + (1 + \theta_{hs}^b)(\delta - \gamma)}\left[\Delta p_{rg}^f - \Delta w_{rg} + \Delta w_{hs}\right]$***)***

As mentioned previously, when the supply effect of a cost reduction dominates its demand effect, the cost reduction for the input suppliers of the reference product increases the consumer and producer prices of its substitute product (recall panel 1 of Figure II.4.6 that depicts this scenario in the price-quantity space).

The increased consumer price of the substitute product, p_{hs}^c, reduces the utility associated with the consumption of this product and further increases the number of consumers that find it optimal to switch their consumption to the reference product (see equation (I.30)). Figure II.4.7 depicts these market and welfare effects as well as the asymmetric impacts of the cost change on the welfare of consumers in the consumer utility space. In addition, the figure shows that the consumers benefiting the most from the cost reduction are those consuming the reference product both before and after the cost reduction (i.e., consumers with $\alpha \in (\alpha_{ls}, \alpha_{rg}]$) followed by consumers who find it optimal to switch to the reference product (i.e., consumers with $\alpha \in (\alpha_{ls}', \alpha_{ls}]$ and $\alpha \in (\alpha_{rg}, \alpha_{rg}'')$). Consumers of the substitute product in the presence of the cost reduction (i.e., consumers with $\alpha \in (\alpha_{rg}', 1]$) as well as some consumers that find it optimal to switch their consumption from the substitute product to the reference good (i.e., consumers with $\alpha \in (\alpha_{rg}^{''}, \alpha_{rg}^{'}]$ in Figure II.4.7) lose from the cost reduction, with the magnitude of their loss determined by their preference parameter/differentiating attribute α. The consumer gains and losses in this case are given by

$$G_c = \int_{\alpha_{ls}^{s'}}^{\alpha_{ls}} (U_{rg}^{'} - U_{ls}) d\alpha + \int_{\alpha_{ls}}^{\alpha_{rg}} (U_{rg}^{'} - U_{rg}) d\alpha + \int_{\alpha_{rg}}^{\alpha_{rg}^{'}} (U_{rg}^{'} - U_{hs}) d\alpha \text{ and}$$

$$L_c = \int_{\alpha_{rg}^{''}}^{\alpha_{rg}^{'}} (U_{hs} - U_{rg}^{'}) d\alpha + \int_{\alpha_{rg}^{'}}^{1} (U_{hs} - U_{hs}^{'}) d\alpha \text{, respectively.}$$

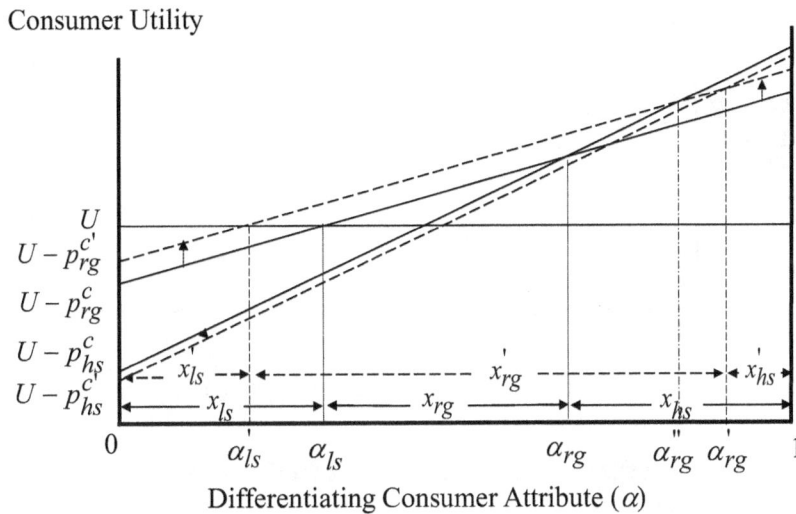

Figure II.4.7. Total Effects of a Cost Reduction on Consumption Decisions and Welfare under Scenario I

While the increased p_{hs}^c reduces the desirability of the substitute product for consumers, the increased p_{hs}^f under Scenario I increases the net returns associated with the production of the substitute product and reduces the incentives for switching to the production of the reference product. Figure II.4.8 depicts these market and welfare effects in the producer net returns space. Producers benefiting the most from the cost reduction are those producing the reference product both before and after the introduction of the change in costs (i.e., producers with $A \in (A_{hs}, A_{rg}]$), followed by producers who find it optimal to switch to the reference product (i.e., producers with $A \in (A_{rg}, A_{rg}']$ and $A \in (A_{hs}', A_{hs}])$ and producers who continue to produce the substitute after the cost reduction (i.e., producers with $A \in (0, A_{hs}']$). Total producer benefits in this case are given by

$$G_p = \int_0^{A_{hs}'} (NR_{hs}' - NR_{hs})dA + \int_{A_{hs}'}^{A_{hs}} (NR_{rg}' - NR_{hs})dA + \int_{A_{hs}}^{A_{rg}} (NR_{rg}' - NR_{rg})dA + \int_{A_{rg}}^{A_{rg}'} (NR_{rg}' - NR_a)dA$$

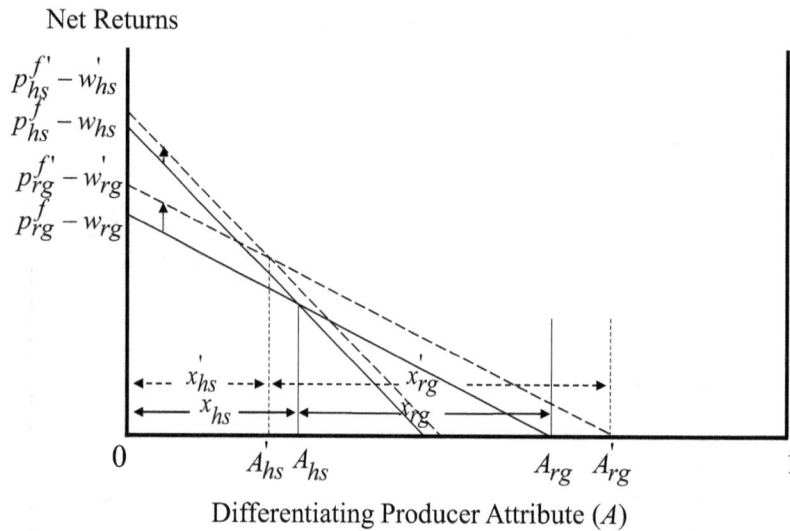

Figure II.4.8. Total Effects of a Cost Reduction on Producer Decisions and Welfare under Scenarios I & II

Market and Welfare Effects of the Cost Reduction under Scenario II (i.e., when

$$\frac{\mu - \lambda}{\theta_{hs}^s(\mu - \lambda) + (1 + \theta_{hs}^b)(\delta - \gamma)} \left[\Delta p_{rg}^f - \Delta w_{rg} + \Delta w_{hs} \right] < \left| \Delta p_{rg}^c \right| < \frac{(1 + \theta_{hs}^s)(\mu - \lambda) + \theta_{hs}^b(\delta - \gamma)}{\delta - \gamma} \left[\Delta p_{rg}^f - \Delta w_{rg} + \Delta w_{hs} \right])$$

As shown in panel 2 of Figure II.4.6, under Scenario II the consumer price of the substitute product falls while the producer price increases making consumers and producers of the substitute product better off.

Predictably, the ramifications of the cost reduction for the producers of the different products are similar to those under Scenario I (described in the previous section and graphed in Figure II.4.8), as p_{hs}^f increases under both Scenarios I and II. Thus, the cost reduction under Scenario II benefits all reference and substitute product producers with the greater benefits enjoyed by those individuals who produce the reference product both before and after the cost reduction.

Unlike Scenario I, consumers of the substitute product gain under Scenario II as the cost reduction for the reference product input suppliers causes the consumer price of the substitute product, p_{hs}^c, to fall. The reduced p_{hs}^c increases the utility associated with the consumption of this product and reduces the number of consumers who switch to the reference product (see equation (I.30)). Figure II.4.9 depicts these market and welfare effects in the consumer utility space. In addition, the figure shows that the consumers benefiting the most from the cost reduction are those consuming the reference product both before and after the cost reduction (i.e., consumers with $\alpha \in (\alpha_{ls}, \alpha_{rg}]$), followed by consumers who find it optimal to switch to the reference product (i.e., consumers with $\alpha \in (\alpha_{ls}', \alpha_{ls}]$ and $\alpha \in (\alpha_{rg}, \alpha_{rg}']$) and consumers who continue to consume the substitute after the cost reduction (i.e., consumers with $\alpha \in (\alpha_{rg}', 1]$). Total consumer benefits from the input suppliers' cost reduction in this case are given by

$$G_c = \int_{\alpha_{ls}'}^{\alpha_{ls}} (U_{rg}' - U_{ls}) d\alpha + \int_{\alpha_{ls}}^{\alpha_{rg}} (U_{rg}' - U_{rg}) d\alpha + \int_{\alpha_{rg}}^{\alpha_{rg}'} (U_{rg}' - U_{hs}) d\alpha + \int_{\alpha_{rg}'}^{1} (U_{hs}' - U_{hs}) d\alpha .$$

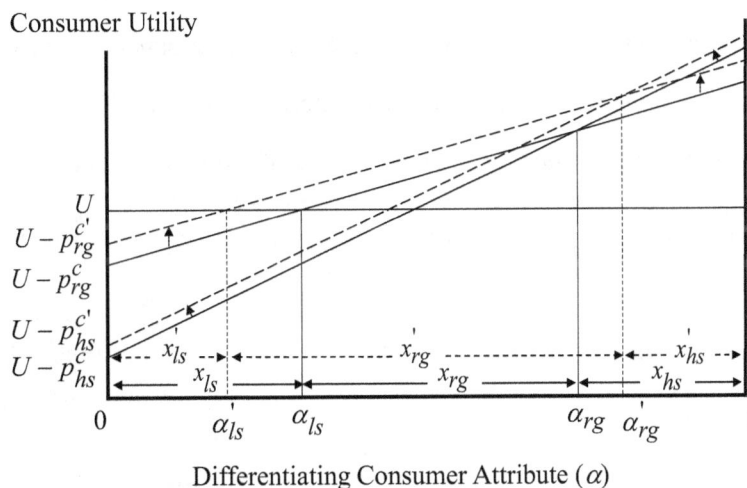

Figure II.4.9. Total Effects of a Cost Reduction on Consumption Decisions and Welfare under Scenarios II & III

Market and Welfare Effects of a Cost Reduction under Scenario III

(i.e., when $\left|\Delta p_{rg}^c\right| > \dfrac{(1+\theta_{hs}^s)(\mu-\lambda)+\theta_{hs}^b(\delta-\gamma)}{\delta-\gamma}\left[\Delta p_{rg}^f - \Delta w_{rg} + \Delta w_{hs}\right]$)

When the demand effect of the cost reduction dominates the supply effect, a reduction in the cost faced by the suppliers of the inputs used in the production of the reference product causes the consumer and producer prices of the substitute product to fall. While the effects of the reduced p_{hs}^c on consumer decisions and welfare are similar to those under Scenario II (described in the previous section and graphed in Figure II.4.9), the effects of the cost reduction on producers are different than those under Scenarios I and II.

Specifically, the reduced p_{hs}^f reduces the net returns associated with the production of the substitute product and increases the incentives for switching to the production of the reference product (see equation (I.30)). Figure II.4.10 depicts these market and welfare effects as well as the asymmetric impacts of the cost reduction on producer welfare in the producer net returns space. Producers benefiting the most from the cost reduction are those producing the reference product both before and after this change (i.e., producers with $A \in (A_{hs}, A_{rg}]$), followed by producers who find it optimal to switch to the reference product from the alternative crop and the substitute product (i.e., producers with $A \in (A_{rg}, A_{rg}']$ and $A \in (A_{hs}'', A_{hs}]$). Producers who continue to produce the substitute after the cost reduction (i.e., producers with $A \in (0, A_{hs}']$) lose, as do some of the substitute product producers who switch to the reference product (i.e., producers with $A \in (A_{hs}', A_{hs}'')$), with the magnitude of this loss determined by the efficiency parameter/differentiating attribute of these producers. The producer gains and losses in this case are given by $G_p = \displaystyle\int_{A_{hs}''}^{A_{hs}} (NR_{rg}' - NR_{hs})dA + \int_{A_{hs}'}^{A_{rg}} (NR_{rg}' - NR_{rg})dA + \int_{A_{rg}}^{A_{rg}'} (NR_{rg}' - NR_a)dA$

and $L_p = \displaystyle\int_{0}^{A_{hs}'} (NR_{hs} - NR_{hs}')dA + \int_{A_{hs}'}^{A_{hs}''} (NR_{hs} - NR_{rg}')dA$, respectively.

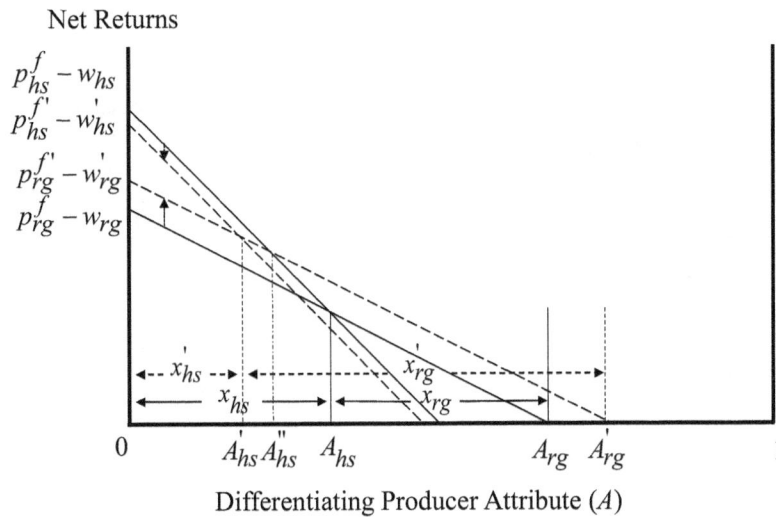

Figure II.4.10. Total Effects of a Cost Reduction on Producer Decisions and Welfare under Scenario III

In addition to affecting the decisions and welfare of consumers and producers of the substitute product, the changes in p_{hs}^c and p_{hs}^f have a feedback effect on the market for the reference product (recall equations (I.24), (I.25) and (I.30)). In particular, an increase (decrease) in p_{hs}^c shifts the demand for the reference product D_{rg} upwards (downwards), while an increase (decrease) in p_{hs}^f causes an upward (downward) shift of the supply of the reference product S_{rg} (recall equations (I.8) and (I.18) and Figures I.3 and I.5). The total effects of the cost reduction on the final consumer market for the reference product under the three scenarios considered here are depicted in Figure II.4.11. In all cases, the cost reduction causes an increase in the reference product supplier profits with the change given by $\Delta \Pi_{rg} = (p_{rg}^f - p_{rg}^{f'})x_{rg} + (p_{rg}^{c'} - p_{rg}^{f'})(x_{rg}' - x_{rg}) - (p_{rg}^c - p_{rg}^{c'})x_{rg} > 0$.

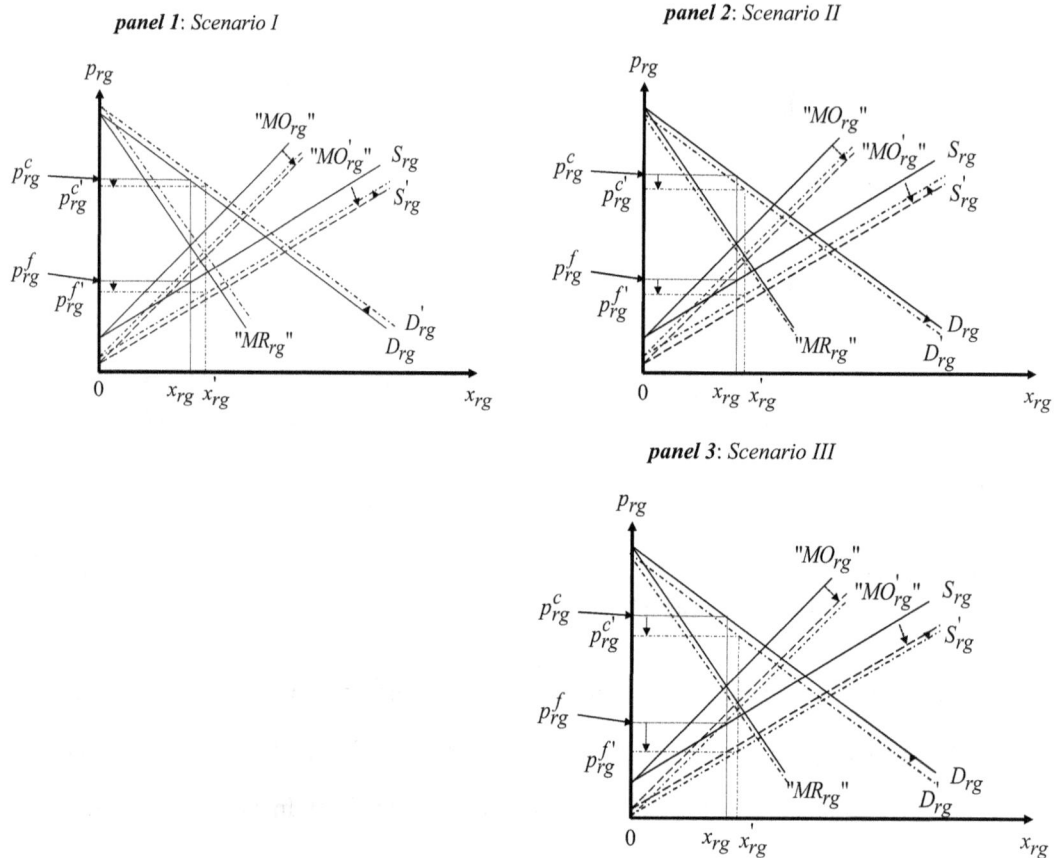

Figure II.4.11. Overall Impact of the Cost Reduction on the *rg* Product Market

Regarding the impact of the cost reduction in the market for the reference input on the inputs used in the production of the substitute product, no matter its effect on p_{hs}^c and p_{hs}^f, the reduction in the costs faced by the suppliers of the inputs used in the production of the reference product reduces the demand for inputs used in the production of its substitute (as the equilibrium quantity of the substitute product falls after the cost reduction). The reduced demand for *hs* inputs results, then, in lower equilibrium input price and quantity (see equations (I.29) and (I.31)), and reduced profits of the supplier of these inputs, with the change in profits given by $\Delta\Pi_{hs}^I = -\left[(w_{hs} - c_{hs}^I)x_{hs} - (w_{hs}' - c_{hs}^I)x_{hs}'\right] < 0$. Figure II.4.12, panel b graphs the changes in the market for the input used in the production of the substitute product due to the cost reduction in the market for the reference input.

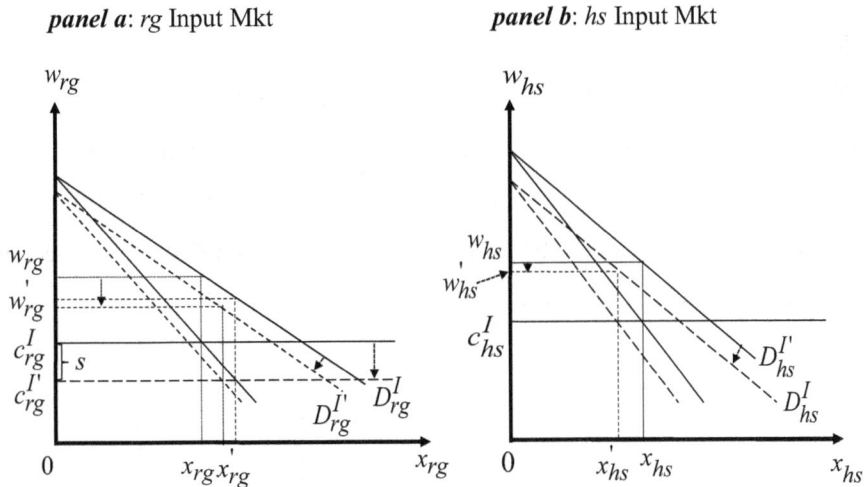

panel a: *rg* Input Mkt   **panel b**: *hs* Input Mkt

Figure II.4.12. Total Effect of a Cost Reduction on the Input Markets

Finally, the change in w_{hs} has a feedback effect on the market of the reference input. Specifically, the decrease in w_{hs} reduces the demand for the reference input D_{rg}^I (see equation (I.20) and Figure I.6) which, in turn, (a) bolsters the impact of the cost reduction on the price of this input, and (b) lessens the impact of the cost change on the quantity of the reference input (see equations (I.28) and (I.30)). The total effects of the cost reduction on the input markets are depicted in Figure II.4.12.

Overall, the analysis on the market and welfare effects of a cost reduction in the market of the input used in the production of the reference product indicates that: (a) the qualitative nature of the welfare effects on the consumers and producers of the substitute product is scenario-specific and depends on the conditions in the market for both the reference product and the substitute product; (b) the impacts of the reduced c_{rg}^I are asymmetric across the different consumers and producers affected by the cost reduction; (c) determination of these asymmetric impacts requires a disaggregation of the benefits and costs to the level of the individual agent; and (d) in Scenarios I and III, some of the consumers (Scenario I) or some of the producers (Scenario III) who find it optimal to switch from the substitute product to the reference good after the decrease in c_{rg}^{I} realize welfare losses.

The asymmetric impact of the cost change on the welfare of all relevant interest groups is summarized in Table II.4.1, while Figures II.4.13-II.4.15 summarize the system-wide market and welfare impacts of this cost reduction under the different scenarios considered in this study. For simplicity, the feedback effects described above (Figures II.4.11 and II.4.12) are not included in Figures II.4.13-II.4.15.

Table II.4.1. System-Wide Welfare Impacts of a Reduction in the Cost of the Suppliers of Inputs used in the Production of the Reference Product, c_{rg}^I

	Consumers of ls switching to rg	Consumers of rg	Consumers of hs switching to rg	Consumers of hs	Producers of rg	Producers of hs switching to rg	Producers of hs	Suppliers of rg	Suppliers of hs	Input Suppliers rg	Input Suppliers hs
Scenario I	+	+	some + some –	–	+	+	+	+	–	+	–
Scenario II	+	+	+	+	+	+	+	+	–	+	–
Scenario III	+	+	+	+	+	some – some +	–	+	–	+	–

+ denotes welfare gains
– denotes welfare losses

Condition for Scenario I: $\left|\Delta p_{rg}^c\right| < \dfrac{\mu - \lambda}{\theta_{hs}^s(\mu-\lambda)+(1+\theta_{hs}^b)(\delta-\gamma)}\left[\Delta p_{rg}^f - \Delta w_{rg} + \Delta w_{hs}\right]$

Condition for Scenario II: $\dfrac{\mu-\lambda}{\theta_{hs}^s(\mu-\lambda)+(1+\theta_{hs}^b)(\delta-\gamma)}\left[\Delta p_{rg}^f - \Delta w_{rg} + \Delta w_{hs}\right] < \left|\Delta p_{rg}^c\right| < \dfrac{(1+\theta_{hs}^s)(\mu-\lambda)+\theta_{hs}^b(\delta-\gamma)}{\delta-\gamma}\left[\Delta p_{rg}^f - \Delta w_{rg} + \Delta w_{hs}\right]$

Condition for Scenario III: $\left|\Delta p_{rg}^c\right| > \dfrac{(1+\theta_{hs}^s)(\mu-\lambda)+\theta_{hs}^b(\delta-\gamma)}{\delta-\gamma}\left[\Delta p_{rg}^f - \Delta w_{rg} + \Delta w_{hs}\right]$

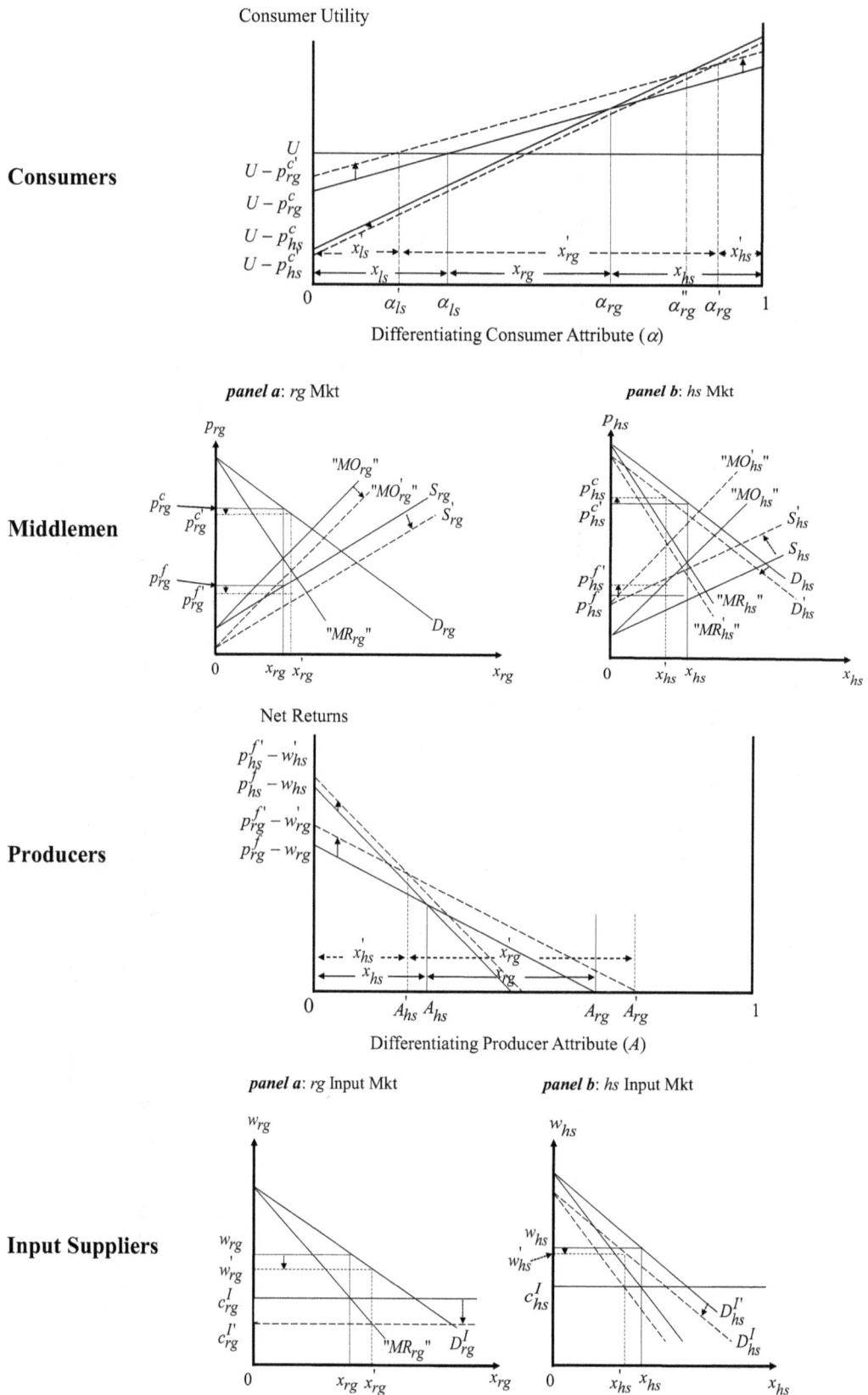

- 110 -

Figure II.4.13. System-Wide Market and Welfare Impacts of a Cost Reduction under Scenario I

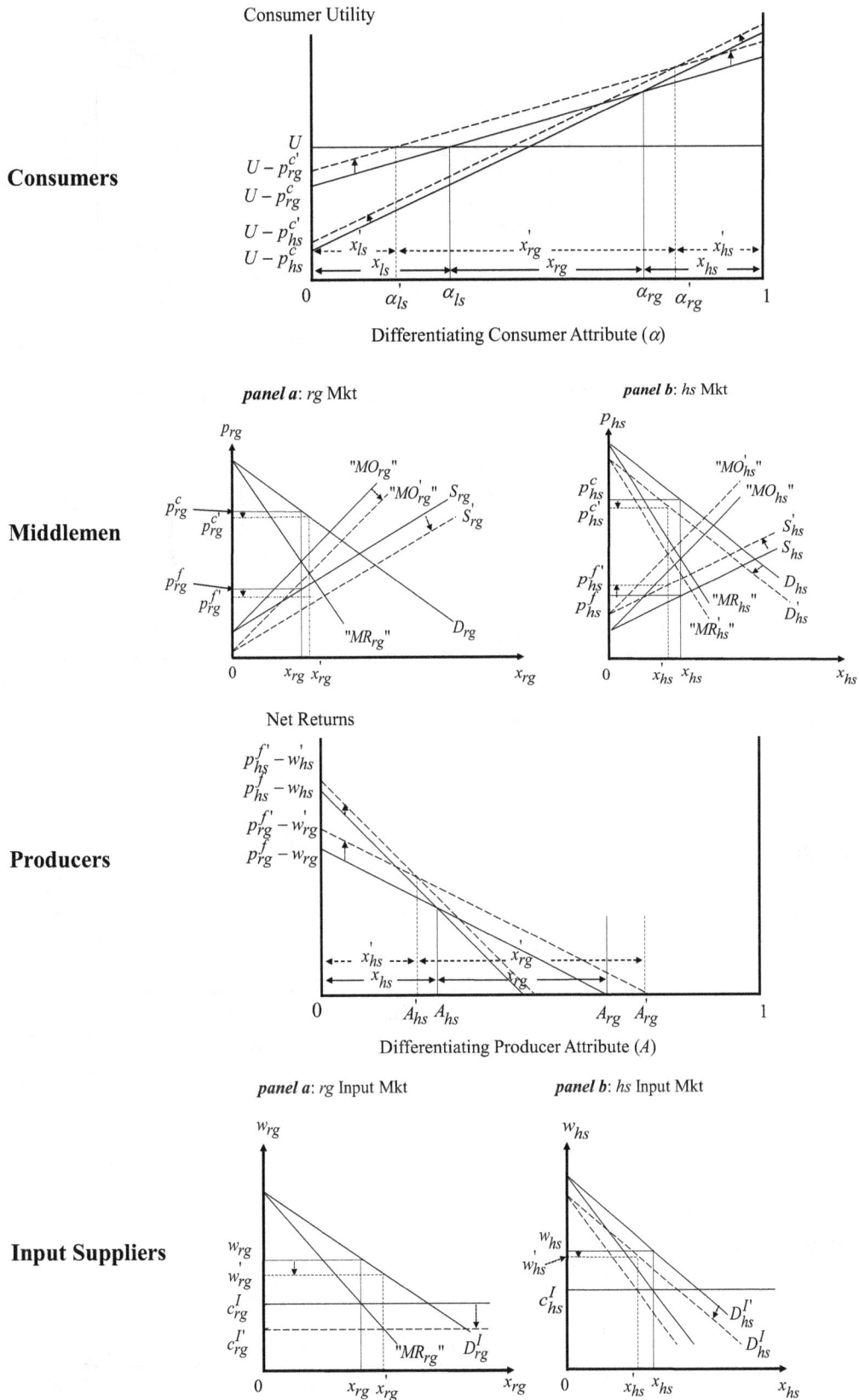

Figure II.4.14. System-Wide Market and Welfare Impacts of a Cost Reduction under Scenario II

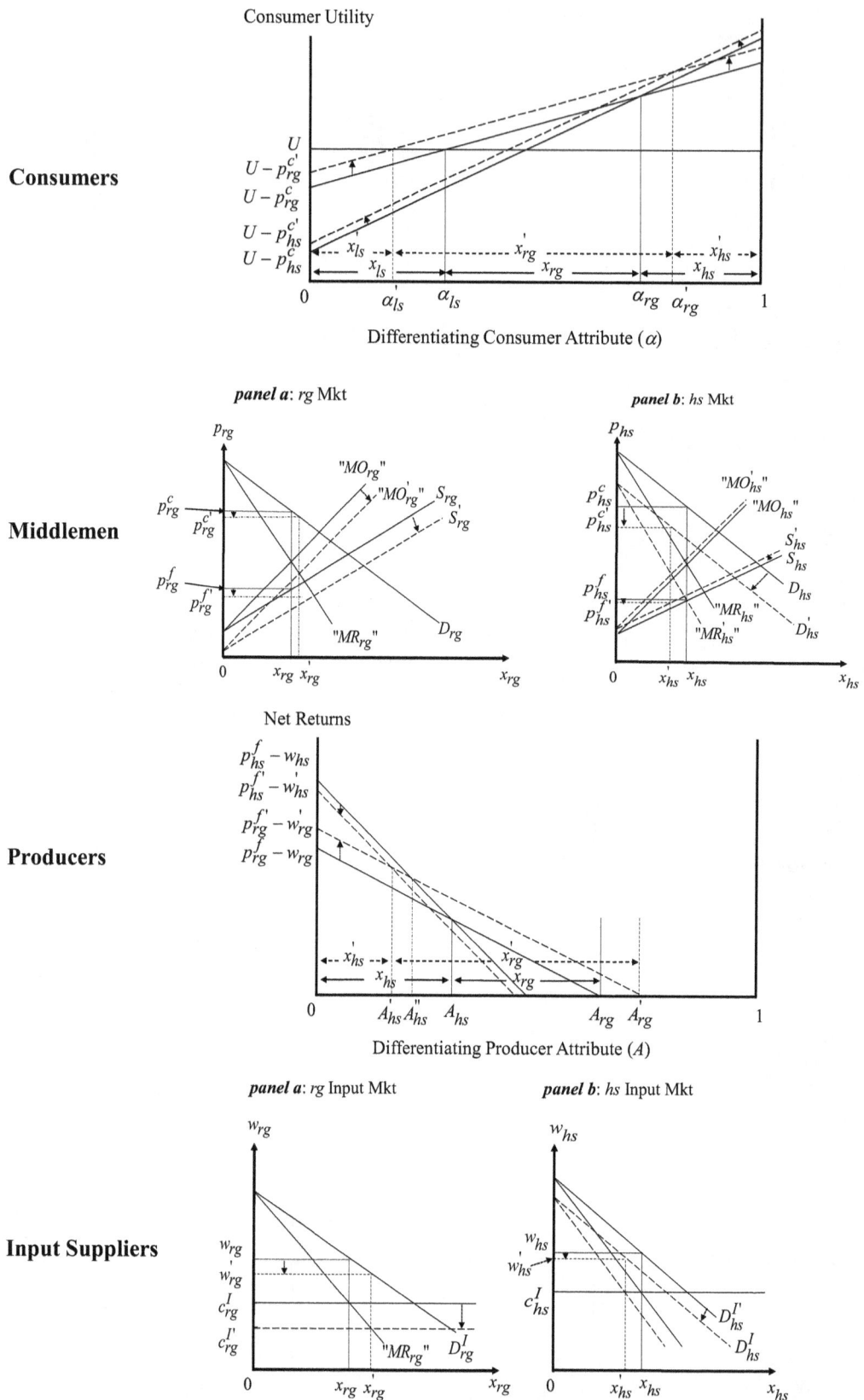

Figure II.4.15. System-Wide Market and Welfare Impacts of a Cost Reduction under Scenario III

Disaggregation of Welfare Changes and Comparison with Conventional Analysis

The conclusions outlined above are important because they indicate that a proper accounting of the differential welfare impacts of a decrease in c_{rg}^I requires a disaggregated analysis, particularly in Scenarios I and III where some of the consumers (Scenario I) or some of the producers (Scenario III) of the substitute product realize welfare losses after they have optimally switched to the reference good. As was pointed out earlier in the book, the aggregate welfare changes can be determined using the calculation of producer and consumer surplus from the supply and demand curves. As will be shown in this section, however, the proper allocation of these surplus changes to different consumers and producers requires an additional disaggregation.

To illustrate the issues involved in properly disaggregating the welfare changes, consider Scenario I where the consumer price of the reference good decreases and the consumer price of the substitute good increases (a similar analysis could be undertaken for producers in Scenario III). Figure II.4.16 (which is the same as Figure II.4.7) shows the utility curves for the reference and substitute goods with the welfare changes disaggregated. The solid lines show the utility curves before the decrease in c_{rg}^I, while the dotted lines show the utility curves after the prices have taken their new equilibrium values as a result of the cost reduction.

Figure II.4.17 shows the demand curves derived from the utility curves (these demand curves were presented earlier in Figure I.3). Before the cost is reduced, the consumer price of the reference good is p_{rg}^c, while the consumer price of the substitute good is p_{hs}^c. The corresponding quantities purchased are x_{rg} and x_{hs}. The decrease in c_{rg}^I reduces the consumer price of the reference good to $p_{rg}^{c'}$. This reduced price, in turn, shifts in the demand curve for the substitute product from $D_{hs}(p_{rg}^c)$ to $D_{hs}(p_{rg}^{c'})$. Recall that the price of the substitute product increases because of the shift in of the supply curve (not shown here; see Figure II.4.6, panel 1) – the resulting equilibrium price is $p_{hs}^{c'}$. At this price, consumption of the substitute good is x_{hs}'. The increase in the price of the substitute good causes the demand curve for the reference good to shift upward from $D_{rg}(p_{hs}^c)$ to $D_{rg}(p_{hs}^{c'})$. Given price $p_{rg}^{c'}$, consumption of the reference good is x_{rg}'.

As shown in Figure II.4.16, the decrease in c_{rg}^I results in a gain of area a for the consumers that enter the market of the reference good (those located between α_{ls}' and α_{ls}) and a gain of area b to those that continue to purchase the reference good (those located between α_{ls} and α_{rg}). Of those that switch from the high quality substitute to the reference good, some gain (those located between α_{rg} and α_{rg}''; the magnitude of the gain is area c plus area d) while some lose (those located between α_{rg}'' and α_{rg}'; the magnitude of the loss is area m). Finally, the consumers that originally purchased the high quality substitute lose (these consumers are located between α_{rg}' and 1; the size of the loss is area n). At the aggregate level, the welfare change is thus $(a + b + c + d) - (m + n)$.

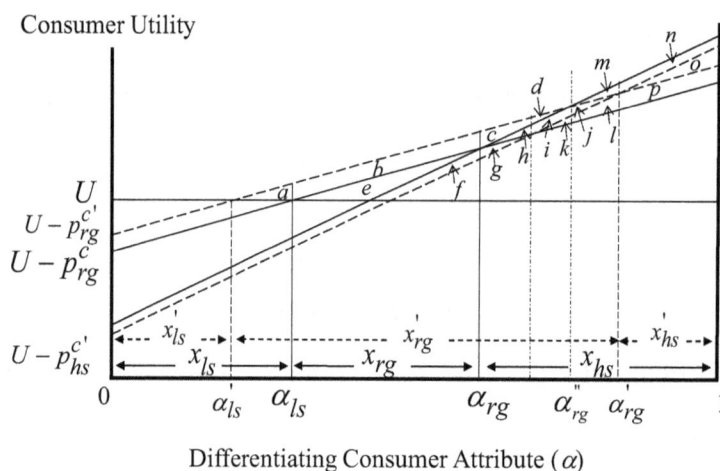

Total consumer welfare change: $(a + b + c + d) - (m + n)$
hs consumers that switch to *rg*:   - some gain (area $c + d$)
                                     - some lose (area m)
hs consumers net gain = $(c + d) - (m + n)$
rg consumers net gain = b
ls consumers net gain = a

rg consumers* net gain = $(a + b + c + d) - m$
hs consumers* net loss = n *ex post* (i.e., after the cost reduction)

Figure II.4.16. Consumer Welfare Impacts of Reduced c_{rg}^I under Scenario I:
Consumer Utility Space

These aggregate welfare changes can also be obtained from the demand curves presented in Figure II.4.17 (the various welfare areas have been labeled so that they match the utility areas in Figure II.4.16). As noted earlier, there are two methods of calculating the welfare change. The first method is to calculate the overall change in consumer surplus (denote this as ΔCS_1) given by the change in consumer surplus in the reference market evaluated at the new equilibrium price of the substitute good, plus the change in consumer surplus in the substitute market evaluated at the original price of the reference good. The second method is to calculate the aggregate change in consumer surplus (denote this as ΔCS_2) as the change in consumer surplus in the reference market evaluated at the original price of the substitute good, plus the change in consumer surplus in the substitute market evaluated at the new equilibrium price of the reference good.

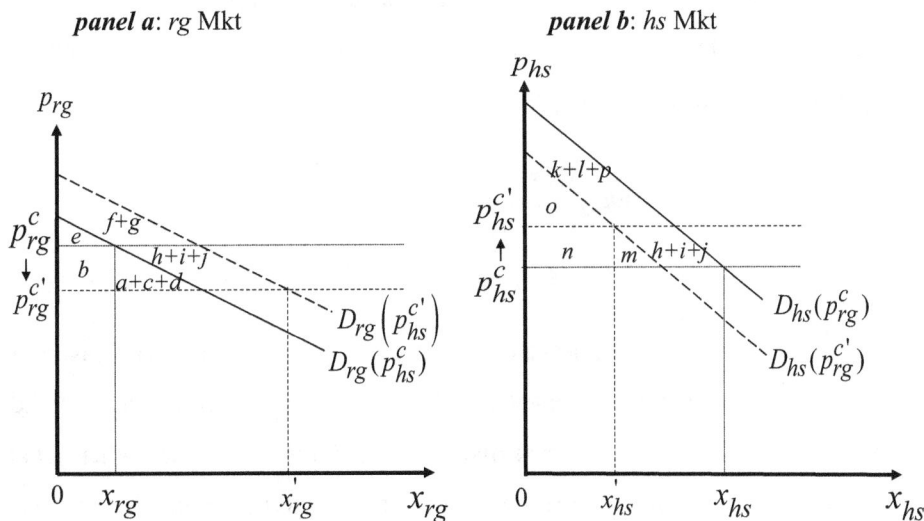

Figure II.2.16. Consumer Welfare Impacts of Reduced c_{rg}^I under Scenario I: Price-Quantity Space

Using the first method, the overall change in consumer surplus ΔCS_1 is given by:

$$\Delta CS_1 = \int_{p_{rg}^{c'}}^{p_{rg}^{c}} x_{rg}(p_{rg}, p_{hs}^{c'})dp_{rg} - \int_{p_{hs}^{c}}^{p_{hs}^{c'}} x_{hs}(p_{hs}, p_{rg}^{c})dp_{hs} = (a+b+c+d)-(m+n)$$

The above expression allocates a gain of utility equal to $(a + b + c + d)$ to the reference market and a loss in utility equal to $(m + n)$ to the substitute market. However, while the aggregate change is correct, the allocation to the two markets is neither correct nor particularly insightful. While most of the original consumers of the substitute good lose utility – this amount is equal to area $(m + n)$ – there are some of these consumers that gain; this gain is given by area $(c + d)$. As well, the original consumers of the reference good and those that were not consuming any of the two products and entered the market of the reference good after the cost reduction gain an amount equal to areas b and a, respectively. Allocating the cost and benefits according to the demand curves in each market overstates the benefits to those that originally consumed the reference product and overstates the costs to those that originally consumed the substitute product. In short, the calculation of consumer surplus from the demand curves does not provide a proper allocation of the costs and benefits to the various consumer groups.

A similar problem emerges if the second method is used. Using this method, the aggregate change in consumer surplus ΔCS_2 is:

$$\Delta CS_2 = \int_{p_{rg}^{c'}}^{p_{rg}^{c}} x_{rg}(p_{rg}, p_{hs}^{c}) dp_{rg} - \int_{p_{hs}^{c}}^{p_{hs}^{c'}} x_{hs}(p_{hs}, p_{rg}^{c'}) dp_{hs}$$

$$= (a + b + c + d + h + i + j) - (m + n + h + i + j) = (a + b + c + d) - (m + n)$$

While calculation of the welfare change in this way also yields the correct measure of the aggregate welfare change, it also overstates both the gain in the reference market and the loss in the substitute market. While these overstated amounts cancel each other out at the aggregate level, they yield incorrect results if they are used to determine the distributional impacts of a reduction in the costs faced by the reference product input suppliers.

The need to disaggregate the consumer surplus measures is clearly important in Scenario I, since in this scenario some consumers gain and others lose from the decrease in c_{rg}^{I}. However, if it is believed that the magnitude of the gain realized by consumers is also important, then disaggregating the gains that occur in Scenarios II and III may also be required as the effects of the cost reduction were shown to vary among consumers. The same conclusions, of course, can be drawn regarding the need to disaggregate producer welfare. In this case, there is a clear need to disaggregate producer welfare in Scenario III, since in this case some of the producers that switch to producing the reference good will be worse off than they were originally in producing the substitute product. There may also be a need to disaggregate the changes in producer welfare in Scenarios I and II, since, as was shown in the previous sections, the welfare changes are not symmetric among producers.

II.5 Additional Considerations/Market Studies

In addition to enabling the analysis of changing market structure, costs and consumer preferences, our framework can also be utilized to analyze the **market and welfare impacts of the introduction of new products in the market**. This is particularly important/relevant in the increasingly industrialized agri-food marketing system where the provision of an ever increasing variety of close but imperfect substitute products has been a key consumer demand (and food company strategy) (Giannakas, 2011). Specifically, the framework can be (and has been) used to (a) identify the exact conditions under which a new product/new technology will end up being ineffective, non-drastic (i.e., will coexist with the existing products/technologies), or drastic (i.e., successful enough to drive its competing products/technologies out of the market), and (b) determine the market and welfare impacts in each case. Examples of new product introductions that have been analyzed using variants/adaptations of our methodological framework are the producer-oriented first-generation GM products (Fulton and Giannakas, 2004), consumer-oriented second-generation GM products (Giannakas and Yiannaka, 2008), and products of food nanotechnology (Tran, Yiannaka and Giannakas, 2018).

The framework can also be utilized to analyze the **optimal strategies of firms** under different structures of the costs associated with these strategies. For instance, the framework can be used to determine optimal cost-reducing or/and quality-enhancing innovation activity – process and product innovation activity, respectively, affecting the production costs (as in Section II.4) and consumer preferences/valuation of the good (as in Section II.1) – and advertising strategies (also affecting consumer preferences) by equating the marginal innovation or advertising costs with the marginal benefits of these activities (identified in the aforementioned sections). Similarly, it can be used to determine whether the benefits from innovation or/and advertising activities (due to an increased consumer valuation of a product or reduced costs of production) justify the high fixed (and, often, sunk) costs associated with such strategies. A similar analysis could also reveal whether benefits from mergers and acquisitions (due to increased market power and/or reduced costs resulting from these activities) exceed the (search, negotiation, bargaining, information, and adjustment) costs of such activities.

III. Policy Analysis

This part of the book utilizes the methodological framework developed in Section I to analyze the market and (disaggregated) welfare impacts of standard, textbook policy mechanisms like subsidies and taxes. In particular, the following sections focus on the analysis of:

1. Output (producer/consumer) subsidy under perfect competition
2. Consumption tax under imperfect competition
3. Input subsidy under imperfect competition

The section concludes with a discussion of other food and energy policies that can be (and have been) analyzed using our framework of analysis.

III.1. Output Subsidy under Perfect Competition

To determine the system-wide market and welfare impacts of the output subsidy, we compare and contrast the equilibrium prices, quantities, and welfare of the interest groups involved before and after the introduction of the policy.

Pre-Subsidy Equilibrium under Perfect Competition

The pre-subsidy equilibrium conditions under perfect competition in the output and input markets can be derived by substituting $\theta_{rg}^s = \theta_{rg}^b = \theta_{rg}^I = \theta_{hs}^s = \theta_{hs}^b = \theta_{hs}^I = 0$ in equations (I.24)-(I.31) of Section I, and are given by:

$$p_{rg}^c = p_{rg}^f = p_{rg}^e = \frac{\frac{\lambda(\mu-\lambda)}{\mu}\left[w_{rg} + \frac{\gamma}{\delta}(p_{hs}^f - w_{hs})\right] + \frac{\lambda\gamma(\delta-\gamma)}{\mu\delta}p_{hs}^c}{\frac{\lambda(\mu-\lambda)}{\mu} + \frac{\gamma(\delta-\gamma)}{\delta}} \quad \text{(III.1.1)}$$

$$p_{hs}^c = p_{hs}^f = p_{hs}^e = \frac{(p_{rg}^c + \mu - \lambda)(\delta-\gamma) + (\mu-\lambda)\left[w_{hs} + (p_{rg}^f - w_{rg})\right]}{(\mu-\lambda) + (\delta-\gamma)} \quad \text{(III.1.2)}$$

$$w_{rg} = c_{rg}^I \quad \text{(III.1.3)}$$

$$w_{hs} = c_{hs}^I \quad \text{(III.1.4)}$$

$$x_{rg} = \frac{\frac{\lambda}{\mu} p_{hs}^c - \left[w_{rg} + \frac{\gamma}{\delta}(p_{hs}^f - w_{hs}) \right]}{\frac{\lambda(\mu - \lambda)}{\mu} + \frac{\gamma(\delta - \gamma)}{\delta}} \qquad (III.1.5)$$

$$x_{hs} = \frac{p_{rg}^c + \mu - \lambda - \left[w_{hs} + (p_{rg}^f - w_{rg}) \right]}{(\mu - \lambda) + (\delta - \gamma)} \qquad (III.1.6)$$

Equilibrium Conditions under the Subsidy

Consider now the equilibrium conditions after the introduction of an output subsidy, s. As shown in Figure III.1.1 below, the subsidy results in (a) increased price received by the producers of the regulated product (compare the producer price with and without the output subsidy, p_{rg}^{fs} and p_{rg}^e, respectively); (b) reduced consumer price (compare p_{rg}^{cs} and p_{rg}^e); and (c) increased equilibrium quantity of the regulated product (compare x_{rg}^s and x_{rg}^e). Producer surplus increases by $\Delta PS = \frac{1}{2}(p_{rg}^{fs} - p_{rg}^e)(x_{rg}^e + x_{rg}^s)$, consumer surplus increases by $\Delta CS = \frac{1}{2}(p_{rg}^e - p_{rg}^{cs})(x_{rg}^e + x_{rg}^s)$, and the deadweight welfare losses of the program (distortionary costs of market intervention) are given by the difference between the taxpayer costs, $TC = (p_{rg}^{fs} - p_{rg}^{cs})x_{rg}^s = sx_{rg}^s$, and the consumer and producer gains, and equal $DWL = \frac{1}{2}(x_{rg}^s - x_{rg}^e)(p_{rg}^{fs} - p_{rg}^{cs}) = \frac{1}{2}(x_{rg}^s - x_{rg}^e)s$.

panel a: rg Mkt

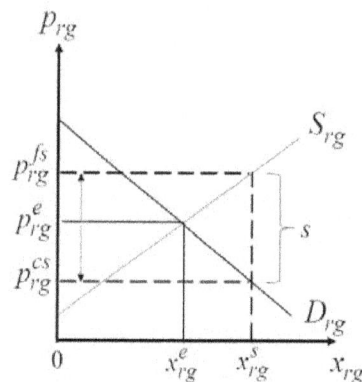

Figure III.1.1. Output Subsidy in the *rg* Market under Perfect Competition

In addition to affecting the market for the regulated product, the introduction of the subsidy has an effect on the vertically, horizontally and diagonally related markets and our integrated framework of analysis can help identify the system-wide market and welfare impacts of this policy. Indeed, the market reaction functions in the presence of the subsidy become:

$$p_{rg}^{cs} = \frac{\frac{\lambda(\mu-\lambda)}{\mu}\left[w_{rg} + \frac{\gamma}{\delta}(p_{hs}^{fs} - w_{hs})\right] + \frac{\lambda\gamma(\delta-\gamma)}{\mu\delta}p_{hs}^{cs} - \frac{\lambda(\mu-\lambda)}{\mu}s}{\frac{\lambda(\mu-\lambda)}{\mu} + \frac{\gamma(\delta-\gamma)}{\delta}} \qquad (III.1.7)$$

$$p_{rg}^{fs} = \frac{\frac{\lambda(\mu-\lambda)}{\mu}\left[w_{rg} + \frac{\gamma}{\delta}(p_{hs}^{fs} - w_{hs})\right] + \frac{\lambda\gamma(\delta-\gamma)}{\mu\delta}p_{hs}^{cs} + \frac{\gamma(\delta-\gamma)}{\delta}s}{\frac{\lambda(\mu-\lambda)}{\mu} + \frac{\gamma(\delta-\gamma)}{\delta}} \qquad (III.1.8)$$

$$p_{hs}^{cs} = p_{hs}^{fs} = \frac{(p_{rg}^{cs} + \mu - \lambda)(\delta-\gamma) + (\mu-\lambda)\left[w_{hs} + (p_{rg}^{fs} - w_{rg})\right]}{(\mu-\lambda) + (\delta-\gamma)} \qquad (III.1.9)$$

$$w_{rg} = c_{rg}^{I} \qquad (III.1.10)$$

$$w_{hs} = c_{hs}^{I} \qquad (III.1.11)$$

$$x_{rg}^{s} = \frac{\frac{\lambda}{\mu}p_{hs}^{cs} - \left[w_{rg} + \frac{\gamma}{\delta}(p_{hs}^{fs} - w_{hs})\right] + s}{\frac{\lambda(\mu-\lambda)}{\mu} + \frac{\gamma(\delta-\gamma)}{\delta}} \qquad (III.1.12)$$

$$x_{hs}^{s} = \frac{p_{rg}^{cs} + \mu - \lambda - \left[w_{hs} + (p_{rg}^{fs} - w_{rg})\right]}{(\mu-\lambda) + (\delta-\gamma)} \qquad (III.1.13)$$

As mentioned earlier, solving the equations for the equilibrium prices simultaneously allows the expression of the output prices as functions of the exogenous variables of the model (i.e., subsidy, preference and cost parameters). Substituting these prices into the expressions for the equilibrium quantities, consumer welfare and producer net returns enables the expression of all equilibrium conditions as functions of the exogenous variables of the model. Perhaps more importantly, the nature of the interdependence of markets captured by these expressions provide, along with the related graphical representation, valuable insights on the mechanism through which the policy affects the different markets. The rest of this section discusses the market and welfare impacts of the output subsidy using the integrated heterogeneous agent framework presented in Section I.

System-Wide Market and Welfare Effects of an Output Subsidy

The analysis in this part focuses on the impact of the subsidy on the input and output markets for the regulated product and its substitute, as well as its effects on the welfare of all interest groups involved (i.e., consumers, producers, middlemen and input suppliers in the markets for the two products). In addition to determining changes in the aggregate consumer and producer welfare, our integrated heterogeneous agent framework enables us to (a) determine the effects of the subsidy on different consumers and producers of the two products and (b) capture relevant indirect and feedback effects of the policy that are not accounted for when focusing solely on the market of the regulated product.

Beginning with the *direct consumer effects* of the subsidy, we see that the reduction in the consumer price of the regulated/subsidized product (a) increases the utility associated with the consumption of this product (see equation (I.1)) and (b) attracts previous consumers of substitute products to the regulated product. Graphically, the reduction in p_{rg}^c causes an upward parallel shift of U_{rg} and the switching of consumers with differentiating attributes $\alpha \in (\alpha_{ls}^s, \alpha_{ls}^e]$ and $\alpha \in (\alpha_{rg}^e, \alpha_{rg}^s]$ in Figure III.1.2 to the regulated product.

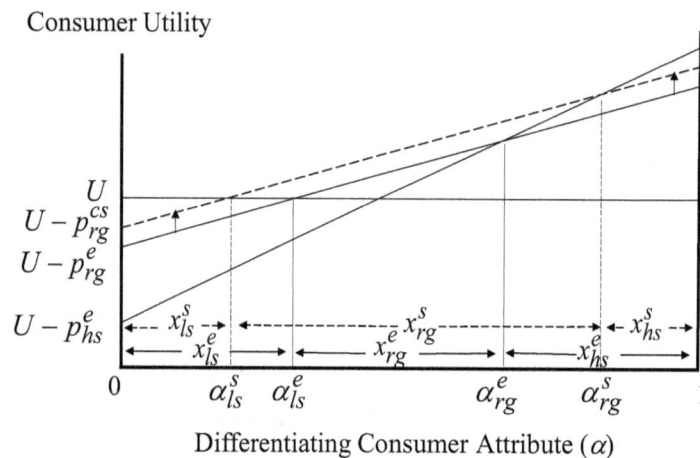

Figure III.1.2. Direct Effects of the Output Subsidy on Consumption Decisions

Similar to consumers, the introduction of the subsidy benefits the producers of the regulated product and results in producers of alternative crops switching to the regulated product. Graphically, the increased p_{rg}^f causes an upward parallel shift of the net returns curve associated with the production of the regulated product and the switching of producers with $A \in (A_{hs}^s, A_{hs}^e]$ and $A \in (A_{rg}^e, A_{rg}^s]$ in Figure III.1.3 to the regulated product.

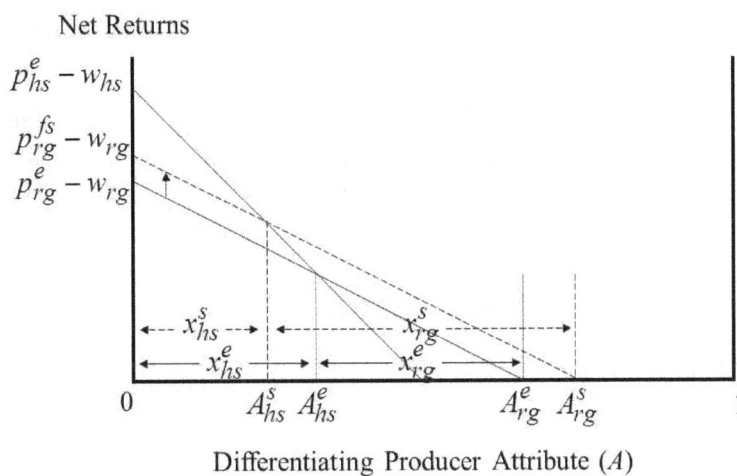

Figure III.1.3. Direct Effects of the Output Subsidy on Producer Decisions

In addition to affecting the market for the regulated product, the changes in the consumer and producer prices of the regulated product caused by the output subsidy have a direct impact on the market for the substitute product (see equations (III.1.9) and (III.1.13)). Specifically, the reduced consumer price and the increased producer price of the regulated product in the presence of the subsidy attract to the regulated product previous consumers and producers of the substitute, affecting, this way, both the demand for and supply of the substitute product.

Formally, the reduced p_{rg}^c causes a downward parallel shift of the demand for the substitute product D_{hs} (see equation (I.9) and Figure III.1.4), while the increased p_{rg}^f causes an upward parallel shift of the supply of the substitute product S_{hs} (see equation

(I.19) and Figure III.1.4). While the reduced demand for, and supply of the substitute product always reduce the equilibrium quantity of this product, the effect on the equilibrium price is determined by the relative magnitude of the demand and supply effects of the output subsidy on the market for the substitute product. In particular, since a *ceteris paribus* decrease in D_{hs} (due to reduced p_{rg}^c) causes p_{hs} to fall, while a similar decrease in S_{hs} (due to increased p_{rg}^f) results in increased p_{hs}, when the demand effect dominates the supply effect so that $\left|\Delta p_{rg}^c\right| > \dfrac{\mu - \lambda}{\delta - \gamma} \Delta p_{rg}^f$, the price of the substitute product falls after the introduction of the output subsidy in the market for the regulated product (Scenario I), while when the supply effect of the subsidy dominates the demand effect (i.e., when $\left|\Delta p_{rg}^c\right| < \dfrac{\mu - \lambda}{\delta - \gamma} \Delta p_{rg}^f \Rightarrow \Delta p_{rg}^f > \dfrac{\delta - \gamma}{\mu - \lambda}\left|\Delta p_{rg}^c\right|$), the subsidization of the regulated product causes the price of the substitute product to increase (Scenario II). Panels 1 and 2 of Figure III.1.4 graph the effects of the output subsidy on the market of the substitute product under these two scenarios.

panel 1: Scenario I   *panel 2:* Scenario II

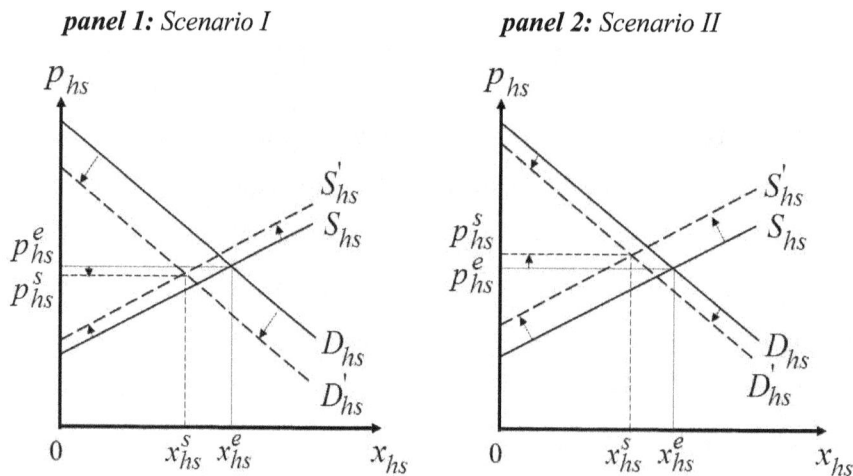

Figure III.1.4. Effects of the Output Subsidy on the Market for the Substitute *hs* Product

Since the equilibrium price of the substitute product affects the welfare of both consumers and producers of this product, our analysis considers the system-wide market and welfare impacts of the output subsidy under both possible effects on the price of the substitute product. The case where the introduction of the output subsidy in the market of the regulated product causes the price of its substitute product to fall (i.e., the case in which the demand effect dominates the supply effect of the subsidy) is analyzed first followed by the case in which the price of the substitute increases as the result of the policy.

Market and Welfare Effects of the Output Subsidy under Scenario I

(i.e., when $\left| \Delta p_{rg}^{c} \right| > \dfrac{\mu - \lambda}{\delta - \gamma} \Delta p_{rg}^{f}$ ***)***

As mentioned previously, when the demand effect dominates the supply effect on the market for the substitute product, the introduction of the output subsidy for the regulated product reduces both the quantity and the price of its substitute product.

The reduced price of the substitute product, p_{hs}, increases the utility associated with its consumption and reduces the number of consumers switching to the regulated product. Figure III.1.5 depicts these market and welfare effects in the consumer utility space. In addition, the figure shows that the consumers benefiting the most from the output subsidy are those consuming the regulated product both before and after the introduction of the policy (i.e., consumers with $\alpha \in (\alpha_{ls}^{e}, \alpha_{rg}^{e}]$), followed by consumers who find it optimal to switch to the regulated product (i.e., consumers with $\alpha \in (\alpha_{ls}^{s}, \alpha_{ls}^{e}]$ and $\alpha \in (\alpha_{rg}^{e}, \alpha_{rg}^{s'}]$) and consumers who continue to consume the substitute after the policy introduction (i.e., consumers with $\alpha \in (\alpha_{rg}^{s'}, 1]$). Total consumer benefits are given

by $G_{c} = \displaystyle\int_{\alpha_{ls}^{s}}^{\alpha_{ls}^{e}} (U_{rg}^{s} - U_{ls}) d\alpha + \int_{\alpha_{ls}^{e}}^{\alpha_{rg}^{e}} (U_{rg}^{s} - U_{rg}) d\alpha + \int_{\alpha_{rg}^{e}}^{\alpha_{rg}^{s'}} (U_{rg}^{s} - U_{hs}) d\alpha + \int_{\alpha_{rg}^{s'}}^{1} (U_{hs}^{s} - U_{hs}) d\alpha$.

Consumer Utility

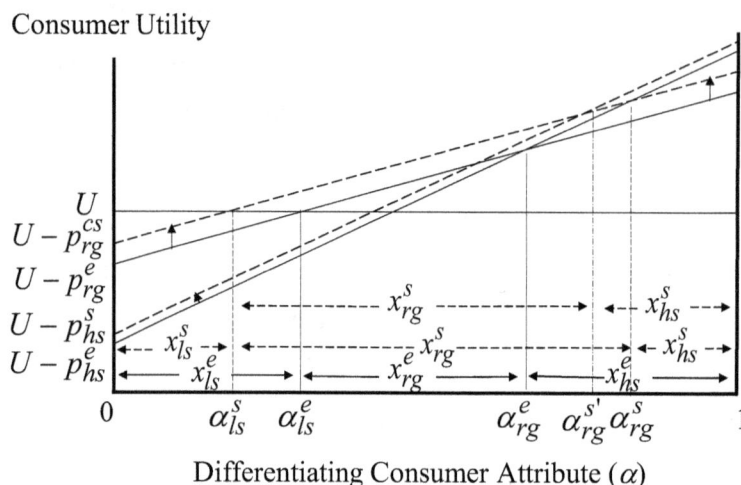

Figure III.1.5. Total Effects of Output Subsidy on Consumption Decisions and Welfare under Scenario I

While increasing the desirability of the substitute product for consumers, the reduced p_{hs} reduces the net returns associated with the production of the substitute product and increases the incentives for switching to the production of the regulated product (see equation (III.1.12)). Figure III.1.6 depicts these market and welfare effects as well as the asymmetric impacts of the policy on producer welfare in the producer net returns space. Producers benefiting the most from the output subsidy are those producing the regulated product both before and after the introduction of the policy (i.e., producers with $A \in (A_{hs}^e, A_{rg}^e])$, followed by producers who find it optimal to switch to the regulated product from the alternative crop (i.e., producers with $A \in (A_{rg}^e, A_{rg}^s])$. Producers who continue to produce the substitute product after the policy introduction (i.e., producers with $A \in (0, A_{hs}^{s'}])$ lose, as do some of the substitute product producers who switch to the regulated product (i.e., producers with $A \in (A_{hs}^{s'}, A_{hs}^s))$, with the magnitude of this loss determined by the differentiating attribute of these producers. The producer gains and losses are given by

$$G_p = \int\limits_{A_{hs}^s}^{A_{hs}^e} (NR_{rg}^s - NR_{hs})dA + \int\limits_{A_{hs}^e}^{A_{rg}^e} (NR_{rg}^s - NR_{rg})dA + \int\limits_{A_{rg}^e}^{A_{rg}^s} (NR_{rg}^s - NR_a)dA \text{ and}$$

$$L_p = \int\limits_{0}^{A_{hs}^{s'}} (NR_{hs} - NR_{hs}^s)dA + \int\limits_{A_{hs}^{s'}}^{A_{hs}^s} (NR_{hs} - NR_{rg}^s)dA \text{ , respectively.}$$

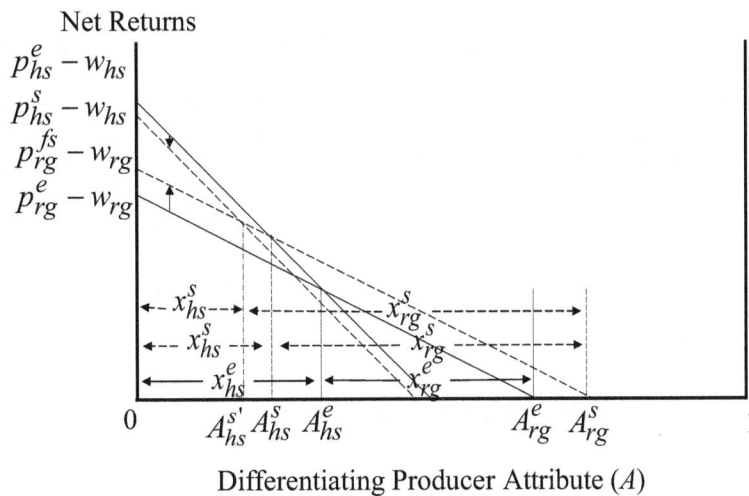

Figure III.1.6. Total Effects of Output Subsidy on Producer Decisions and Welfare under Scenario I

Market and Welfare Effects of the Output Subsidy under Scenario II (i.e., when $\left|\Delta p_{rg}^c\right| < \frac{\mu - \lambda}{\delta - \gamma}\Delta p_{rg}^f$)

When the supply effect of an output subsidy dominates its demand effect on the market for the substitute product, the introduction of the output subsidy for the regulated product reduces the quantity *but* increases the price of its substitute product (recall panel 2 of Figure III.1.4 that depicts this scenario in the price-quantity space).

The increased price of the substitute product, p_{hs}, reduces the utility associated with the consumption of this product and further increases the number of consumers that find it optimal to switch to the regulated product (see equation (III.1.12)). Figure III.1.7 depicts these market and welfare effects as well as the asymmetric impacts of the policy on the welfare of consumers in the consumer utility space. Similar to the case where the demand effect of the policy dominates, the consumers benefiting the most from the output subsidy are those consuming the regulated product both before and after the introduction of the policy (i.e., consumers with $\alpha \in (\alpha_{ls}^e, \alpha_{rg}^e]$). Unlike the case of the dominant demand effect, however, all consumers of the substitute product in the presence of the policy (i.e., consumers with $\alpha \in (\alpha_{rg}^{s'}, 1]$) as well as some consumers that find it optimal to switch from the substitute product to the regulated good (i.e., consumers with $\alpha \in (\alpha_{rg}^s, \alpha_{rg}^{s'}]$ in Figure III.1.7) lose from the introduction of the policy, with the magnitude of their loss determined by their preference parameter α. The consumer gains and losses in this case are given by

$$G_c = \int_{\alpha_{ls}^s}^{\alpha_{ls}^e} (U_{rg}^s - U_{ls}) d\alpha + \int_{\alpha_{ls}^e}^{\alpha_{rg}^e} (U_{rg}^s - U_{rg}) d\alpha + \int_{\alpha_{rg}^e}^{\alpha_{rg}^s} (U_{rg}^s - U_{hs}) d\alpha \text{ and}$$

$$L_c = \int_{\alpha_{rg}^s}^{\alpha_{rg}^{s'}} (U_{hs} - U_{rg}^s) d\alpha + \int_{\alpha_{rg}^{s'}}^{1} (U_{hs} - U_{hs}^s) d\alpha \text{, respectively.}$$

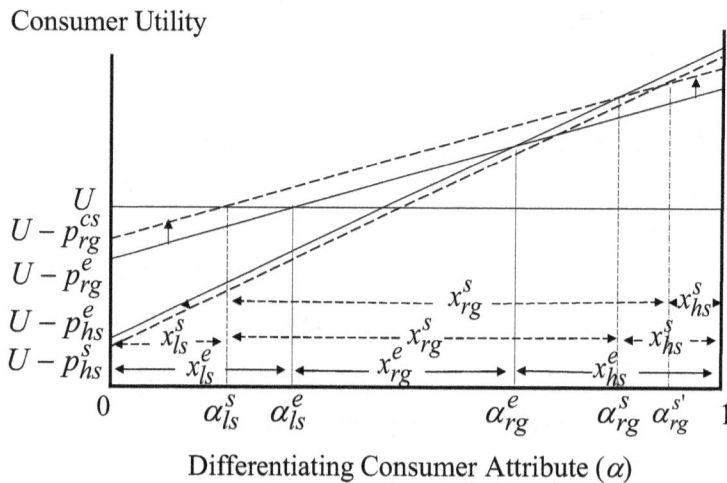

Figure III.1.7. Total Effects of Output Subsidy on Consumption Decisions and Welfare under Scenario II

While decreasing the desirability of the substitute product for consumers, the increased p_{hs} increases the net returns associated with the production of the substitute product and reduces the incentives for switching to the production of the regulated product. Figure III.1.8 depicts these market and welfare effects in the producer net returns space. Producers benefiting the most from the output subsidy are those producing the regulated product both before and after the introduction of the policy (i.e., producers with $A \in (A_{hs}^e, A_{rg}^e]$), followed by producers who find it optimal to switch to the regulated product (i.e., producers with $A \in (A_{rg}^e, A_{rg}^s]$ and $A \in (A_{hs}^{s'}, A_{hs}^e]$) and producers who continue to produce the substitute after the policy introduction (i.e., producers with $A \in (0, A_{hs}^{s'}]$). Total producer benefits when $\left| \Delta p_{rg}^c \right| < \dfrac{\mu - \lambda}{\delta - \gamma} \Delta p_{rg}^f$ are given by

$$G_p = \int_0^{A_{hs}^{s'}} (NR_{hs}^s - NR_{hs}) dA + \int_{A_{hs}^{s'}}^{A_{hs}^e} (NR_{rg}^s - NR_{hs}) dA + \int_{A_{hs}^e}^{A_{rg}^e} (NR_{rg}^s - NR_{rg}) dA + \int_{A_{rg}^e}^{A_{rg}^s} (NR_{rg}^s - NR_a) dA \; .$$

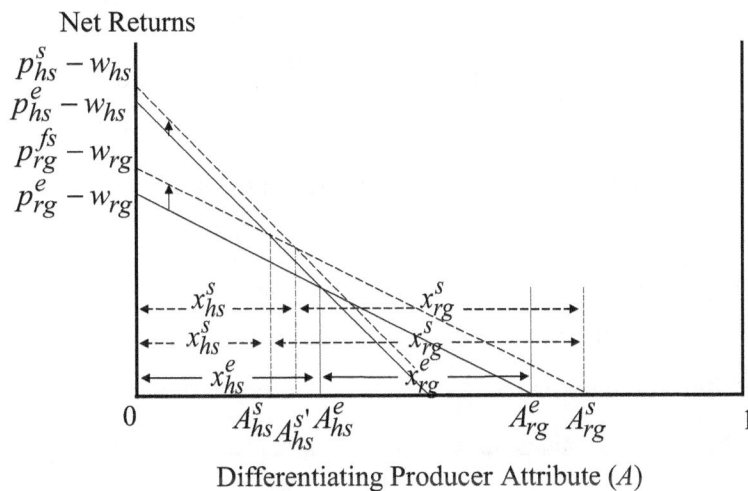

Figure III.1.8. Total Effects of Output Subsidy on Producer Decisions and Welfare under Scenario II

In addition to affecting the decisions and welfare of consumers and producers of the substitute product, the changes in p_{hs} have a feedback effect on the market for the regulated product. In particular, a reduction (increase) in p_{hs} reduces (increases) the demand and increases (reduces) the supply of the regulated product (see equations (I.8), (I.9), (I.18), (I.19) and Figures I.3 and I.5). The total effects of the output subsidy on the final consumer market for the regulated product under the two scenarios considered here are depicted in panels 1 and 2 of Figure III.1.9.

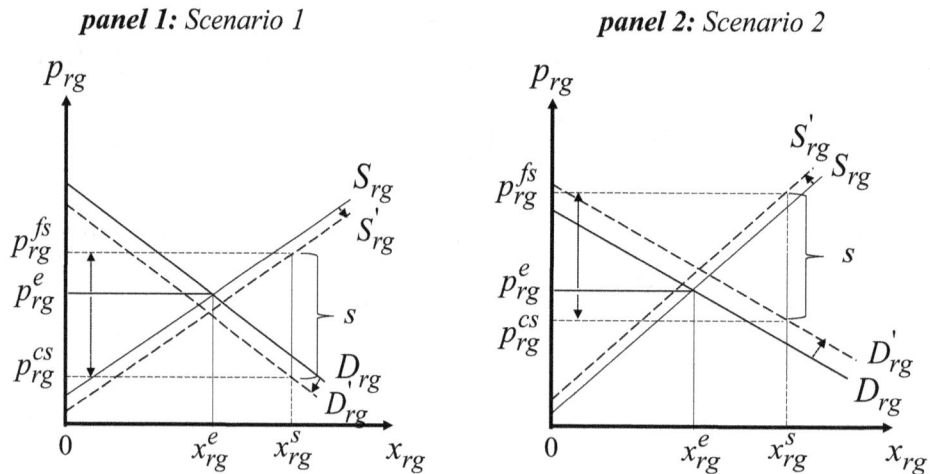

panel 1: *Scenario 1*   **panel 2:** *Scenario 2*

Figure III.1.9. Overall Effects of an Output Subsidy on the *rg* Market

Finally, regarding the impact of the output subsidy on the markets for the inputs used in the production of the regulated product and its substitute, no matter the relative magnitude of its demand and supply effects on the market for the substitute product (and its effect on p_{hs}), the introduction of an output subsidy in the market for the regulated product increases the demand for inputs used in the production of the regulated product (so that the increased production of this product in the presence of the subsidy can be facilitated) and reduces the demand for inputs used in the production of the substitute product (see equations (III.1.12) and (III.1.13)). The effects of the subsidy on the input markets are depicted in Figure III.1.10.

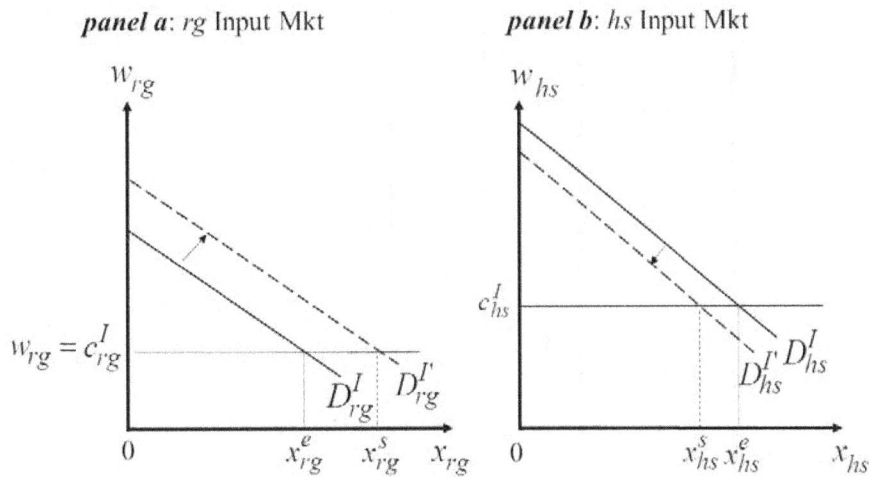

Figure III.1.10. Output Subsidy Impact on the Input Markets

Overall, the analysis of the system-wide market and welfare effects of the output subsidy
indicates that: (a) the qualitative nature of the welfare effects on the consumers and
producers of the substitute product is scenario-specific and depends on the conditions in
the market for both the regulated product and the substitute product; (b) the impacts of
the output subsidy are asymmetric across the different consumers and producers affected
by the policy; (c) determination of these asymmetric impacts requires a disaggregation of
the benefits and costs to the level of the individual agent; and (d) some of the producers
(Scenario I) or some of the consumers (Scenario II) who find it optimal to switch from
the substitute product to the regulated good after the introduction of the subsidy realize
welfare losses.

The asymmetric impact of the policy on the welfare of all relevant interest groups
is summarized in Table III.1.1, while Figures III.1.11 and III.1.12 summarize the system-
wide market and welfare impacts of the output subsidy under the two scenarios
considered in this study.

Table III.1.1. System-Wide Welfare Impacts of an Output Subsidy

	Consumers of ls switching to rg	Consumers of rg	Consumers of hs switching to rg	Consumers of hs	Producers of rg	Producers of hs switching to rg	Producers of hs	Suppliers of rg	Suppliers of hs	Input Suppliers rg	Input Suppliers hs
Scenario I	+	+	+	+	+	some – some +	–	nc	nc	nc	nc
Scenario II	+	+	some + some –	–	+	+	+	nc	nc	nc	nc

+ denotes welfare gains
– denotes welfare losses
nc denotes no change

Condition for Scenario I: $\left|\Delta p_{rg}^c\right| > \dfrac{\mu - \lambda}{\delta - \gamma}\,\Delta p_{rg}^f$

Condition for Scenario II: $\left|\Delta p_{rg}^c\right| < \dfrac{\mu - \lambda}{\delta - \gamma}\,\Delta p_{rg}^f$

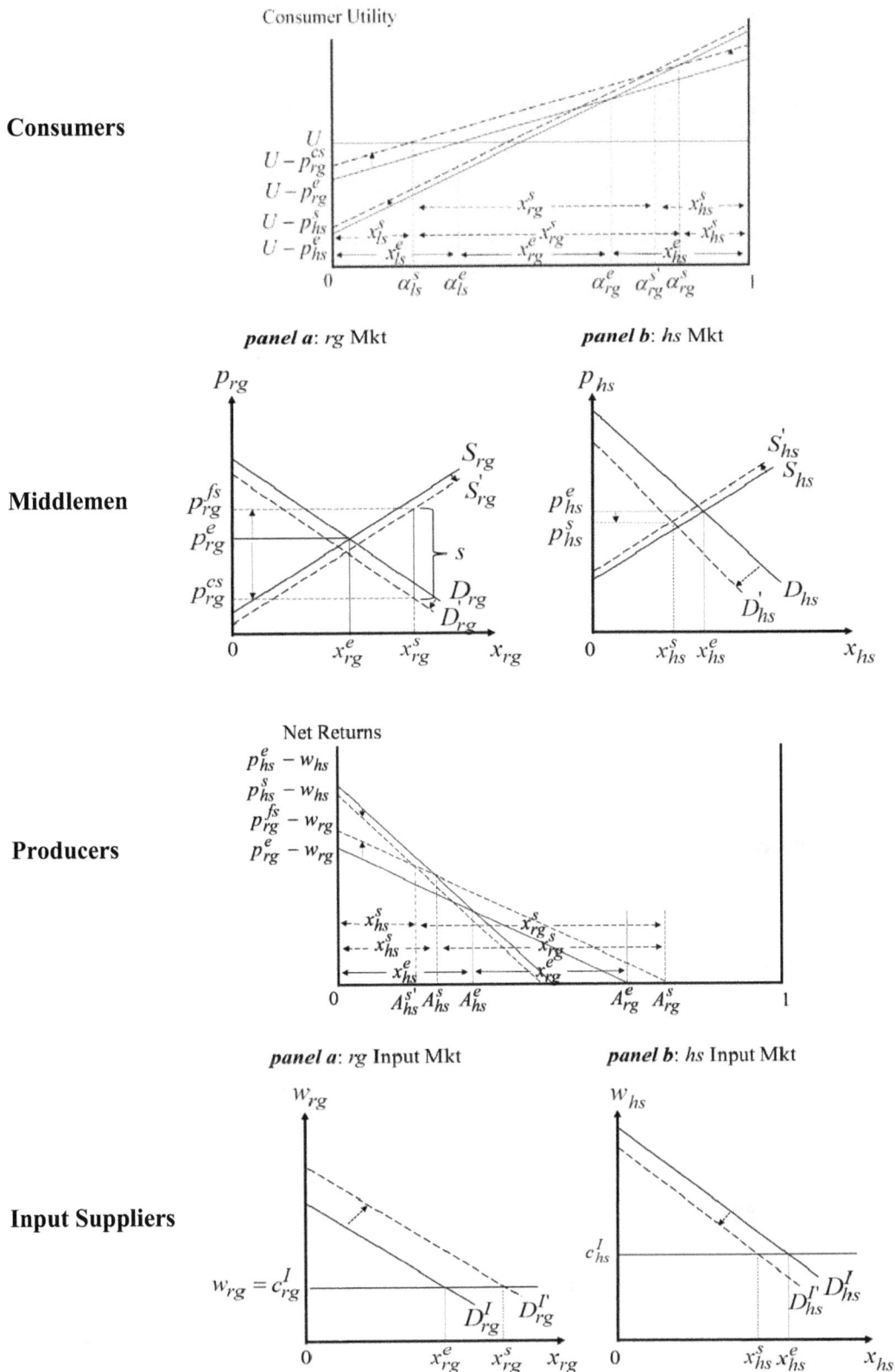

Figure III.1.11. System-Wide Market and Welfare Impacts of an Output Subsidy under Scenario I

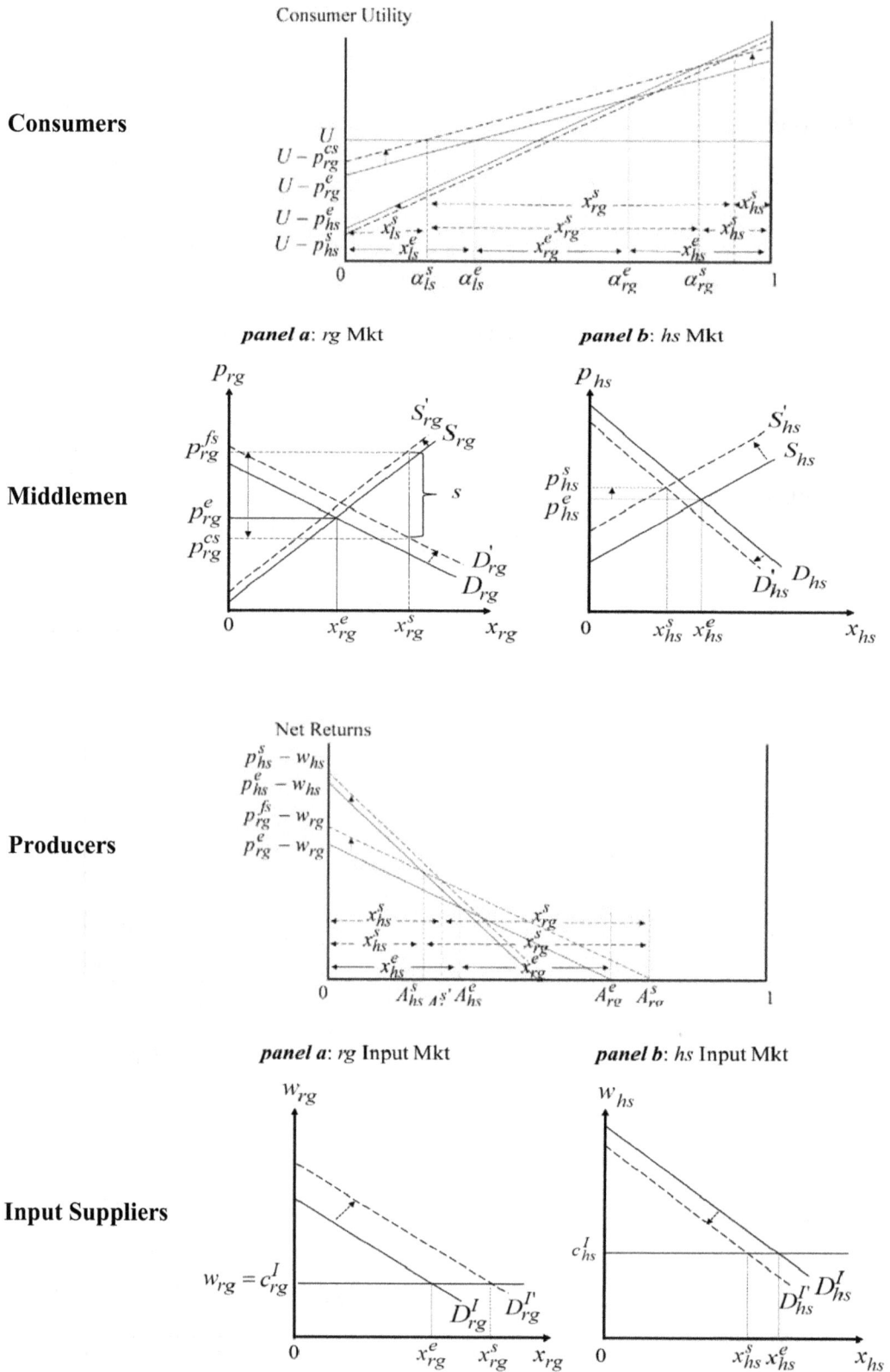

Figure III.1.12. System-Wide Market and Welfare Impacts of an Output Subsidy under Scenario II

Disaggregation of Welfare Changes and Comparison with Conventional Analysis

Before concluding the analysis of this policy, it is important to note that the key findings outlined above are important because they indicate that a proper accounting of the differential welfare impacts of an output subsidy requires a disaggregated analysis, as some of the consumers (Scenario II) or some of the producers (Scenario I) of the substitute product realize welfare losses after they have optimally switched to the regulated good. While, as was pointed out earlier, the aggregate welfare changes can be determined using the calculation of producer and consumer surplus from the supply and demand curves, the allocation of the welfare changes to the two markets is incorrect.

Following the same approach developed in the analysis of the reduced c_{rg}^{I} in Section II.4 (as in both cases the changes in the consumer prices of the different products are qualitatively the same), it can be shown that, similar to the case of reduced c_{rg}^{I} Scenario I, allocating the cost and benefits according to the demand curves in each market overstates the benefits to those that originally consumed the regulated product and overstates the costs to those that originally consumed the substitute product (i.e., overstates both the gain in the regulated market and the loss in the substitute market). In short, the calculation of consumer surplus from the demand curves does not provide a proper allocation of the costs and benefits to the various consumer groups. While these overstated amounts cancel each other out at the aggregate level, they yield incorrect results if they are used to determine the distributional impacts of an output subsidy.

The need to disaggregate the consumer surplus measures is clearly important in Scenario II, since in this scenario some consumers gain and others lose from the introduction of the output subsidy. However, if it is believed that the magnitude of the gain realized by consumers is also important, then disaggregating the gains that occur in Scenario I may also be required as the effects of the subsidy were shown to vary among consumers. The same conclusions, of course, can be drawn regarding the need to disaggregate producer welfare. In this case, there is a clear need to disaggregate producer welfare in Scenario I, since in this case some of the producers that switch to the regulated good will be worse off than they were originally in producing the substitute product.

There may also be a need to disaggregate the changes in producer welfare in Scenario II, since, as was shown in the previous sections, the welfare changes are not symmetric among producers.

III.2. Consumption Tax under Imperfect Competition

Similar to the output subsidy case, to determine the system-wide market and welfare impacts of a consumption tax, we compare and contrast the equilibrium prices, quantities, and welfare of the interest groups involved before and after the introduction of the tax. With the pre-tax equilibrium conditions derived in Section I (and graphed in Figure I.9), our focus here is on the (system-wide) equilibrium conditions under the tax. Once the effects of the tax on the market where it is introduced have been determined (i.e., the final consumer market for the regulated product), we proceed in discussing the impacts of the policy on the vertically, horizontally and diagonally related markets and interest groups involved (i.e., consumers, producers, middlemen and input suppliers in the supply channels of the regulated and substitute products).

Equilibrium Conditions under a Consumption Tax

The introduction of a consumption tax for a product creates a difference/margin between the price paid by consumers and the price actually received by the suppliers of this product; the difference being the unit tax, t. With the demand curve depicting the consumer valuation of (and maximum willingness to pay for) a product, a tax can be viewed/conceptualized as creating a difference between the maximum consumer willingness to pay for (different units of) a product and the maximum price suppliers can charge for (the different units of) this product. Graphically, the tax t can be depicted as creating an inward parallel shift of the demand schedule faced by the suppliers of the product (and a difference between the actual consumer demand D_{rg} and the demand curve faced by the product suppliers, D_{rg}').

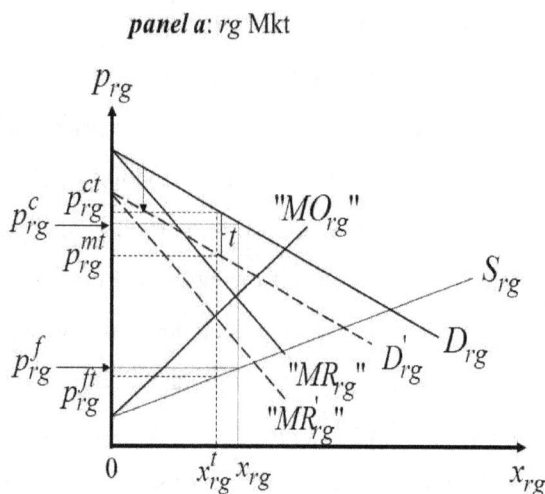

panel a: *rg* Mkt

Figure II.2.1. Consumption Tax under Imperfect Competition (Monempory/Oligempory)

As shown in Figure III.2.1 above, the introduction of a consumption tax results in (a) increased consumer price of the regulated product (compare the consumer price before and after the tax, p_{rg}^{c} and p_{rg}^{ct}, respectively); (b) reduced supplier/middlemen price (compare p_{rg}^{c} and p_{rg}^{mt}); (c) reduced price received by the producers of the regulated product (compare p_{rg}^{f} and p_{rg}^{ft}); and (d) reduced equilibrium quantity of the regulated product (compare x_{rg} and x_{rg}^{t}). Consumers, middlemen and producers of the regulated product lose while taxpayers receive the tax revenues on the equilibrium quantity under the tax regime.

In addition to affecting the market for the regulated product, the introduction of the tax has an effect on the vertically, horizontally and diagonally related markets and our integrated framework of analysis can help identify the system-wide market and welfare impacts of this policy. Indeed, the equilibrium conditions/ market reaction functions in the presence of the tax become:

$$p_{rg}^{ct} = \frac{\frac{\lambda}{\mu} p_{hs}^{ct} \left[\theta_{rg}^s \frac{\lambda(\mu-\lambda)}{\mu} + (1+\theta_{rg}^b) \frac{\gamma(\delta-\gamma)}{\delta} \right] + \frac{\lambda(\mu-\lambda)}{\mu} \left[t + w_{rg} + \frac{\gamma}{\delta}(p_{hs}^{ft} - w_{hs}) \right]}{(1+\theta_{rg}^s) \frac{\lambda(\mu-\lambda)}{\mu} + (1+\theta_{rg}^b) \frac{\gamma(\delta-\gamma)}{\delta}} \qquad \text{(III.2.1)}$$

$$p_{rg}^{mt} = \frac{\left(\frac{\lambda}{\mu} p_{hs}^{ct} - t \right) \left[\theta_{rg}^s \frac{\lambda(\mu-\lambda)}{\mu} + (1+\theta_{rg}^b) \frac{\gamma(\delta-\gamma)}{\delta} \right] + \frac{\lambda(\mu-\lambda)}{\mu} \left[w_{rg} + \frac{\gamma}{\delta}(p_{hs}^{ft} - w_{hs}) \right]}{(1+\theta_{rg}^s) \frac{\lambda(\mu-\lambda)}{\mu} + (1+\theta_{rg}^b) \frac{\gamma(\delta-\gamma)}{\delta}} \qquad \text{(III.2.2)}$$

$$p_{rg}^{ft} = \frac{\left[w_{rg} + \frac{\gamma}{\delta}(p_{hs}^{ft} - w_{hs}) \right] \left[(1+\theta_{rg}^s) \frac{\lambda(\mu-\lambda)}{\mu} + \theta_{rg}^b \frac{\gamma(\delta-\gamma)}{\delta} \right] + \frac{\gamma(\delta-\gamma)}{\delta} \left(\frac{\lambda}{\mu} p_{hs}^{ct} - t \right)}{(1+\theta_{rg}^s) \frac{\lambda(\mu-\lambda)}{\mu} + (1+\theta_{rg}^b) \frac{\gamma(\delta-\gamma)}{\delta}} \qquad \text{(III.2.3)}$$

$$p_{hs}^{ct} = \frac{(p_{rg}^{ct} + \mu - \lambda) \left[\theta_{hs}^s (\mu-\lambda) + (1+\theta_{hs}^b)(\delta-\gamma) \right] + (\mu-\lambda) \left[w_{hs} + (p_{rg}^{ft} - w_{rg}) \right]}{(1+\theta_{hs}^s)(\mu-\lambda) + (1+\theta_{hs}^b)(\delta-\gamma)} \qquad \text{(III.2.4)}$$

$$p_{hs}^{ft} = \frac{\left[w_{hs} + (p_{rg}^{ft} - w_{rg}) \right] \left[(1+\theta_{hs}^s)(\mu-\lambda) + \theta_{hs}^b (\delta-\gamma) \right] + (\delta-\gamma)(p_{rg}^{ct} + \mu - \lambda)}{(1+\theta_{hs}^s)(\mu-\lambda) + (1+\theta_{hs}^b)(\delta-\gamma)} \qquad \text{(III.2.5)}$$

$$w_{rg} = \frac{\theta_{rg}^I \left[p_{rg}^{ft} - \frac{\gamma}{\delta}(p_{hs}^{ft} - w_{hs}) \right] + c_{rg}^I}{(1+\theta_{rg}^I)} \qquad \text{(III.2.6)}$$

$$w_{hs} = \frac{\theta_{hs}^I \left[p_{hs}^{ft} - (p_{rg}^{ft} - w_{rg}) \right] + c_{hs}^I}{(1+\theta_{hs}^I)} \qquad \text{(III.2.7)}$$

$$x_{rg}^t = \frac{\frac{\lambda}{\mu} p_{hs}^c - t - \left[w_{rg} + \frac{\gamma}{\delta}(p_{hs}^f - w_{hs}) \right]}{(1+\theta_{rg}^s) \frac{\lambda(\mu-\lambda)}{\mu} + (1+\theta_{rg}^b) \frac{\gamma(\delta-\gamma)}{\delta}} \qquad \text{(III.2.8)}$$

$$x_{hs}^t = \frac{p_{rg}^c + \mu - \lambda - \left[w_{hs} + (p_{rg}^f - w_{rg}) \right]}{(1+\theta_{hs}^s)(\mu-\lambda) + (1+\theta_{hs}^b)(\delta-\gamma)} \qquad \text{(III.2.9)}$$

As mentioned earlier, solving the equations for the equilibrium prices simultaneously allows the expression of the output and input prices as functions of the exogenous variables of the model (i.e., tax, preference, market power and cost parameters).

Substituting these prices into the expressions for the equilibrium quantities, firm profits, consumer welfare and producer net returns enables the expression of all equilibrium conditions as functions of the exogenous variables of the model. The nature of the interdependence of markets captured by these expressions provides, along with the related graphical representation, valuable insights on the mechanism through which the policy affects the different vertically, horizontally, and diagonally related markets. The section below discusses the market and welfare impacts of the consumption tax using the integrated heterogeneous agent framework presented in Section I.

System-Wide Market and Welfare Effects of a Consumption Tax

The analysis in this part focuses on the impact of the tax on the input and output markets for the regulated product and its substitute, as well as its effects on the welfare of all interest groups involved (i.e., consumers, producers, middlemen and input suppliers in the markets for the two products). In addition to determining changes in aggregate consumer and producer welfare, our integrated heterogeneous agent framework enables us to (a) determine the effects of the tax on different consumers and producers of the two products and (b) capture indirect and feedback effects of the policy that are not accounted for when focusing solely on the market of the regulated product.

Beginning with the *direct consumer effects* of the tax, we see that the increase in the consumer price of the regulated/taxed product (a) reduces the utility associated with the consumption of this product and (b) drives consumers of the regulated product to substitute products. Graphically, the increase in p_{rg}^c causes a downward parallel shift of U_{rg} and the exit of consumers with differentiating attributes $\alpha \in (\alpha_{ls}, \alpha_{ls}^t]$ and $\alpha \in (\alpha_{rg}^t, \alpha_{rg}]$ in Figure III.2.2 from the market for the regulated product.

Consumer Utility

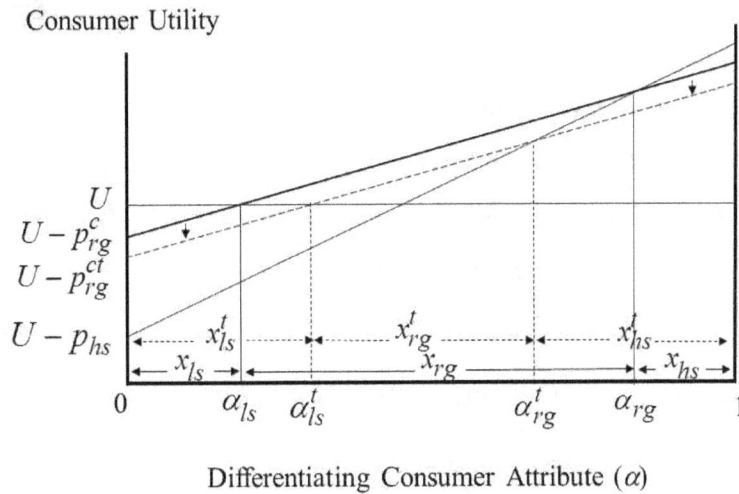

Differentiating Consumer Attribute (α)

Figure III.2.2. Direct Effects of the Tax on Consumption Decisions and Welfare

Similar to consumers, the introduction of the tax hurts the producers of the regulated product and results in a number of them switching to alternative crops. Graphically, the reduced p_{rg}^{f} causes an downward parallel shift of the net returns curve associated with the production of the regulated product and the switching of producers with $A \in (A_{hs}, A_{hs}^{t}]$ and $A \in (A_{rg}^{t}, A_{rg}]$ in Figure III.2.3 to alternative products.

Net Returns

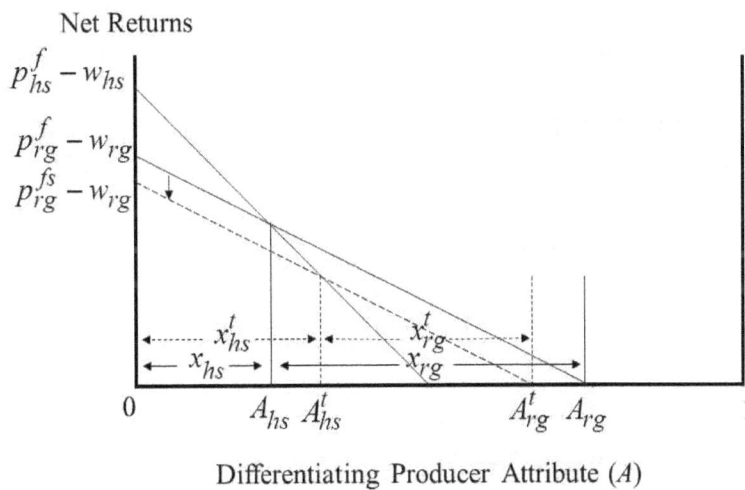

Differentiating Producer Attribute (A)

Figure II.2.3. Direct Effects of the Tax on Producer Decisions and Welfare

As expected, in addition to affecting the market for the regulated product, the changes in the consumer and producer prices of the regulated product caused by the tax have a direct impact on the market for the substitute product. The increased consumer price and the reduced producer price of the regulated product in the presence of the tax drive a number of consumers and producers out of the market for the regulated product affecting, this way, both the demand for and supply of the substitute product.

Formally, the increased p_{rg}^c causes an upward parallel shift of the demand for the substitute product, D_{hs} (see equation (I.9) and Figure III.2.4), while the reduced p_{rg}^f causes a downward parallel shift of the supply of the substitute product, S_{hs} (see equation (I.19) and Figure III.2.4). While the increased demand for, and supply of the substitute product always increase the equilibrium quantity and profits of the suppliers of this product, the effect on the equilibrium consumer and producer prices (p_{hs}^c and p_{hs}^f, respectively) is determined by the relative magnitude of the demand and supply effects of the tax on the market for the substitute product. In particular, since a *ceteris paribus* increase in D_{hs} causes p_{hs}^c and p_{hs}^f to increase, while a similar increase in S_{hs} results in reduced p_{hs}^c and p_{hs}^f, when the demand effect dominates the supply effect so that

$$\Delta p_{rg}^c > \frac{(1+\theta_{hs}^s)(\mu-\lambda)+\theta_{hs}^b(\delta-\gamma)}{\delta-\gamma}\left[-\Delta p_{rg}^f+\Delta w_{rg}-\Delta w_{hs}\right] \text{ (where, as noted above,}$$

$\Delta p_{rg}^c > 0$ and $\Delta p_{rg}^f < 0$, while, as shown in Figure III.2.11 below, $\Delta w_{rg} < 0$ and $\Delta w_{hs} > 0$), the consumer and producer prices of the substitute product increase after the introduction of the tax (Scenario I); when

$$\frac{\mu-\lambda}{\theta_{hs}^s(\mu-\lambda)+(1+\theta_{hs}^b)(\delta-\gamma)}\left[-\Delta p_{rg}^f+\Delta w_{rg}-\Delta w_{hs}\right]<\Delta p_{rg}^c<$$
$$<\frac{(1+\theta_{hs}^s)(\mu-\lambda)+\theta_{hs}^b(\delta-\gamma)}{\delta-\gamma}\left[-\Delta p_{rg}^f+\Delta w_{rg}-\Delta w_{hs}\right]$$

the consumer price of the substitute product increases while the producer price falls (Scenario II); while when the supply effect of the tax dominates the demand effect so that

$$\Delta p^c_{rg} < \frac{\mu - \lambda}{\theta^s_{hs}(\mu - \lambda) + (1 + \theta^b_{hs})(\delta - \gamma)}\left[-\Delta p^f_{rg} + \Delta w_{rg} - \Delta w_{hs}\right], \text{ the taxation of the regulated}$$

product causes the consumer and producer prices of the substitute product to fall
(Scenario III). Figure III.2.4 provides a graphical representation of the conditions leading
to the three scenarios while panels 1, 2 and 3 of Figure III.2.5 graph the effects of the tax
on the market of the substitute product under these three scenarios.

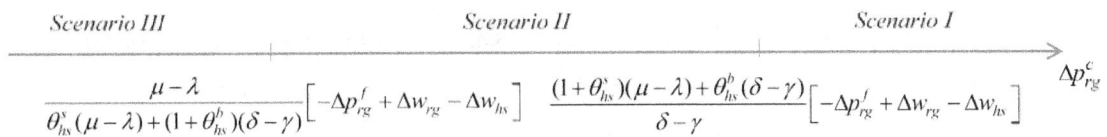

Figure II.2.4. Scenarios on the Effects of the Tax on Prices of the Substitute *hs* Product

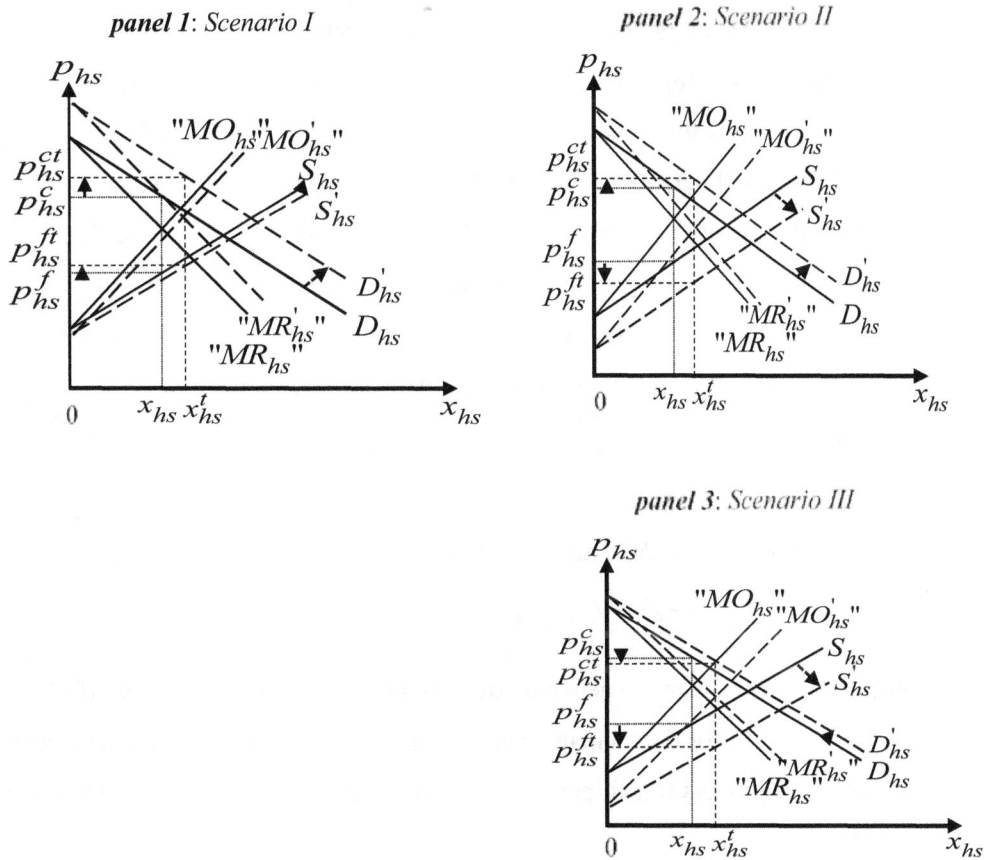

Figure III.2.5. Effects of the Tax on the Market for the Substitute *hs* Product

It is important to note that for Scenario II to occur, the middlemen in the substitute product market should be able to exercise market power. If $\theta_{hs}^s = \theta_{hs}^b = 0$, the condition for Scenario I becomes $\Delta p_{rg}^c > \dfrac{\mu - \lambda}{\delta - \gamma}\left[-\Delta p_{rg}^f + \Delta w_{rg} - \Delta w_{hs}\right]$ and the condition for

Scenario III becomes $\Delta p_{rg}^c < \dfrac{\mu - \lambda}{\delta - \gamma}\left[-\Delta p_{rg}^f + \Delta w_{rg} - \Delta w_{hs}\right]$. Intuitively, under perfectly competitive middlemen in the substitute product market, the consumer and producer prices of this product will always move in the same direction. While the presence of middlemen market power is necessary for the consumer and producer prices of the substitute product to move in different directions, it is not sufficient for the emergence of Scenario II – as shown above, both Scenarios I and III can emerge in the presence of middlemen market power.

Since the equilibrium prices of the substitute product affect the welfare of the consumers and producers of this product, our analysis considers the market and welfare impacts of the tax under the three scenarios outlined above. The case where the introduction of the tax in the market of the regulated product causes the consumer and producer prices of its substitute to increase (i.e., the case in which the demand effect dominates the supply effect of the tax) is analyzed first followed by the other two scenarios considered here. In all cases, suppliers of the substitute product see their profits increase after the introduction of the tax, with the change in profits given by

$$\Delta\Pi_{hs} = (p_{hs}^{ct} - p_{hs}^c)x_{hs} + (p_{hs}^{ct} - p_{hs}^{ft})(x_{hs}^t - x_{hs}) - (p_{hs}^{ft} - p_{hs}^f)x_{hs} > 0.$$

Market and Welfare Effects of the Tax under Scenario I

(i.e., when $\Delta p_{rg}^c > \dfrac{(1 + \theta_{hs}^s)(\mu - \lambda) + \theta_{hs}^b(\delta - \gamma)}{\delta - \gamma}\left[-\Delta p_{rg}^f + \Delta w_{rg} - \Delta w_{hs}\right]$)

As mentioned previously, when the demand effect of a tax dominates its supply effect, the introduction of the tax for the regulated product increases the consumer and producer prices of its substitute product (recall panel 1 of Figure III.2.5 that depicts this scenario in the price-quantity space).

The increased consumer price of the substitute product, p_{hs}^c, reduces the utility associated with the consumption of this product and limits the number of consumers of the regulated product switching to the substitute product. Figure III.2.6 depicts these market and welfare effects in the consumer utility space. In addition, the figure shows that the consumers hurt the most from the tax are those consuming the regulated product both before and after the introduction of the policy (i.e., consumers with $\alpha \in (\alpha_{ls}^t, \alpha_{rg}^{t'}]$), followed by consumers who find it optimal to turn away from the regulated product (i.e., consumers with $\alpha \in (\alpha_{rg}^{t'}, \alpha_{rg}]$ and $\alpha \in (\alpha_{ls}, \alpha_{ls}^t]$), and consumers who consume the substitute before and after the policy introduction (i.e., consumers with $\alpha \in (\alpha_{rg}, 1]$). Total consumer losses from the tax are given by

$$L_c = \int_{\alpha_{ls}}^{\alpha_{ls}^t} (U_{rg} - U_{ls}) d\alpha + \int_{\alpha_{ls}^t}^{\alpha_{rg}^{t'}} (U_{rg} - U_{rg}^t) d\alpha + \int_{\alpha_{rg}^{t'}}^{\alpha_{rg}} (U_{rg} - U_{hs}^t) d\alpha + \int_{\alpha_{rg}}^{1} (U_{hs} - U_{hs}^t) d\alpha .$$

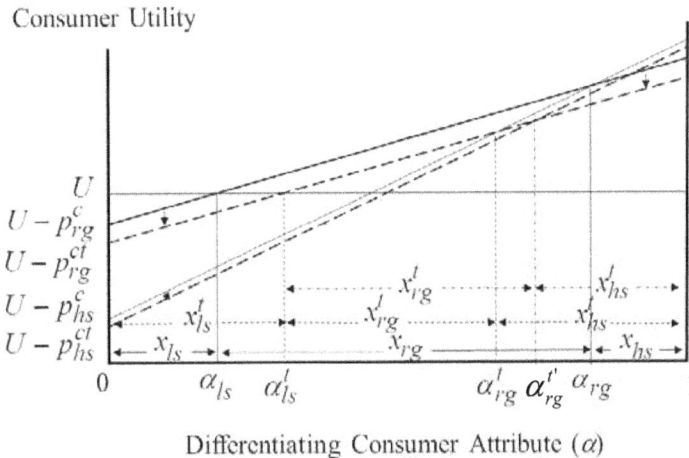

Figure III.2.6. Total Effects of the Tax on Consumption Decisions and Welfare under Scenarios I & II

While the increased p_{hs}^c reduces the desirability of the substitute product for consumers, the increased p_{hs}^f increases the net returns associated with the production of the substitute product and, thus, increases the incentives for switching to the production of this product. Figure III.2.7 depicts these market and welfare effects as well as the asymmetric impacts of the policy in the producer net returns space. Producers losing the most from the tax are those producing the regulated product both before and after the introduction of the policy (i.e., producers with $A \in (A_{hs}^t, A_{rg}^t]$), followed by producers who find it optimal to switch from the regulated product to the alternative crop (i.e., producers with $A \in (A_{rg}^t, A_{rg}]$), and the producers with $A \in (A_{hs}^{t'}, A_{hs}^t]$) who switch from the regulated product to the substitute.

Producers who produce the substitute before and after the policy introduction (i.e., producers with $A \in [0, A_{hs}]$) gain, as do some of the regulated product producers who switch to the substitute (i.e., producers with $A \in (A_{hs}, A_{hs}^{t'})$), with the magnitude of this gain determined by the efficiency parameter/differentiating attribute of these producers. Producer gains and losses in this case are given by

$$G_p = \int_0^{A_{hs}} (NR_{hs}^{t'} - NR_{hs})dA + \int_{A_{hs}}^{A_{hs}^{t'}} (NR_{hs}^{t'} - NR_{rg})dA \text{ and}$$

$$L_p = \int_{A_{hs}^{t'}}^{A_{hs}^t} (NR_{rg} - NR_{hs}^{t'})dA + \int_{A_{hs}^t}^{A_{rg}^t} (NR_{rg} - NR_{rg}^{t'})dA + \int_{A_{rg}^t}^{A_{rg}} (NR_{rg} - NR_a)dA, \text{ respectively.}$$

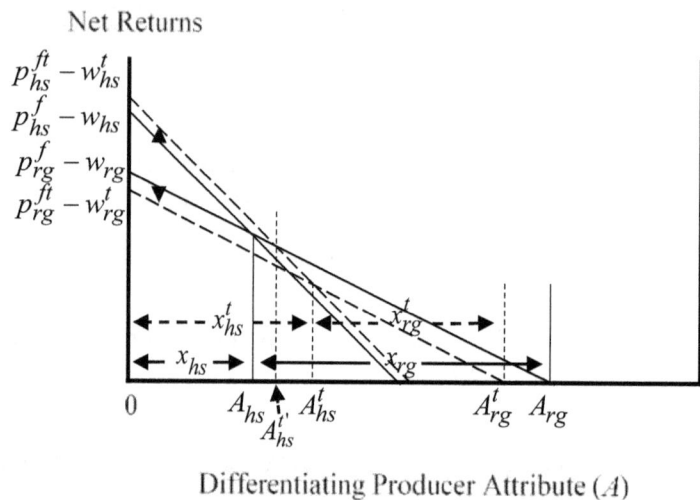

Figure II.2.7. Total Effects of the Tax on Producer Decisions and Welfare under Scenario I

Market and Welfare Effects of the Tax under Scenario II (i.e., when

$$\frac{\mu - \lambda}{\theta_{hs}^s(\mu - \lambda) + (1 + \theta_{hs}^b)(\delta - \gamma)} \left[-\Delta p_{rg}^f + \Delta w_{rg} - \Delta w_{hs} \right] < \Delta p_{rg}^c <$$

$$< \frac{(1 + \theta_{hs}^s)(\mu - \lambda) + \theta_{hs}^b(\delta - \gamma)}{\delta - \gamma} \left[-\Delta p_{rg}^f + \Delta w_{rg} - \Delta w_{hs} \right])$$

As shown in panel 2 of Figure III.2.5, under Scenario II the consumer price of the substitute product increases while the producer price falls causing both consumers and producers of this product to lose.

Predictably, the ramifications of the policy for the consumers of the different products are similar to those under Scenario I (described in the previous section and graphed in Figure III.2.6), as p_{hs}^c increases under both Scenarios I and II. Thus, the tax under Scenario II hurts all regulated and substitute product consumers with the greater losses incurred by those consumers who buy the regulated product both before and after the introduction of the tax.

Unlike Scenario I, producers of the substitute product lose under Scenario II as the introduction of a tax for the regulated product causes the producer price of the substitute product, p_{hs}^f, to fall. The reduced p_{hs}^f reduces the net returns associated with the production of this product and limits the number of producers who find it optimal to switch to the substitute product after the introduction of the tax (recall that the reduction in the price received by the producers of the regulated product creates incentives for a number of them to switch to the substitute and alternative crops; see Figure III.2.3).

Figure III.2.8 depicts these market and welfare effects in the producer net returns space. In addition, the figure shows that the producers losing the most from the tax are those producing the regulated product both before and after the introduction of the policy (i.e., producers with $A \in (A_{hs}^t, A_{rg}^t]$), followed by producers who switch from the regulated to the alternative and substitute crops (i.e., producers with $A \in (A_{rg}^t, A_{rg}]$ and $A \in (A_{hs}, A_{hs}^t]$), and producers who continue to produce the substitute product after the policy introduction (i.e., producers with $A \in [0, A_{hs}]$). Total producer losses from the tax in this case are given by

$$L_p = \int\limits_{0}^{A_{hs}} (NR_{hs} - NR_{hs}^t)dA + \int\limits_{A_{hs}^t}^{A_{hs}^t} (NR_{rg} - NR_{hs}^t)dA + \int\limits_{A_{hs}^t}^{A_{rg}^t} (NR_{rg} - NR_{rg}^t)dA + \int\limits_{A_{rg}^t}^{A_{rg}} (NR_{rg} - NR_a)dA$$

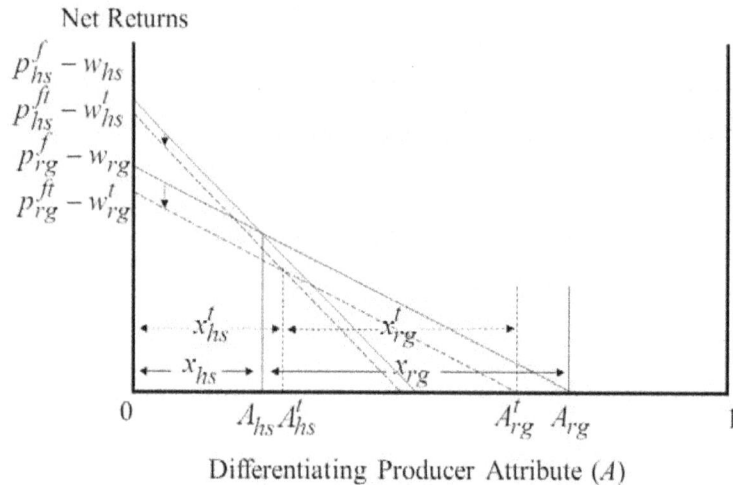

Figure III.2.8. Total Effects of the Tax on Producer Decisions and Welfare under Scenarios II and III

Market and Welfare Effects of the Tax under Scenario III

(i.e., when $\Delta p_{rg}^c < \dfrac{\mu - \lambda}{\theta_{hs}^s (\mu - \lambda) + (1 + \theta_{hs}^b)(\delta - \gamma)} \left[-\Delta p_{rg}^f + \Delta w_{rg} - \Delta w_{hs} \right]$**)**

When the supply effect of the tax dominates the demand effect, the taxation of the regulated product causes the consumer and producer prices of the substitute good to fall. While the effects of the reduced p_{hs}^f on producer decisions and welfare are similar to those under Scenario II (described in the previous section and graphed in Figure III.2.8), the effects of the tax on consumers are different than those under Scenarios I and II.

Specifically, the reduced p_{hs}^c increases the utility associated with the consumption of the substitute product and increases the number of consumers switching from the regulated product. Figure III.2.9 depicts these market and welfare effects as well as the asymmetric impacts of the tax on consumer welfare in the consumer utility space. Similar to Scenarios I and II, consumers losing the most from the tax are those consuming the regulated product both before and after the introduction of the policy (i.e., consumers with $\alpha \in (\alpha_{ls}^t, \alpha_{rg}^t]$), followed by consumers who find it optimal to turn away

from the regulated product (i.e., consumers with $\alpha \in (\alpha_{rg}^t, \alpha_{rg}^{t'}]$ and $\alpha \in (\alpha_{ls}, \alpha_{ls}^t]$).

Unlike Scenarios I and II, however, consumers who prefer the substitute product before

and after the policy introduction (i.e., consumers with $\alpha \in (\alpha_{rg}, 1]$) gain, as do some of

the regulated product consumers who switch to the substitute (i.e., consumers with

$\alpha \in (\alpha_{rg}^{t'}, \alpha_{rg}]$), with the magnitude of this gain determined by the differentiating

attribute of these consumers. Consumer gains and losses in this case are given by

$$G_c = \int_{\alpha_{rg}^{t'}}^{\alpha_{rg}} (U_{hs}^t - U_{rg}) d\alpha + \int_{\alpha_{rg}}^{1} (U_{hs}^t - U_{hs}) d\alpha \text{ and}$$

$$L_c = \int_{\alpha_{ls}}^{\alpha_{ls}^t} (U_{rg} - U_{ls}) d\alpha + \int_{\alpha_{ls}^t}^{\alpha_{rg}^t} (U_{rg} - U_{rg}^t) d\alpha + \int_{\alpha_{ls}^t}^{\alpha_{rg}^{t'}} (U_{rg} - U_{hs}^t) d\alpha \text{, respectively.}$$

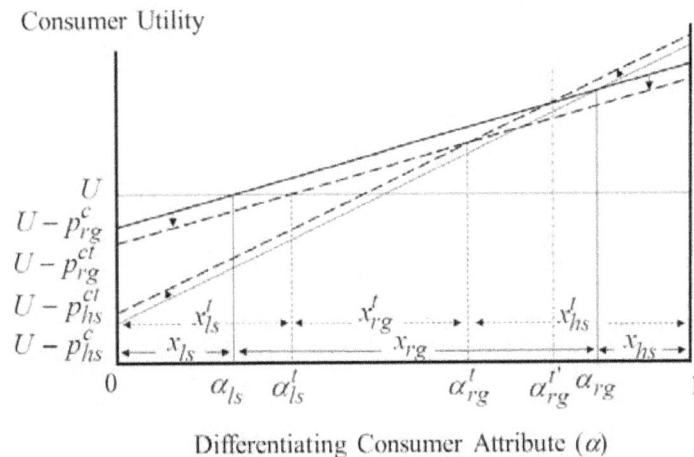

Figure III.2.9. Total Effects of the Tax on Consumption Decisions and Welfare
under Scenario III

In addition to affecting the decisions and welfare of consumers and producers of the

substitute product, the changes in p_{hs}^c and p_{hs}^f have a feedback effect on the market for

the regulated product. In particular, an increase (decrease) in p_{hs}^c shifts the demand for the regulated product D_{rg} upwards (downwards), while an increase (decrease) in p_{hs}^f

causes an upward (downward) shift of the supply of the regulated product S_{rg} (recall

equations (I.8) and (I.18) and Figures I.3 and I.5). The total effects of the tax on the final

consumer market for the regulated product under the three scenarios considered here are

depicted in panels 1-3 of Figure III.2.10. In all cases, the policy causes a reduction in the

regulated product supplier profits, with the change in profits given by

$$\Delta\Pi_{rg} = (p_{rg}^c - p_{rg}^{mt})x_{rg}^t + (p_{rg}^c - p_{rg}^f)(x_{rg} - x_{rg}^t) - (p_{rg}^f - p_{rg}^{ft})x_{rg}^t > 0.$$

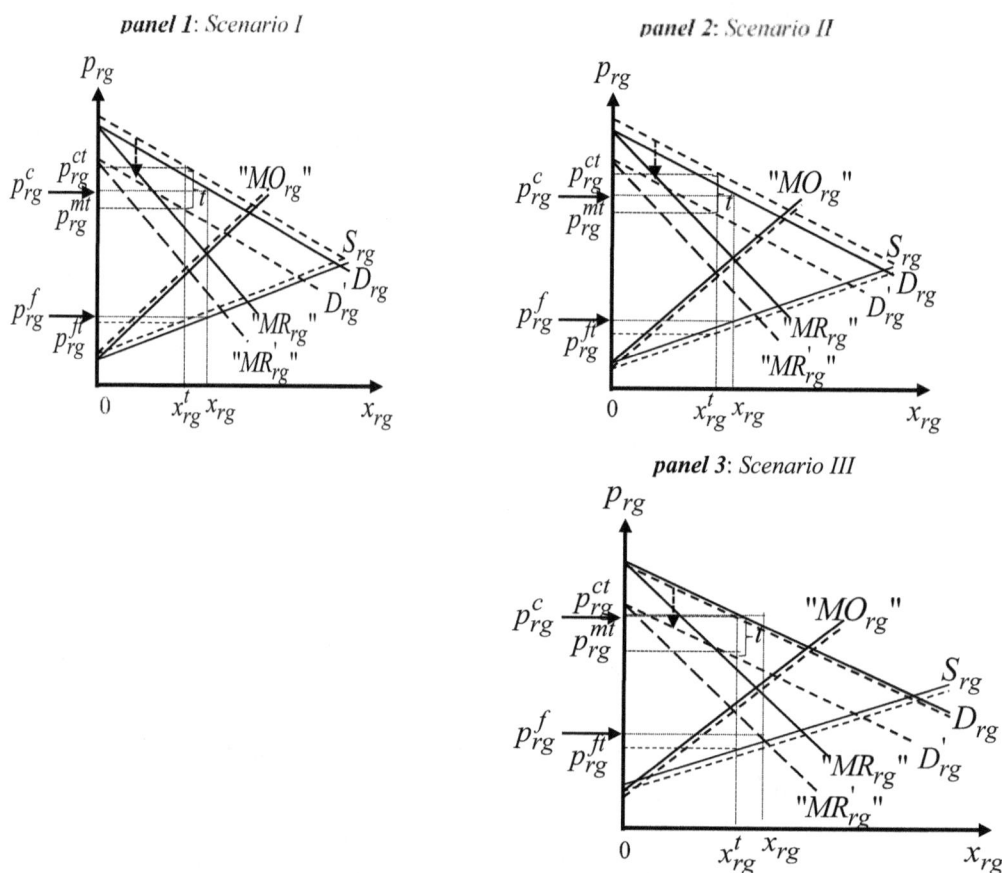

Figure III.2.10. Overall Impact of the Tax on the *rg* Market

Finally, regarding the impact of the tax on the markets for the inputs used in the production of the regulated product and its substitute, no matter the effect of the policy on p_{hs}^c and p_{hs}^f, the introduction of a tax in the market for the regulated product reduces the demand for inputs used in the production of this product (as the equilibrium quantity of the regulated product falls in the presence of the tax; see equation (III.2.8)) and increases the demand for inputs used in the production of the substitute (so that the increased production of this product in the presence of the tax can be facilitated).

The reduced equilibrium price and quantity of the inputs used in the production of the regulated product result in reduced profits for the suppliers of these inputs, while the increased price and quantity of the inputs used in the production of the substitute increase the profits of the suppliers of these inputs. The change in the profits of the rg input suppliers is given by $\Delta\Pi_{rg}^I = -\left[(w_{rg} - c_{rg}^I)x_{rg} - (w_{rg}^t - c_{rg}^I)x_{rg}^t \right] < 0$, while the change in the profits of the hs input suppliers is $\Delta\Pi_{hs}^I = (w_{hs}^t - c_{hs}^I)x_{hs}^t - (w_{hs} - c_{hs}^I)x_{hs} > 0$. The market and welfare effects of the tax on the input markets are depicted in Figure III.2.11.

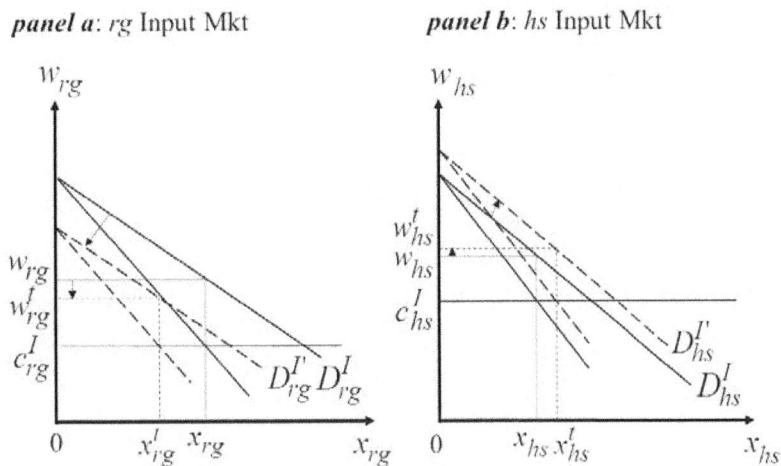

Figure III.2.11. Tax Impact on the Input Markets

Overall, the analysis of the system-wide market and welfare effects of the consumption tax indicates that: (a) the qualitative nature of the welfare effects on the consumers and producers of the substitute product is scenario-specific and depends on the conditions in the market for both the regulated product and the substitute product; (b) the impacts of the consumption tax are asymmetric across the different consumers and producers affected by the policy; (c) determination of these asymmetric impacts requires a disaggregation of the benefits and costs to the level of the individual agent; and (d) in Scenarios I and III, some of the consumers (Scenario III) or some of the producers (Scenario I) who find it optimal to switch from the regulated product to its substitute after the introduction of the consumption tax realize welfare gains.

Table III.2.1 summarizes the asymmetric effects of the policy on the welfare of all relevant interest groups, while Figures III.2.12-III.2.14 summarize the system-wide market and welfare impacts of the tax under the different scenarios considered in this study. For simplicity, the feedback effect on the rg market (depicted in Figure III.2.10) is not included in Figures III.2.12-III.2.14.

Table III.2.1. System-Wide Welfare Impacts of a Consumption Tax

	Consumers of rg switching to ls	Consumers of rg	Consumers of rg switching to hs	Consumers of hs	Producers of rg	Producers of rg switching to hs	Producers of hs	Suppliers of rg	Suppliers of hs	Input Suppliers rg	Input Suppliers hs
Scenario I	−	−	−	−	−	some + some −	+	−	+	−	+
Scenario II	−	−	−	−	−	−	−	−	+	−	+
Scenario III	−	−	some − some +	+	−	−	−	−	+	−	+

+ denotes welfare gains
− denotes welfare losses

Condition for Scenario I: $\Delta p_{rg}^c > \dfrac{(1+\theta_{hs}^s)(\mu-\lambda)+\theta_{hs}^b(\delta-\gamma)}{\delta-\gamma}\left[-\Delta p_{rg}^f + \Delta w_{rg} - \Delta w_{hs}\right]$

Condition for Scenario II: $\dfrac{\mu-\lambda}{\theta_{hs}^s(\mu-\lambda)+(1+\theta_{hs}^b)(\delta-\gamma)}\left[-\Delta p_{rg}^f + \Delta w_{rg} - \Delta w_{hs}\right] < \Delta p_{rg}^c < \dfrac{(1+\theta_{hs}^s)(\mu-\lambda)+\theta_{hs}^b(\delta-\gamma)}{\delta-\gamma}\left[-\Delta p_{rg}^f + \Delta w_{rg} - \Delta w_{hs}\right]$

Condition for Scenario III: $\Delta p_{rg}^c < \dfrac{\mu-\lambda}{\theta_{hs}^s(\mu-\lambda)+(1+\theta_{hs}^b)(\delta-\gamma)}\left[-\Delta p_{rg}^f + \Delta w_{rg} - \Delta w_{hs}\right]$

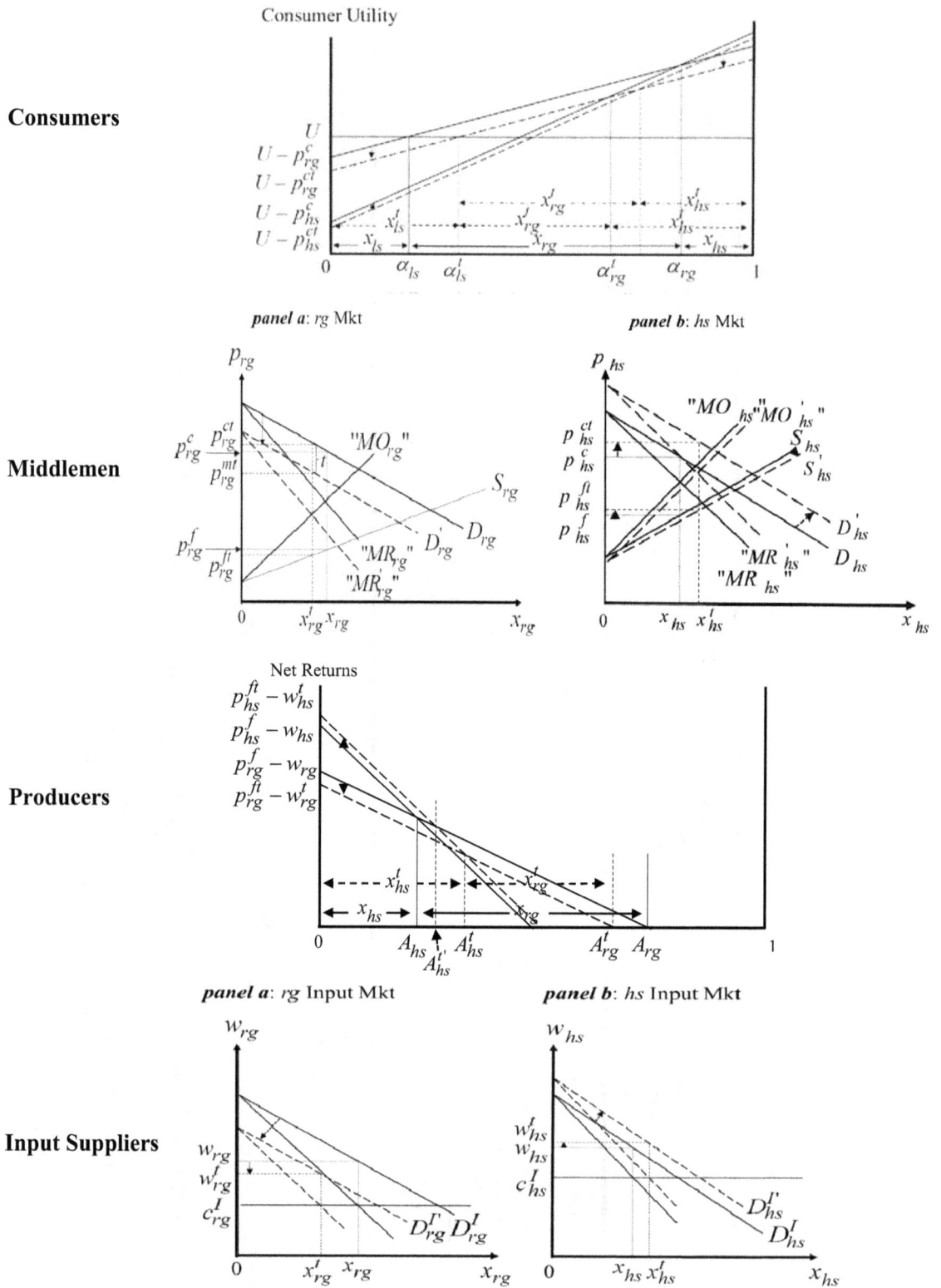

Figure III.2.12. System-Wide Market and Welfare Impacts of a Consumption Tax under Scenario I

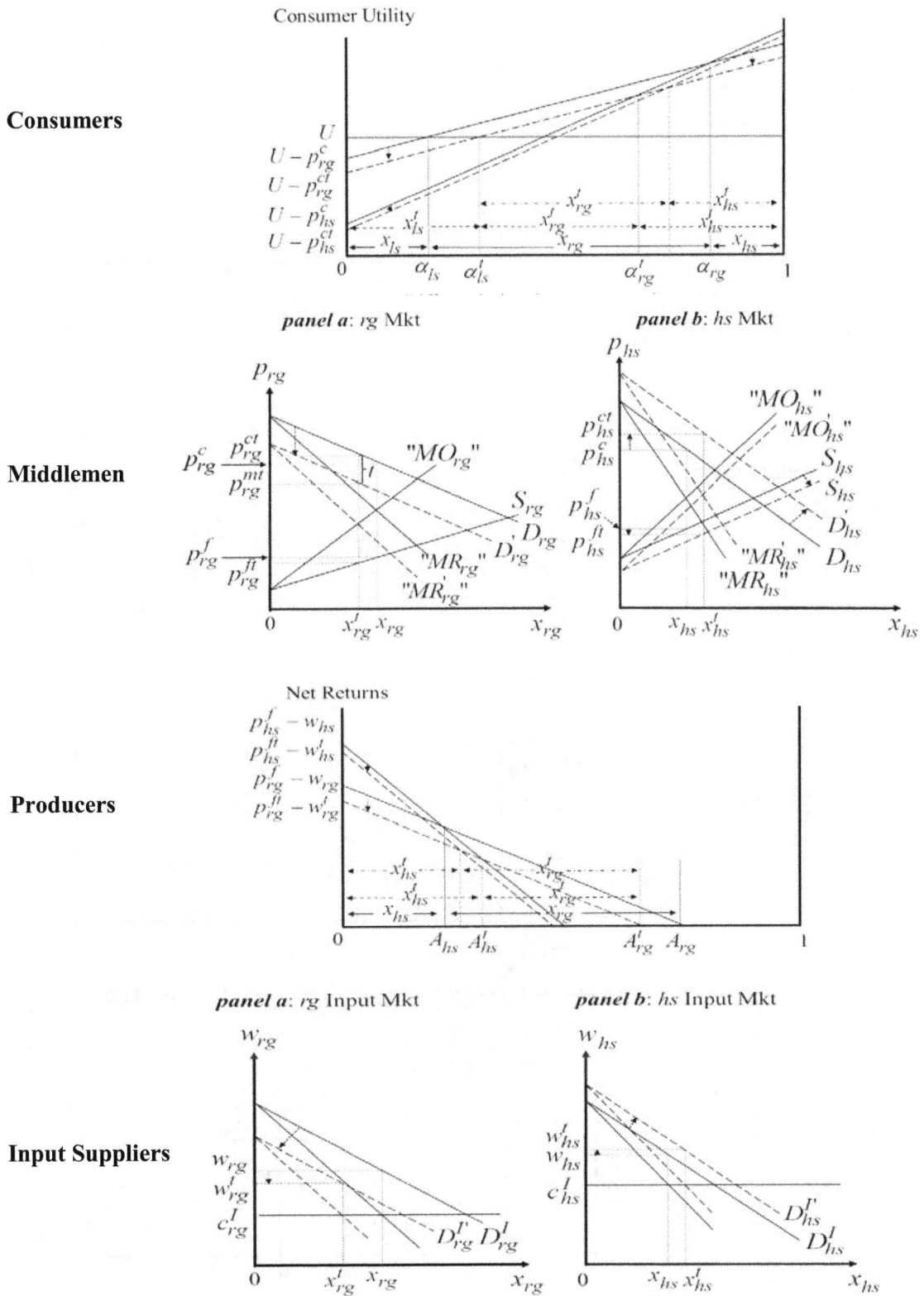

Figure III.2.13. System-Wide Market and Welfare Impacts of a Consumption Tax under Scenario II

Consumer Utility

Consumers

U
$U - p_{rg}^{c}$
$U - p_{rg}^{ct}$
$U - p_{hs}^{ct}$
$U - p_{hs}^{c}$

x_{ls}^{t} x_{rg}^{t} x_{hs}^{t}
x_{ls} x_{rg} x_{hs}

0   α_{ls} α_{ls}^{t} $\alpha_{rg}^{t} \alpha_{rg}$ 1

panel a: rg Mkt   *panel 2*: hs Mkt

Middlemen

p_{rg}

p_{rg}^{c} p_{rg}^{ct}
p_{rg}^{mt}
"MO_{rg}"
S_{rg}
p_{rg}^{f}
p_{rg}^{ft}
"MR_{rg}"
"$MR_{rg}^{'}$"
$D_{rg}^{'}$ D_{rg}

0   $x_{rg}^{t} x_{rg}$ x_{rg}

p_{hs}

"MO_{hs}""$MO_{hs}^{'}$"
p_{hs}^{c}
p_{hs}^{ct}
S_{hs}
S_{hs}
p_{hs}^{f}
p_{hs}^{ft}
"$MR_{hs}^{'}$" $D_{hs}^{'}$
"MR_{hs}" D_{hs}

0   $x_{hs} x_{hs}^{t}$ x_{hs}

Net Returns

Producers

$p_{hs}^{f} - w_{hs}$
$p_{hs}^{ft} - w_{hs}^{t}$
$p_{rg}^{f} - w_{rg}$
$p_{rg}^{ft} - w_{rg}^{t}$

x_{hs}^{t} x_{rg}^{t}
x_{hs} x_{rg}

0   $A_{hs} A_{hs}^{t}$ $A_{rg}^{t} A_{rg}$ 1

panel a: rg Input Mkt   *panel b*: hs Input Mkt

Input Suppliers

w_{rg}

w_{rg}
w_{rg}^{t}
c_{rg}^{I}
$D_{rg}^{I'} D_{rg}^{I}$

0   $x_{rg}^{t} x_{rg}$ x_{rg}

w_{hs}

w_{hs}^{t}
w_{hs}
c_{hs}^{I}
$D_{hs}^{I'}$
D_{hs}^{I}

0   $x_{hs} x_{hs}^{t}$ x_{hs}

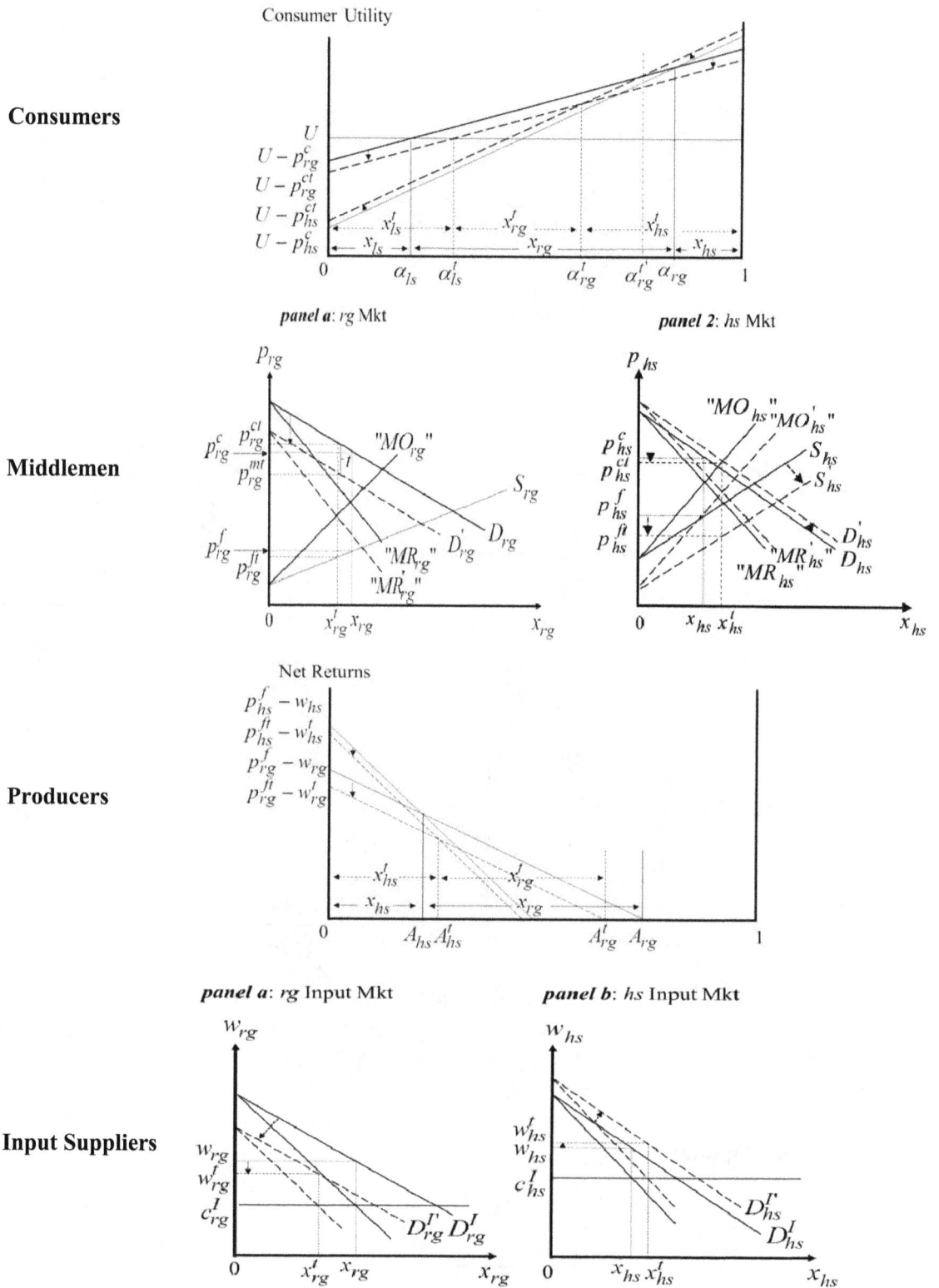

Figure III.2.14. System-Wide Market and Welfare Impacts of a Consumption Tax under Scenario III

Disaggregation of Welfare Changes and Comparison with Conventional Analysis

Before concluding the analysis of this policy, it is important to note that the key findings of this section outlined above are important because they indicate that a proper accounting of the differential welfare impacts of a tax requires a disaggregated analysis, particularly in Scenarios I and III where some of the consumers (Scenario III) or some of the producers (Scenario I) of the regulated product realize welfare gains after they have optimally switched. While, as was pointed out earlier, the aggregate welfare changes can be determined using the calculation of producer and consumer surplus from the supply and demand curves, the allocation of the welfare changes to the two markets is incorrect.

Following the same approach developed in the analysis of the increased θ_{rg} in Section II.2 (as in both cases the changes in the consumer and producer prices of the different products are qualitatively the same), it can be shown that, similar to the case of increased θ_{rg} Scenario III, allocating the costs and benefits according to the demand curves in each market overstates the benefits to those that originally consumed the substitute product and overstates the costs to those that originally consumed the regulated product (i.e., overstates both the loss in the regulated market and the gain in the substitute market). In short, the calculation of consumer surplus from the demand curves does not provide a proper allocation of the costs and benefits of the tax to the various consumer groups. While these overstated amounts cancel each other out at the aggregate level, they yield incorrect results if they are used to determine the distributional impacts of a tax.

The need to disaggregate the consumer surplus measures is clearly important in Scenario III, since in this scenario some consumers gain and others lose from the introduction of a tax. However, if it is believed that the magnitude of the loss felt by consumers is also important (as would be the case if consumers exhibit loss aversion, for instance), then disaggregating the losses that occur in Scenarios I and II may also be required as the effects of the policy were shown to vary among consumers. The same conclusions, of course, can be drawn regarding the need to disaggregate producer welfare. In this case, there is a clear need to disaggregate producer welfare in Scenario I, since in this case the producer price of the substitute good rises and some of the producers that switch to producing the substitute good will be better off than they were originally in producing the regulated product. There may also be a need to disaggregate the changes in producer welfare in Scenarios II and III, since as was shown in the previous sections, the welfare changes are not symmetric among producers.

III.3. Input Subsidy under Imperfect Competition

To determine the system-wide market and welfare impacts of the input subsidy, we compare and contrast the equilibrium prices, quantities, and welfare of the interest groups involved before and after the introduction of the subsidy. With the pre-subsidy equilibrium conditions derived in Section I (and graphed in Figure I.9), our focus here is on the (system-wide) equilibrium conditions under the input subsidy. Once the effects of the input subsidy on the market where it is introduced have been determined (i.e., the input market for the regulated product), we proceed in discussing the impacts of the policy on the vertically, horizontally and diagonally related markets and interest groups involved (i.e., consumers, producers, middlemen and input suppliers in the supply channels of the regulated and its substitute products). Before proceeding with the analysis, it is important to note that, while focusing on input subsidies, the analysis presented below is more general and applies to all input cost-reducing government policies (such as energy and/or R&D subsidies, and public R&D).

Equilibrium Conditions under an Input Subsidy

The introduction of a unit subsidy s in an input market reduces the costs faced by the suppliers of this input by the amount of the subsidy. The lower costs result, then, in a reduction in the price of the input that is dependent on the degree of market power exercised by the suppliers of the regulated input. Graphically, the input subsidy s can be depicted as creating a downward parallel shift of the marginal cost schedule faced by the (imperfectly competitive) suppliers of the regulated input, and a subsequent reduction in the price of this input from w_{rg} to w_{rg}^s in Figure III.3.1.

panel a: rg Input Mkt

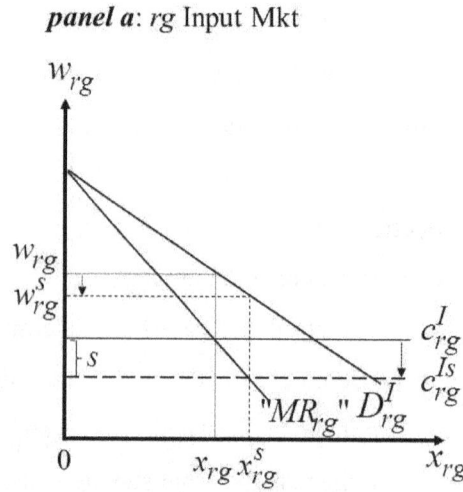

Figure III.3.1. Input Subsidy in an (Imperfectly Competitive) Input Market

In addition to reducing the price of the regulated input, the introduction of an input subsidy results in increased equilibrium quantity (compare x_{rg} and x_{rg}^s in Figure III.3.1) and greater profits for the suppliers of this input (as the cost reduction exceeds the reduction in w_{rg}).

Besides affecting the market for the regulated input, the introduction of the input subsidy has an effect on the vertically, horizontally and diagonally related markets and our integrated framework of analysis can help identify the system-wide market and welfare impacts of this policy. The equilibrium conditions/market reaction functions in the presence of the input subsidy can be derived by introducing the relationship between the costs faced by the input suppliers before and after the subsidy (i.e., $c_{rg}^{Is} = c_{rg}^{I} - s$) in equations (I.24)-(I.31) and are given by:

$$p_{rg}^c = \frac{\lambda}{\mu}\left\{\frac{p_{hs}^c\left[\theta_{rg}^s \frac{\lambda(\mu-\lambda)}{\mu} + (1+\theta_{rg}^b)\frac{\gamma(\delta-\gamma)}{\delta}\right] + (\mu-\lambda)\left[w_{rg} + \frac{\gamma}{\delta}(p_{hs}^f - w_{hs})\right]}{(1+\theta_{rg}^s)\frac{\lambda(\mu-\lambda)}{\mu} + (1+\theta_{rg}^b)\frac{\gamma(\delta-\gamma)}{\delta}}\right\} \quad \text{(III.3.1)}$$

$$p_{rg}^f = \frac{\left[w_{rg} + \frac{\gamma}{\delta}(p_{hs}^f - w_{hs})\right]\left[(1+\theta_{rg}^s)\frac{\lambda(\mu-\lambda)}{\mu} + \theta_{rg}^b\frac{\gamma(\delta-\gamma)}{\delta}\right] + \frac{\lambda\gamma(\delta-\gamma)}{\mu\delta}p_{hs}^c}{(1+\theta_{rg}^s)\frac{\lambda(\mu-\lambda)}{\mu} + (1+\theta_{rg}^b)\frac{\gamma(\delta-\gamma)}{\delta}} \qquad \text{(III.3.2)}$$

$$p_{hs}^c = \frac{(p_{rg}^c + \mu - \lambda)\left[\theta_{hs}^s(\mu-\lambda) + (1+\theta_{hs}^b)(\delta-\gamma)\right] + (\mu-\lambda)\left[w_{hs} + (p_{rg}^f - w_{rg})\right]}{(1+\theta_{hs}^s)(\mu-\lambda) + (1+\theta_{hs}^b)(\delta-\gamma)} \qquad \text{(III.3.3)}$$

$$p_{hs}^f = \frac{\left[w_{hs} + (p_{rg}^f - w_{rg})\right]\left[(1+\theta_{hs}^s)(\mu-\lambda) + \theta_{hs}^b(\delta-\gamma)\right] + (\delta-\gamma)(p_{rg}^c + \mu - \lambda)}{(1+\theta_{hs}^s)(\mu-\lambda) + (1+\theta_{hs}^b)(\delta-\gamma)} \qquad \text{(III.3.4)}$$

$$w_{rg} = \frac{\theta_{rg}^I\left[p_{rg}^f - \frac{\gamma}{\delta}(p_{hs}^f - w_{hs})\right] + c_{rg}^I - s}{(1+\theta_{rg}^I)} \qquad \text{(III.3.5)}$$

$$w_{hs} = \frac{\theta_{hs}^I\left[p_{hs}^f - (p_{rg}^f - w_{rg})\right] + c_{hs}^I}{(1+\theta_{hs}^I)} \qquad \text{(III.3.6)}$$

$$x_{rg} = \frac{\frac{\lambda}{\mu}p_{hs}^c - \left[w_{rg} + \frac{\gamma}{\delta}(p_{hs}^f - w_{hs})\right]}{(1+\theta_{rg}^s)\frac{\lambda(\mu-\lambda)}{\mu} + (1+\theta_{rg}^b)\frac{\gamma(\delta-\gamma)}{\delta}} \qquad \text{(III.3.7)}$$

$$x_{hs} = \frac{p_{rg}^c + \mu - \lambda - \left[w_{hs} + (p_{rg}^f - w_{rg})\right]}{(1+\theta_{hs}^s)(\mu-\lambda) + (1+\theta_{hs}^b)(\delta-\gamma)} \qquad \text{(III.3.8)}$$

As mentioned earlier, solving the equations for the equilibrium prices simultaneously allows the expression of the output and input prices as functions of the exogenous variables of the model (i.e., input subsidy, preference, market power and cost parameters). Substituting these prices into the expressions for the equilibrium quantities, firm profits, consumer welfare and producer net returns enables the expression of all equilibrium conditions as functions of the exogenous variables of the model. The nature of the interdependence of markets captured by these expressions provides, along with the related graphical representation, valuable insights on the mechanism through which the policy affects the different (vertically, horizontally and diagonally related) markets. The rest of this section discusses the market and welfare impacts of the input subsidy using the integrated heterogeneous agent framework developed in this book.

System-Wide Market and Welfare Effects of an Input Subsidy

The analysis in this part focuses on the impact of the input subsidy on the input and output markets for the regulated product and its substitute, as well as its effects on the welfare of all interest groups involved (i.e., consumers, producers, middlemen and input suppliers in the markets for the two products). In addition to determining changes in the aggregate consumer and producer welfare, our integrated heterogeneous agent framework enables us to (a) determine the effects of the input subsidy on different consumers and producers of the two products and (b) capture indirect and feedback effects of the policy that are not accounted for when focusing solely on the market of the regulated input. It turns out that, since the input subsidy reduces the costs of input suppliers, the system-wide market and welfare impacts of the policy are very similar to those of the cost reduction derived and discussed in Section II.4.

Beginning with the *direct producer effects* of the input subsidy, we see that the reduction in the price of the regulated input, w_{rg}, (a) increases the net returns associated with the production of the product utilizing the subsidized input in its production process (regulated product, hereafter), and (b) attracts to the regulated product previous producers of substitute and alternative crops. Graphically, the reduction in w_{rg} causes an upward parallel shift of Π_{rg} and the switching of producers with differentiating attributes $A \in (A_{hs}^{s}, A_{hs}]$ and $A \in (A_{rg}, A_{rg}^{s}]$ in Figure III.3.2 to the regulated product.

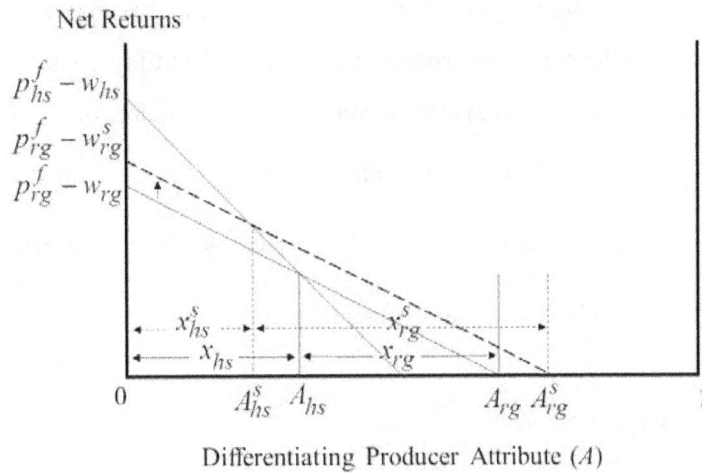

Figure III.3.2. Direct Effects of an Input Subsidy on Producer Decisions

The increased appeal of the regulated product due to its reduced input costs increases the supply of the regulated product and, through this, reduces the consumer and producer prices of this product (see equations (III.3.1), (III.3.2) and (III.3.7)). Figure III.3.3 graphs the downward parallel shift of S_{rg} and consequent increase in x_{rg} and reductions in p_{rg}^c and p_{rg}^f due to the input subsidy.

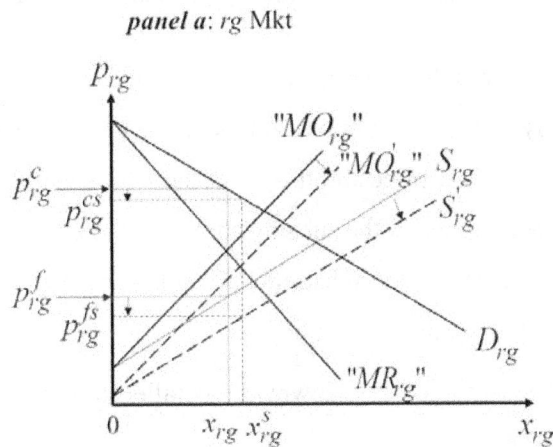

Figure III.3.3. Direct Effects of an Input Subsidy on the Oligemporistic *rg* Market

Moving to the *direct consumer effects* of the input subsidy, we see that the reduction in the consumer price of the regulated product (a) increases the utility associated with the consumption of this product and (b) attracts some of the consumers of substitute products to the regulated product. Graphically, the reduction in p_{rg}^c causes an upward parallel shift of U_{rg} and the switching of consumers with differentiating attributes $\alpha \in (\alpha_{ls}^s, \alpha_{ls}]$ and $\alpha \in (\alpha_{rg}, \alpha_{rg}^s]$ in Figure III.3.4 to the regulated product.

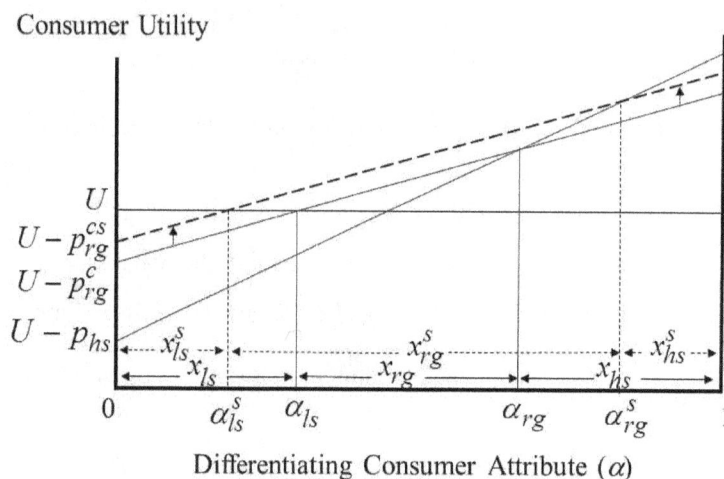

Figure III.3.4. Direct Effects of an Input Subsidy on Consumption Decisions

In addition to affecting the market for the regulated product, the changes in this market caused by the input subsidy have a direct impact on the market for the substitute product. In particular, the reduced consumer price and the increased returns to the production of the regulated product in the presence of the subsidy attract to the regulated product previous consumers and producers of the substitute, affecting, this way, both the demand for and supply of the substitute product.

Formally, the reduced p_{rg}^c causes a downward parallel shift of the demand for the substitute product, D_{hs} (see equation (I.9) and Figure III.3.6), while the reduced w_{rg} and p_{rg}^f cause an upward parallel shift of the supply of the substitute product, S_{hs} (as the reduction in w_{rg} exceeds that in p_{rg}^f; see equation (I.19) and Figure III.3.6). While the reduced demand for, and supply of the substitute product always reduce the equilibrium quantity and profits of the suppliers of this product, the effect on the equilibrium consumer and producer prices (p_{hs}^c and p_{hs}^f, respectively) is determined by the relative magnitude of the demand and supply effects of the input subsidy on the market for the substitute product. In particular, since a *ceteris paribus* decrease in D_{hs} causes p_{hs}^c and p_{hs}^f to fall, while a similar decrease in S_{hs} results in increased p_{hs}^c and p_{hs}^f, when the supply effect dominates the demand effect so that

$$\left| \Delta p_{rg}^c \right| < \frac{\mu - \lambda}{\theta_{hs}^s (\mu - \lambda) + (1 + \theta_{hs}^b)(\delta - \gamma)} \left[\Delta p_{rg}^f - \Delta w_{rg} + \Delta w_{hs} \right] \text{ (where, as noted above,}$$

$\Delta p_{rg}^c < 0$, $\Delta p_{rg}^f < 0$ and $\Delta w_{rg} < 0$, while, as shown in Figure III.3.12 below, $\Delta w_{hs} < 0$), the consumer and producer prices of the substitute product increase after the introduction of the input subsidy (Scenario I); when

$$\frac{\mu - \lambda}{\theta_{hs}^s (\mu - \lambda) + (1 + \theta_{hs}^b)(\delta - \gamma)} \left[\Delta p_{rg}^f - \Delta w_{rg} + \Delta w_{hs} \right] < \left| \Delta p_{rg}^c \right| < \frac{(1 + \theta_{hs}^s)(\mu - \lambda) + \theta_{hs}^b (\delta - \gamma)}{\delta - \gamma} \left[\Delta p_{rg}^f - \Delta w_{rg} + \Delta w_{hs} \right],$$

the producer price of the substitute product increases while the consumer price falls (Scenario II); while when the demand effect of the input subsidy dominates the supply effect so that $\left| \Delta p_{rg}^c \right| > \frac{(1 + \theta_{hs}^s)(\mu - \lambda) + \theta_{hs}^b (\delta - \gamma)}{\delta - \gamma} \left[\Delta p_{rg}^f - \Delta w_{rg} + \Delta w_{hs} \right]$, the input subsidy

causes both the consumer and producer prices of the substitute product to fall (Scenario III). Figure III.3.5 provides a graphical representation of the conditions leading to the three scenarios while panels 1, 2 and 3 of Figure III.3.6 graph the effects of the input subsidy on the market of the substitute product under these three scenarios.

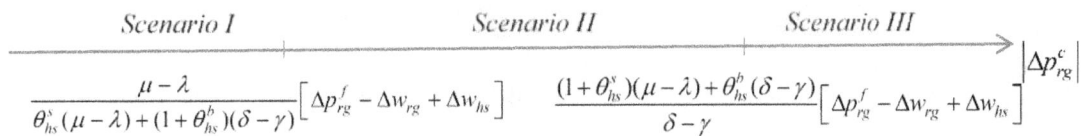

Figure III.3.5. Scenarios on the Effects of an Input Subsidy on Prices of Substitute *hs* Product

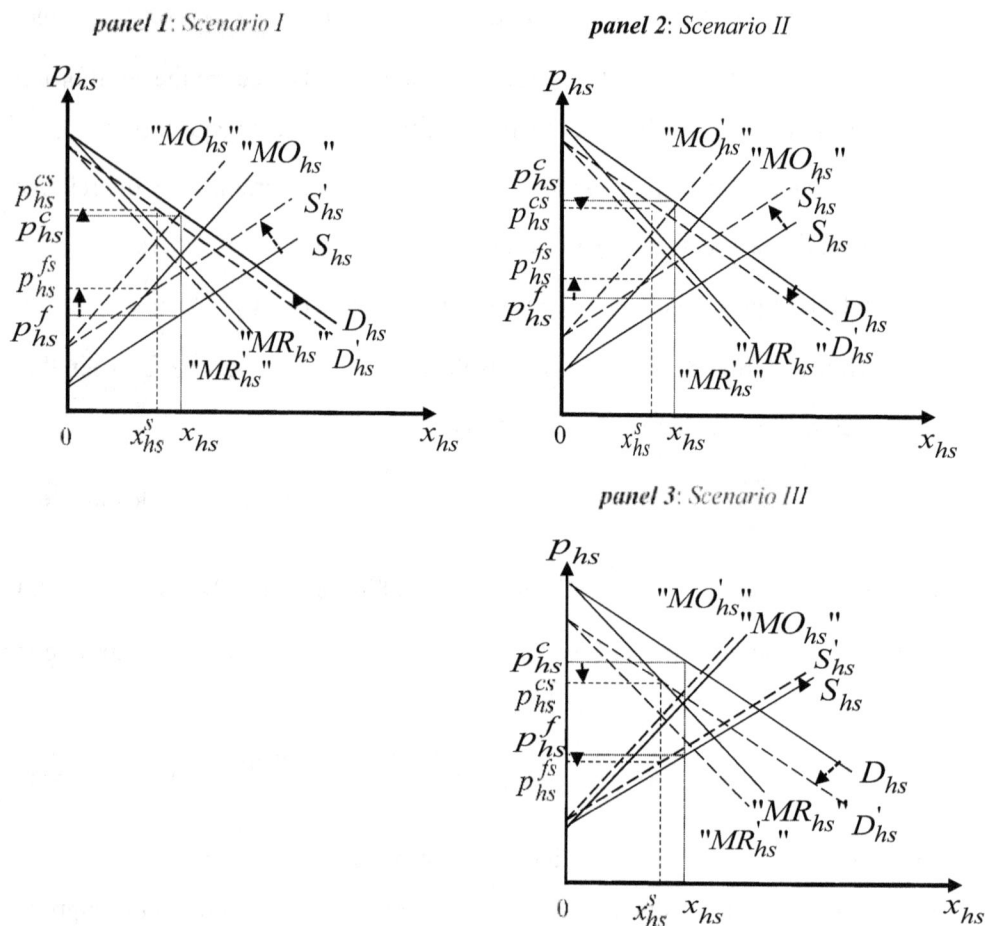

Figure III.3.6. Effects of an Input Subsidy on the Market for the Substitute *hs* Product

It is important to note that for Scenario II to occur, the middlemen in the substitute product market should be able to exercise market power. If $\theta_{hs}^s = \theta_{hs}^b = 0$, the condition for Scenario I becomes $\left| \Delta p_{rg}^c \right| < \frac{\mu - \lambda}{\delta - \gamma} \left[\Delta p_{rg}^f - \Delta w_{rg} + \Delta w_{hs} \right]$ and the condition for Scenario III becomes $\left| \Delta p_{rg}^c \right| > \frac{\mu - \lambda}{\delta - \gamma} \left[\Delta p_{rg}^f - \Delta w_{rg} + \Delta w_{hs} \right]$. Intuitively, under perfectly competitive middlemen in the substitute product market, the consumer and producer prices of this product will always move in the same direction. While the presence of middlemen market power is necessary for the consumer and producer prices of the substitute product to move in different directions, it is not sufficient for the emergence of Scenario II – as shown above, both Scenarios I and III can emerge in the presence of middlemen market power.

Since the equilibrium prices of the substitute product affect the welfare of the consumers and producers of this product, our analysis considers the market and welfare impacts of the input subsidy under the three scenarios outlined above. The case where the introduction of the input subsidy in the market of the regulated product causes the consumer and producer prices of its substitute product to increase (i.e., the case in which the supply effect dominates the demand effect of the subsidy) is analyzed first followed by the two other scenarios considered here. In all cases, suppliers of the substitute product realize a reduction in profits, with the change given by:

$$\Delta\Pi_{hs} = -\left[(p_{hs}^{cs} - p_{hs}^{c})x_{hs}^{s} - (p_{hs}^{fs} - p_{hs}^{f})x_{hs}^{s} - (p_{hs}^{c} - p_{hs}^{f})(x_{hs} - x_{hs}^{s}) \right] < 0.$$

Market and Welfare Effects of the Input Subsidy under Scenario I

(i.e., when $\left|\Delta p_{rg}^{c}\right| < \dfrac{\mu - \lambda}{\theta_{hs}^{s}(\mu - \lambda) + (1 + \theta_{hs}^{b})(\delta - \gamma)}\left[\Delta p_{rg}^{f} - \Delta w_{rg} + \Delta w_{hs}\right]$ ***)***

As mentioned previously, when the supply effect of an input subsidy dominates its demand effect, the introduction of the input subsidy for the regulated product increases the consumer and producer prices of its substitute product (recall panel 1 of Figure III.3.6 that depicts this scenario in the price-quantity space).

The increased consumer price of the substitute product, p_{hs}^{c}, reduces the utility associated with the consumption of this product and further increases the number of consumers that find it optimal to switch to the regulated product (see equation (III.3.1)). Figure III.3.7 depicts these market and welfare effects as well as the asymmetric impacts of the policy on the welfare of consumers in the consumer utility space. In addition, the figure shows that the consumers benefiting the most from the input subsidy are those consuming the regulated product both before and after the introduction of the policy (i.e., consumers with $\alpha \in (\alpha_{ls}, \alpha_{rg}]$) followed by consumers who find it optimal to switch to the regulated product (i.e., consumers with $\alpha \in (\alpha_{ls}^{s}, \alpha_{ls}]$ and $\alpha \in (\alpha_{rg}, \alpha_{rg}^{s'}]$).

Consumers of the substitute product in the presence of the policy (i.e., consumers with $\alpha \in (\alpha_{rg}^s, 1]$) as well as some consumers that find it optimal to switch their consumption from the substitute product to the regulated good (i.e., consumers with $\alpha \in (\alpha_{rg}^{s'}, \alpha_{rg}^s]$ in Figure III.3.7) lose from the introduction of the policy, with the magnitude of their loss determined by their preference parameter/differentiating attribute α. The consumer gains and losses in this case are given by

$$G_c = \int_{\alpha_{ls}^s}^{\alpha_{ls}} (U_{rg}^s - U_{ls})d\alpha + \int_{\alpha_{ls}}^{\alpha_{rg}} (U_{rg}^s - U_{rg})d\alpha + \int_{\alpha_{rg}}^{\alpha_{rg}^{s'}} (U_{rg}^s - U_{hs})d\alpha \text{ and}$$

$$L_c = \int_{\alpha_{rg}^{s'}}^{\alpha_{rg}^s} (U_{hs} - U_{rg}^s)d\alpha + \int_{\alpha_{rg}^s}^{1} (U_{hs} - U_{hs}^s)d\alpha \text{, respectively.}$$

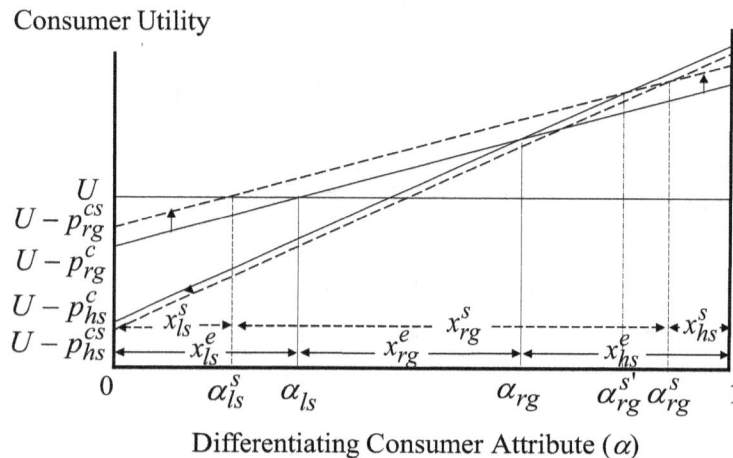

Figure III.3.7. Total Effects of an Input Subsidy on Consumption Decisions and Welfare under Scenario I

While the increased p_{hs}^c reduces the desirability of the substitute product for consumers, the increased p_{hs}^f under Scenario I increases the net returns associated with the production of the substitute product and reduces the incentives for switching to the production of the regulated product. Figure III.3.8 depicts these market and welfare effects in the producer net returns space. Producers benefiting the most from the input subsidy are those producing the regulated product both before and after the introduction of the policy (i.e., producers with $A \in (A_{hs}, A_{rg}]$), followed by producers who find it optimal to switch to the regulated product (i.e., producers with $A \in (A_{rg}, A^s_{rg}]$ and $A \in (A^s_{hs}, A_{hs}]$) and producers who continue to produce the substitute after the policy introduction (i.e., producers with $A \in (0, A^s_{hs}]$). Total producer benefits in this case are given by

$$G_p = \int_0^{A^s_{hs}} (NR^s_{hs} - NR_{hs})dA + \int_{A^s_{hs}}^{A_{hs}} (NR^s_{rg} - NR_{hs})dA + \int_{A_{hs}}^{A_{rg}} (NR^s_{rg} - NR_{rg})dA + \int_{A_{rg}}^{A^s_{rg}} (NR^s_{rg} - NR_a)dA$$

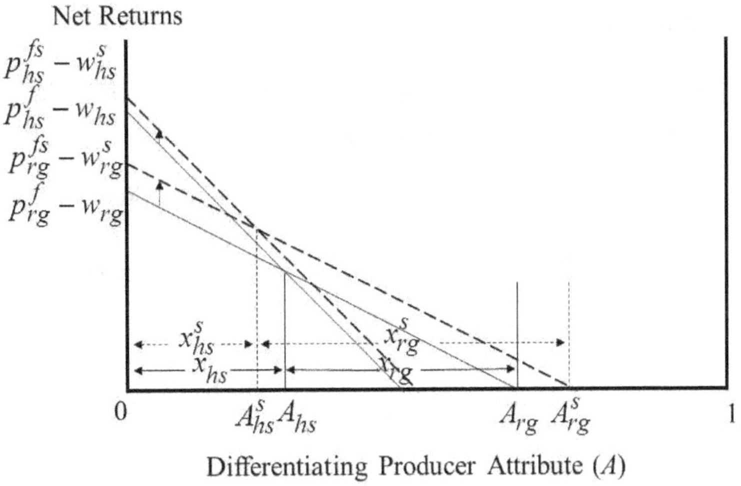

Figure III.3.8. Total Effects of an Input Subsidy on Producer Decisions and Welfare under Scenarios I & II

Market and Welfare Effects of the Input Subsidy under Scenario II (i.e., when $\frac{\mu-\lambda}{\theta^s_{hs}(\mu-\lambda)+(1+\theta^b_{hs})(\delta-\gamma)}\left[\Delta p^f_{rg} - \Delta w_{rg} + \Delta w_{hs}\right] < \left|\Delta p^c_{rg}\right| < \frac{(1+\theta^s_{hs})(\mu-\lambda)+\theta^b_{hs}(\delta-\gamma)}{\delta-\gamma}\left[\Delta p^f_{rg} - \Delta w_{rg} + \Delta w_{hs}\right]$***)***

As shown in panel 2 of Figure III.3.6, under Scenario II the consumer price of the substitute product falls while the producer price increases making consumers and producers of the substitute product better off.

Predictably, the ramifications of the policy for the producers of the different products are similar to those under Scenario I (described in the previous section and graphed in Figure III.3.8), as p^f_{hs} increases under both Scenarios I and II. Thus, the input subsidy under Scenario II benefits all regulated and substitute product producers with the greater benefits enjoyed by those individuals who produce the regulated product both before and after the introduction of the input subsidy.

Unlike Scenario I, consumers of the substitute product gain under Scenario II as the introduction of the input subsidy for the regulated product causes the consumer price of the substitute product, p_{hs}^c, to fall. The reduced p_{hs}^c increases the utility associated with the consumption of this product and reduces the number of consumers switching to the regulated product (see equation (III.3.7)). Figure III.3.9 depicts these market and welfare effects in the consumer utility space. In addition, the figure shows that the consumers benefiting the most from the input subsidy are those consuming the regulated product both before and after the introduction of the policy (i.e., consumers with $\alpha \in (\alpha_{ls}, \alpha_{rg}]$), followed by consumers who find it optimal to switch to the regulated product (i.e., consumers with $\alpha \in (\alpha_{ls}^s, \alpha_{ls}]$ and $\alpha \in (\alpha_{rg}, \alpha_{rg}^s]$) and consumers who continue to consume the substitute product after the policy introduction (i.e., consumers with $\alpha \in (\alpha_{rg}^s, 1]$). Total consumer benefits from the input subsidy in this case are given by $G_c = \int_{\alpha_{ls}^s}^{\alpha_{ls}} (U_{rg}^s - U_{ls}) d\alpha + \int_{\alpha_{ls}}^{\alpha_{rg}} (U_{rg}^s - U_{rg}) d\alpha + \int_{\alpha_{rg}}^{\alpha_{rg}^s} (U_{rg}^s - U_{hs}) d\alpha + \int_{\alpha_{rg}^s}^{1} (U_{hs}^s - U_{hs}) d\alpha$.

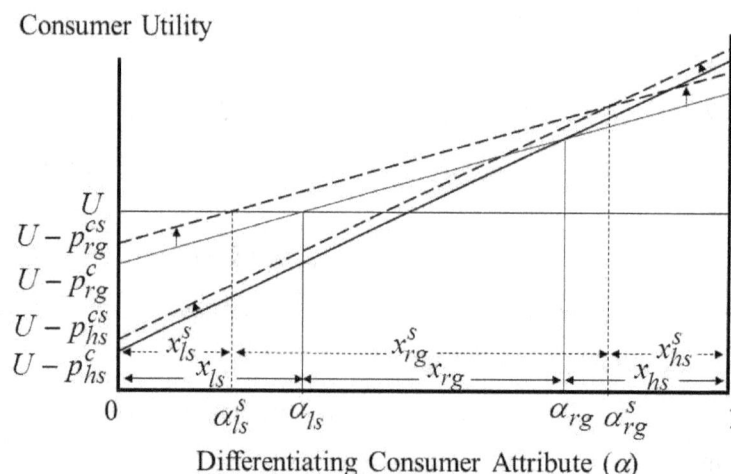

Figure III.3.9. Total Effects of Input Subsidy on Consumption Decisions and Welfare under Scenarios II & III

Market and Welfare Effects of the Tax under Scenario III

(i.e., when $\left|\Delta p_{rg}^c\right| > \dfrac{(1+\theta_{hs}^s)(\mu-\lambda)+\theta_{hs}^b(\delta-\gamma)}{\delta-\gamma}\left[\Delta p_{rg}^f - \Delta w_{rg} + \Delta w_{hs}\right]$*)*

When the demand effect of the input subsidy dominates the supply effect, subsidizing the input used in the production of the regulated product causes the consumer and producer prices of the substitute product to fall. While the effects of the reduced p_{hs}^c on consumer decisions and welfare are similar to those under Scenario II (described in the previous section and graphed in Figure III.3.9), the effects of the input subsidy on producers are different than those under Scenarios I and II.

Specifically, the reduced p_{hs}^f reduces the net returns associated with the production of the substitute product and increases the incentives for switching to the production of the regulated product (see equation (III.3.1)). Figure III.3.10 depicts these market and welfare effects as well as the asymmetric impacts of the policy on producer welfare in the producer net returns space. Producers benefiting the most from the input subsidy are those producing the regulated product both before and after the introduction of the policy (i.e., producers with $A \in (A_{hs}, A_{rg}]$), followed by producers who find it optimal to switch to the regulated product from the alternative crop and the substitute product (i.e., producers with $A \in (A_{rg}, A_{rg}^s]$ and $A \in (A_{hs}^{s'}, A_{hs}]$). Producers who continue to produce the substitute after the policy introduction (i.e., producers with $A \in (0, A_{hs}^s]$) lose, as do some of the substitute product producers who switch to the regulated product (i.e., producers with $A \in (A_{hs}^s, A_{hs}^{s'})$), with the magnitude of this loss determined by the efficiency parameter/differentiating attribute of these producers. The producer gains and losses in this case are given by

$$G_p = \int_{A_{hs}^{s'}}^{A_{hs}} (NR_{rg}^s - NR_{hs})dA + \int_{A_{hs}}^{A_{rg}} (NR_{rg}^s - NR_{rg})dA + \int_{A_{rg}}^{A_{rg}^s} (NR_{rg}^s - NR_a)dA \text{ and}$$

$$L_p = \int_0^{A_{hs}^s} (NR_{hs} - NR_{hs}^s)dA + \int_{A_{hs}^s}^{A_{hs}^{s'}} (NR_{hs} - NR_{rg}^s)dA \text{, respectively.}$$

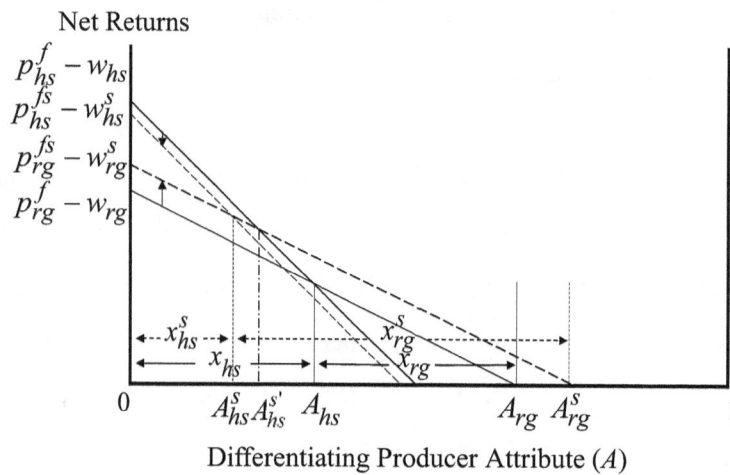

Net Returns

$p_{hs}^f - w_{hs}$
$p_{hs}^{fs} - w_{hs}^s$
$p_{rg}^{fs} - w_{rg}^s$
$p_{rg}^f - w_{rg}$

x_{hs}^s
x_{hs}
x_{rg}^s
x_{rg}

0     $A_{hs}^s A_{hs}^{s'}$ A_{hs} A_{rg} A_{rg}^s 1

Differentiating Producer Attribute (A)

Figure III.3.10. Total Effects of an Input Subsidy on Producer Decisions and Welfare under Scenario III

In addition to affecting the decisions and welfare of consumers and producers of the substitute product, the changes in p_{hs}^c and p_{hs}^f have a feedback effect on the market for the regulated product (recall equations (III.3.1), (III.3.2), and (III.3.7)). In particular, an increase (decrease) in p_{hs}^c shifts the demand for the regulated product D_{rg} upwards (downwards), while an increase (decrease) in p_{hs}^f causes an upward (downward) shift of the supply of the regulated product S_{rg} (recall equations (I.8) and (I.18) and Figures I.3 and I.5). The total effects of the input subsidy on the final consumer market for the regulated product under the three scenarios considered here are depicted in Figure III.3.11. In all cases, the policy causes an increase in the regulated product supplier profits given by $\Delta\Pi_{rg} = (p_{rg}^f - p_{rg}^{fs})x_{rg} + (p_{rg}^{cs} - p_{rg}^{fs})(x_{rg}^s - x_{rg}) - (p_{rg}^c - p_{rg}^{cs})x_{rg} > 0$.

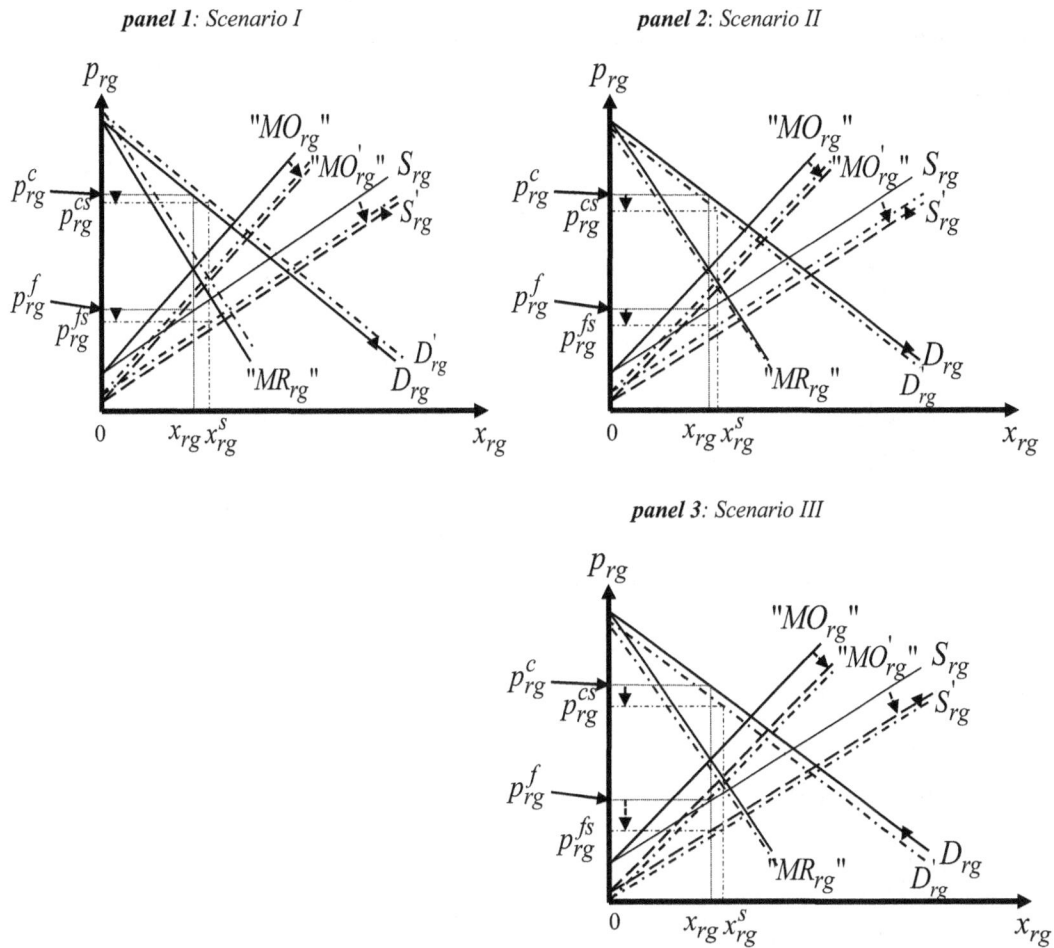

panel 1: Scenario I

panel 2: Scenario II

panel 3: Scenario III

Figure III.3.11. Overall Impact of the Input Subsidy on the *rg* Product Market

Regarding the impact of the input subsidy on the market for the inputs used in the

production of the substitute product, no matter the effect of the policy on p_{hs}^c and p_{hs}^f,

the introduction of an input subsidy in the market for the regulated product reduces the

demand for inputs used in the production of its substitute (as the equilibrium quantity of

the substitute product falls in the presence of the policy). The reduced demand for *hs*

inputs results, then, in lower equilibrium input price and quantity (see equations (III.3.6)

and (III.3.8)), and a reduction in the profits of the supplier of these inputs, with the

change in profits given by $\Delta\Pi_{hs}^I = -\left[(w_{hs} - c_{hs}^I)x_{hs} - (w_{hs}^s - c_{hs}^I)x_{hs}^s \right] < 0$. Figure

III.3.12, panel b graphs the changes in the market for the input used in the production of the substitute product due to the introduction of an input subsidy for the regulated product.

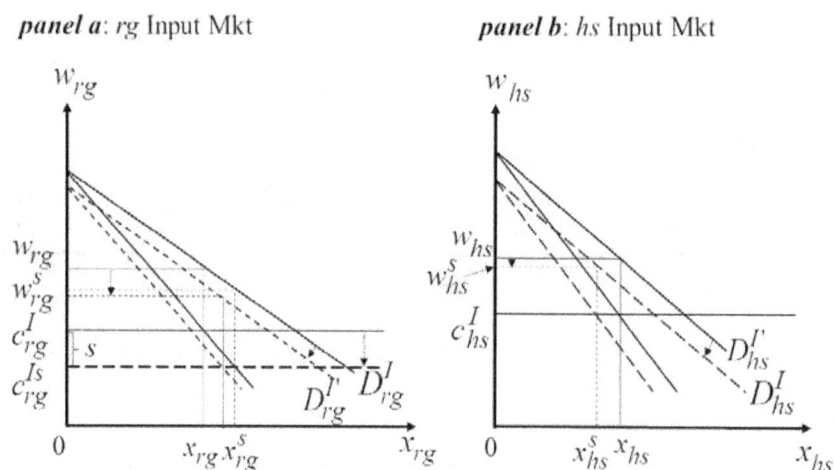

panel a: *rg* Input Mkt   **panel b**: *hs* Input Mkt

Figure III.3.12. Total Effect of an Input Subsidy on the Input Markets

Finally, the change in w_{hs} has a feedback effect on the market of the regulated input. Specifically, the decrease in w_{hs} reduces the demand for the regulated input D_{rg}^I (see equation (I.20) and Figure I.6) which, in turn, (a) bolsters the impact of the cost-reducing input subsidy on the price of this input, and (b) lessens the impact of the policy on the quantity of the subsidized input (see equations (III.3.5) and (III.3.7)). The total effects of the input subsidy on the input markets are depicted in Figure III.3.12.

Overall, the analysis of the system-wide market and welfare impacts of the input subsidy indicates that: (a) the qualitative nature of the welfare effects on the consumers and producers of the substitute product is scenario-specific and depends on the conditions in the market for both the regulated product and the substitute product; (b) the impacts of the input subsidy are asymmetric across the different consumers and producers affected by the policy; (c) determination of these asymmetric impacts requires a disaggregation of the benefits and costs to the level of the individual agent; and (d) in Scenarios I and III, some of the consumers (Scenario I) or some of the producers (Scenario III) who find it optimal to switch from the substitute product to the regulated good after the introduction of the input subsidy realize welfare losses.

The asymmetric impact of the policy on the welfare of all relevant interest groups is summarized in Table III.3.1, while Figures III.3.13-III.3.15 summarize the system-wide market and welfare impacts of this policy under the different scenarios considered in this study. For simplicity, the feedback effects described above (Figures III.3.11 and III.3.12) are not included in Figures III.3.13-III.3.15.

Table III.3.1. System-Wide Welfare Impacts of an Input Subsidy

	Consumers of ls switching to rg	Consumers of rg	Consumers of hs switching to rg	Consumers of hs	Producers of hs switching to rg	Producers of rg	Producers of hs	Suppliers of rg	Suppliers of hs	Input Suppliers rg	Input Suppliers hs
Scenario I	+	+	some + some –	–	+	+	+	+	–	+	–
Scenario II	+	+	+	+	+	+	+	+	–	+	–
Scenario III	+	+	+	+	some – some +	+	–	+	–	+	–

+ denotes welfare gains
– denotes welfare losses

Condition for Scenario I: $\left| \Delta p_{rg}^c \right| < \dfrac{\mu - \lambda}{\theta_{hs}^s (\mu - \lambda) + (1 + \theta_{hs}^b)(\delta - \gamma)} \left[\Delta p_{rg}^f - \Delta w_{rg} + \Delta w_{hs} \right]$

Condition for Scenario II: $\dfrac{\mu - \lambda}{\theta_{hs}^s (\mu - \lambda) + (1 + \theta_{hs}^b)(\delta - \gamma)} \left[\Delta p_{rg}^f - \Delta w_{rg} + \Delta w_{hs} \right] < \left| \Delta p_{rg}^c \right| < \dfrac{(1 + \theta_{hs}^s)(\mu - \lambda) + \theta_{hs}^b (\delta - \gamma)}{\delta - \gamma} \left[\Delta p_{rg}^f - \Delta w_{rg} + \Delta w_{hs} \right]$

Condition for Scenario III: $\left| \Delta p_{rg}^c \right| > \dfrac{(1 + \theta_{hs}^s)(\mu - \lambda) + \theta_{hs}^b (\delta - \gamma)}{\delta - \gamma} \left[\Delta p_{rg}^f - \Delta w_{rg} + \Delta w_{hs} \right]$

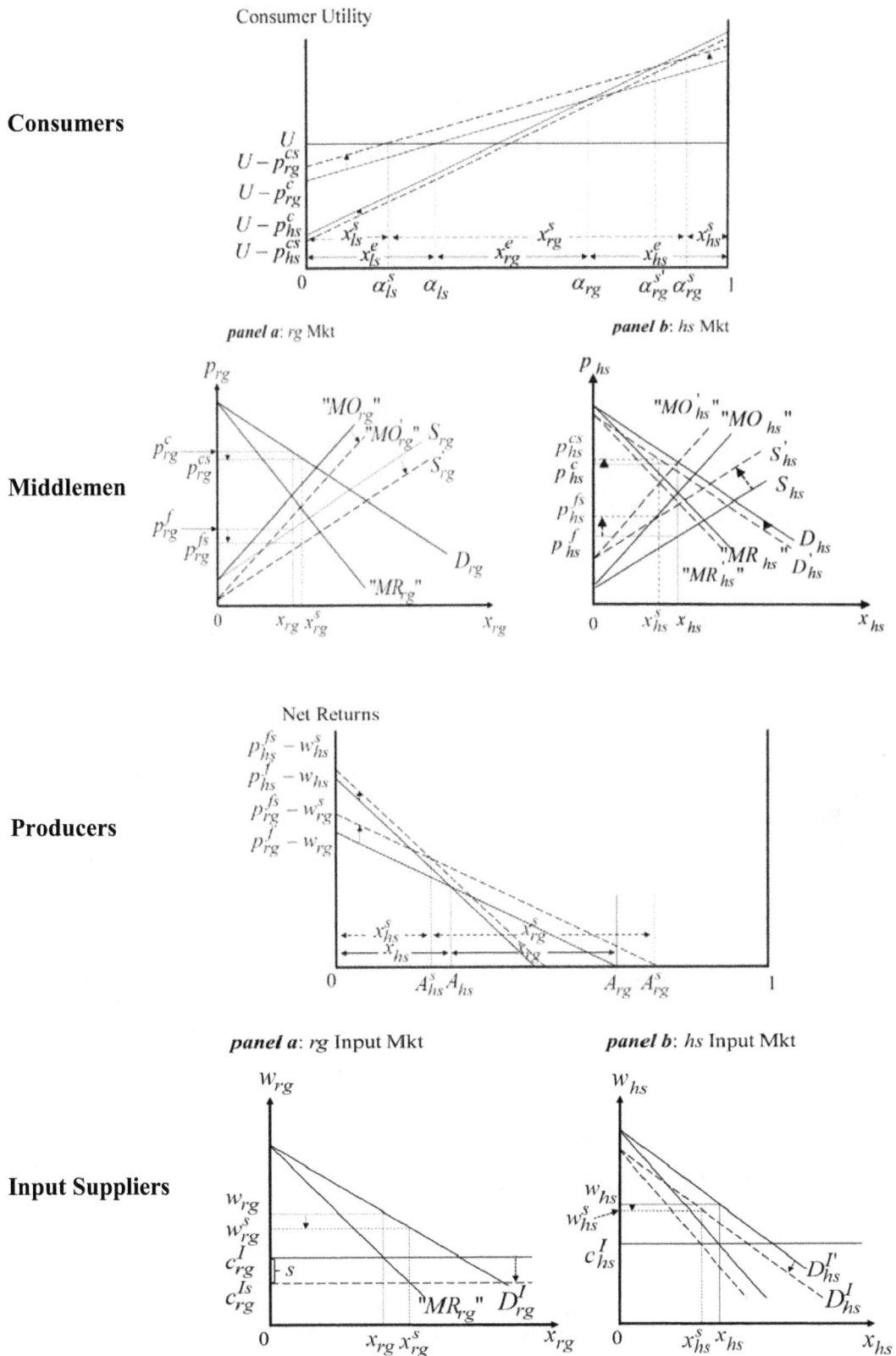

Figure II.3.13. System-Wide Market and Welfare Impacts of an Input Subsidy under Scenario I

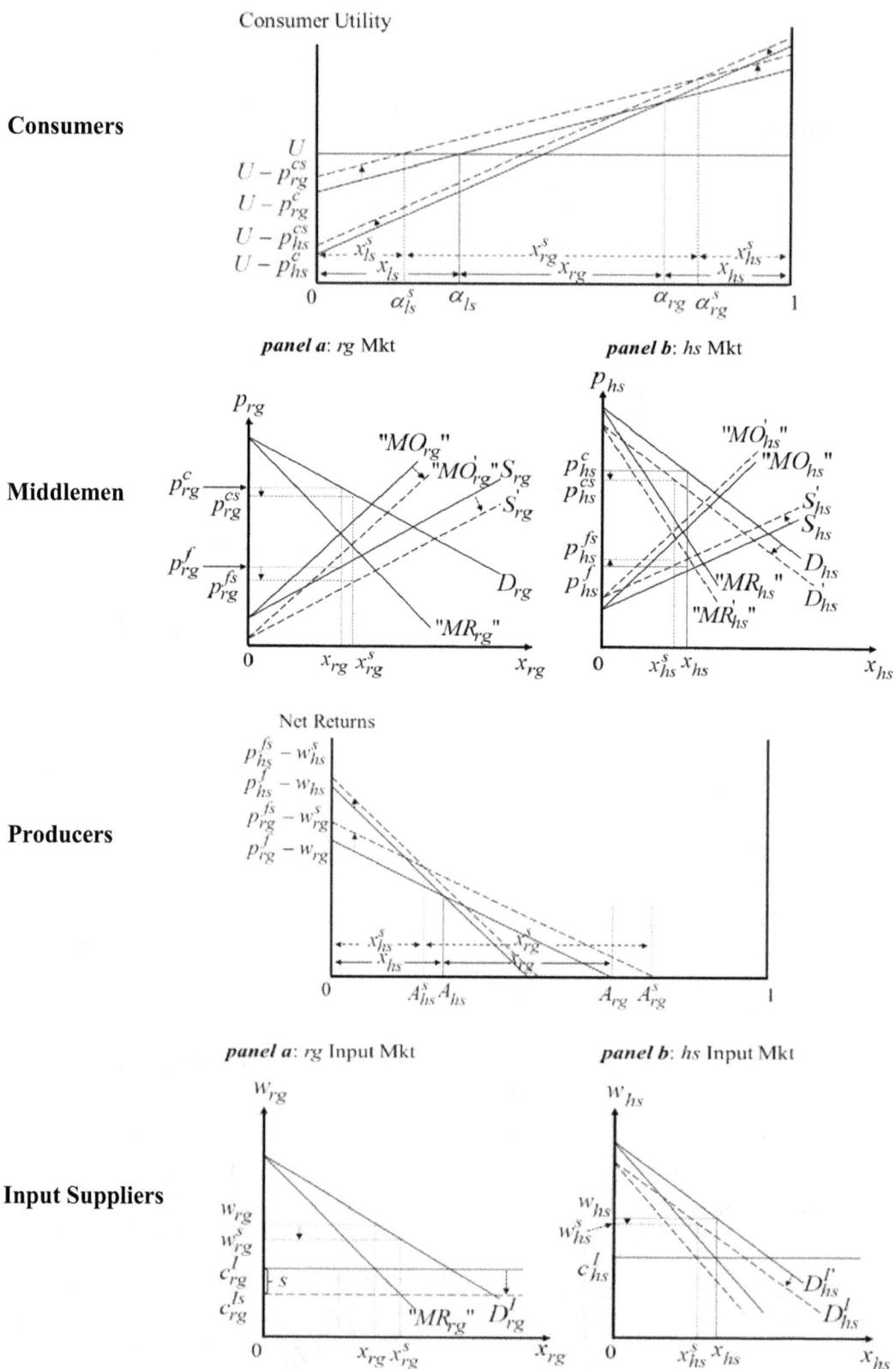

Figure II.3.14. System-Wide Market and Welfare Impacts of an Input Subsidy under Scenario II

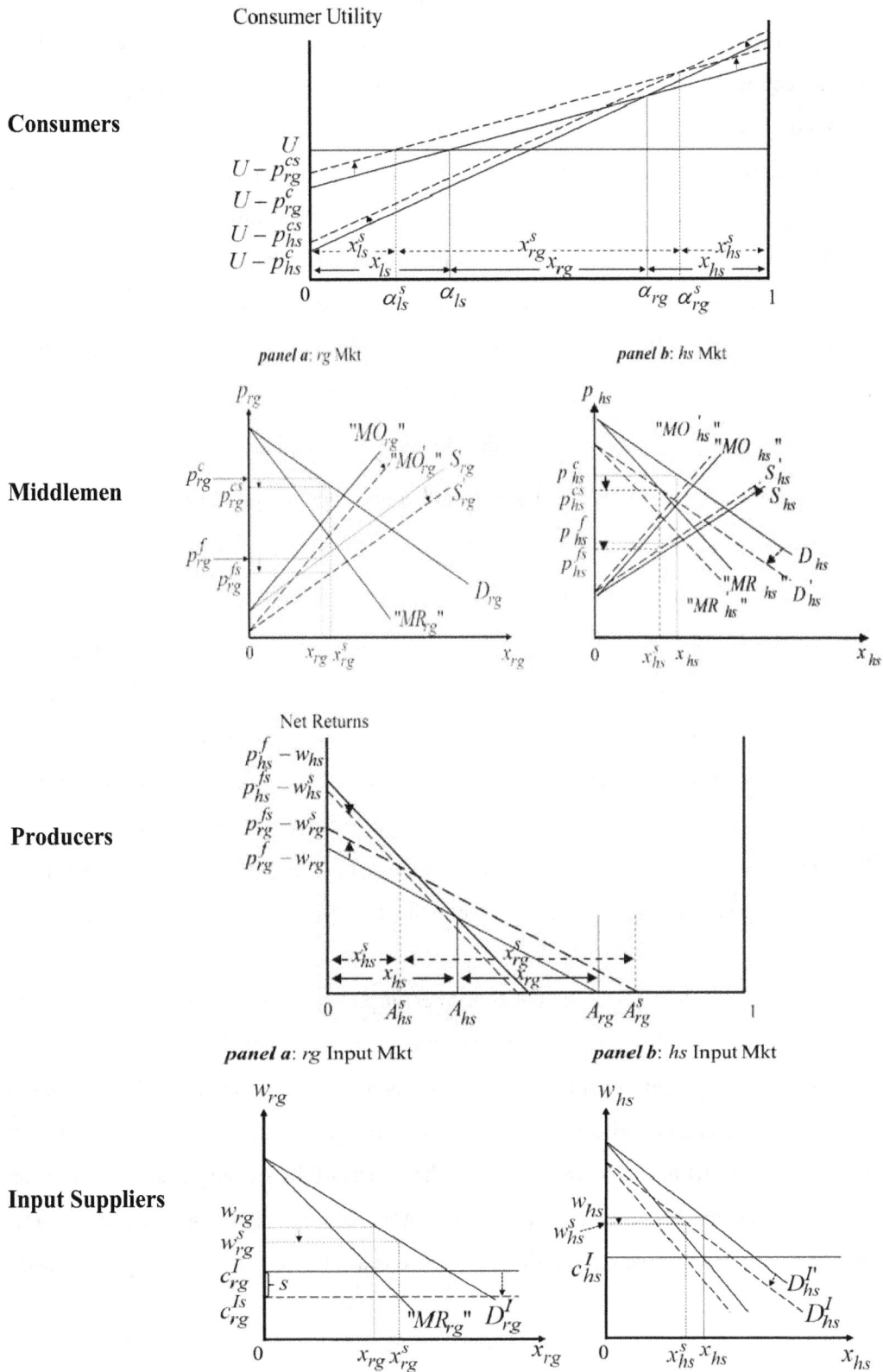

Figure II.3.15. System-Wide Market and Welfare Impacts of an Input Subsidy under Scenario III

Disaggregation of Welfare Changes and Comparison with Conventional Analysis

Before concluding the analysis of this policy, it is important to note that the key findings of this section outlined above are important because they indicate that a proper accounting of the differential welfare impacts of an input subsidy requires a disaggregated analysis, particularly in Scenarios I and III where some of the consumers (Scenario I) or some of the producers (Scenario III) of the substitute product realize welfare losses after they have optimally switched to the regulated good. While, as was pointed out earlier, the aggregate welfare changes can be determined using the calculation of producer and consumer surplus from the supply and demand curves, the allocation of the welfare changes to the two markets is incorrect.

Following the same approach developed in the analysis of the reduced c_{rg}^{I} in Section II.4 (as in both cases the changes in the consumer and producer prices of the different products are qualitatively the same), it can be shown that, similar to the case of reduced c_{rg}^{I} Scenario I, allocating the cost and benefits according to the demand curves in each market overstates the benefits to those that originally consumed the regulated product and overstates the costs to those that originally consumed the substitute product (i.e., overstates both the gain in the regulated market and the loss in the substitute market). In short, the calculation of consumer surplus from the demand curves does not provide a proper allocation of the costs and benefits to the various consumer groups. While these overstated amounts cancel each other out at the aggregate level, they yield incorrect results if they are used to determine the distributional impacts of an input subsidy.

The need to disaggregate the consumer surplus measures is clearly important in Scenario I, since in this scenario some consumers gain and others lose from the introduction of the input subsidy. However, if it is believed that the magnitude of the gain realized by consumers is also important, then disaggregating the gains that occur in Scenarios II and III may also be required as the effects of the subsidy were shown to vary among consumers. The same conclusions, of course, can be drawn regarding the need to disaggregate producer welfare. In this case, there is a clear need to disaggregate producer welfare in Scenario III, since in this case some of the producers that switch to producing the regulated good will be worse off than they were originally in producing the substitute product. There may also be a need to disaggregate the changes in producer welfare in Scenarios I and II, since, as was shown in the previous sections, the welfare changes are not symmetric among producers.

III.4 Additional Considerations, Policy Studies and Empirical Implementation

In addition to enabling the analysis of traditional policy mechanisms like subsidies and taxes, our framework can also be utilized to analyze the market and welfare impacts of other important (and increasingly relevant) policy mechanisms like **food labeling** and the introduction and change of **standards** for various products. Such policies are particularly significant for marketing systems that, like the industrialized agri-food system, are characterized by asymmetric information due to the presence and continuous development of credence goods and concepts (like natural, local, sustainable, low carbon footprint, etc.).

Examples of labeling policies that have been analyzed using various adaptations of our framework include the labeling of GM products (Fulton and Giannakas, 2004; Veyssiere and Giannakas, 2006), country-of-origin-labeling (Plastina, Giannakas and Pick, 2011), and labeling of nanofoods (Tran, Yiannaka and Giannakas, 2019), while examples of studies on regulatory requirements/standards include those on the economic effects of purity standards in biotech labeling laws (Giannakas et al., 2011) and renewable portfolio standards for conventional electricity (Bhattacharya, Giannakas and Schoengold, 2017). In general, labeling policies and standards affect the consumer valuation of the regulated product (preference effect, which is similar to the one studied in Section II.1), while increasing the segregation and identity preservation costs (cost effect, which is the reverse of that studied in Section II.4 and can affect multiple supply channels). The system-wide market and welfare effects of these policies are determined, then, by the relative magnitude of these preference and cost effects.

Regarding the empirical implementation of our theoretical framework, a common finding in the previous analyses and results is that the market and welfare impacts of different policies (and changes in market conditions) depend on the values of the key parameters of our models – the preference, cost and market power parameters. These values can be derived from relevant (stated and revealed) consumer preference studies, studies on cost structure and producer efficiency, and studies on market power in the supply channels of interest. Examples of studies that utilize empirical estimates and simulation methods to quantify analytical results of various adaptations of our framework include Giannakas and Kaplan (2005) who study conservation compliance on highly erodible lands by heterogeneous producers; Plastina, Giannakas and Pick (2011) who analyze the market and welfare impacts of mandatory country-of-origin labeling for specialty crops in the U.S.; and Bhattacharya, Giannakas and Schoengold (2017) who study the impacts of renewable portfolio standards in the U.S. electricity sector.

Finally, it is important to note that, in providing a means of determining the system-wide economic effects and distributional impacts of changes in market conditions and policies, our framework of analysis can provide a valuable theoretical grounding to empirical studies of important market and policy issues. Indeed, by explicitly accounting for consumer and producer heterogeneity, our framework is uniquely equipped to inform behavioral and experimental economic studies that can empirically capture the essence of such heterogeneity, while, by identifying the exact conditions under which different scenarios will emerge, it can help direct a focus of the empirical research efforts on the determination of the relevant scenario at hand. This is particularly important for (*ex ante*) policy design since, as shown in our analysis, the system-wide market and welfare impacts of changes in market conditions and policies tend to be case/scenario specific.

Summary and Concluding Remarks

This book presented a novel, integrated, multi-market framework of market and policy analysis that explicitly accounts for the empirically relevant heterogeneity in consumer preferences or/and incomes; heterogeneous producers; imperfectly competitive input suppliers, processors or/and retailers; and links and interactions between the agri-food supply channels of interest. The explicit consideration of consumer and producer heterogeneity represents a significant departure from the representative consumer and producer that have been at the center of most of the literature on market and policy analysis, and enables the distributional impacts of changes in market conditions and policies to be fully identified.

Once the general framework of analysis was developed, it was used to analyze the system-wide market and welfare impacts of a number of changes in market conditions (like changes in consumer preferences, costs and market structure) and policies (like subsidies and taxes) on one of the products in the system. Consistent with a priori expectations, the use of the framework unveiled impacts masked by the conventional market and policy analysis.

Overall, the analysis of the system-wide economic effects of the changes in market conditions and policies indicated that: (a) the qualitative nature of the welfare effects on the consumers and producers of the substitute products is case-specific and dependent on the conditions in the market for both the reference/regulated product and the substitute product; (b) the impacts of these changes in market conditions and policies are asymmetric across the different consumers and producers involved; (c) determination of these asymmetric impacts requires a disaggregation of the benefits and costs to the level of the individual agent; and (d) the conventional analysis fails to provide a proper allocation of the costs and benefits of these changes in market conditions and policies to the various consumer and producer groups involved.

In particular, the analysis revealed that allocating the costs and benefits according to the demand and supply curves in each market overstates the gains and losses in the markets for the reference/regulated product and its substitute. While these overstated amounts cancel each other out at the aggregate level, they yield incorrect results if they are used to determine the distributional impacts of changes in market conditions and policies.

Thus, in addition to enhancing the empirical relevance of market and policy analysis by allowing the research to account for key elements of the increasingly industrialized agri-food system, the explicit consideration of consumer and producer heterogeneity enables the analysis to disaggregate these interest groups and correctly identify the effects of different market changes and policies on different consumers and producers. This is important as better measures (and understanding) of the economic impacts of changes in market conditions and policies can lead to improved policy design, enhanced efficiency, increased effectiveness, and reduced policy failures.

References

Alston J.M., R.J. Sexton, M. Zhang. "The Effects of Imperfect Competition on the Size and Distribution of Research Benefits." *American Journal of Agricultural Economics* 79(1997): 1252-1265.

Bhattacharya S., K. Giannakas, K. Schoengold. "Market and Welfare Effects of Renewable Portfolio Standards in United States Electricity Markets." *Energy Economics* 64(2017): 384-401.

Boehlje M. "Industrialization of Agriculture: What are the Implications?" *Choices* First Quarter (1996): 30-33.

Buse R.C. "Total Elasticities - A Predictive Device." *Journal of Farm Economics* 40, 4 (1958): 881-891.

Drivas K., K. Giannakas. "The Effect of Cooperatives on Quality-Enhancing Innovation." *Journal of Agricultural Economics* 61, 2(2010): 295-317.

_____. "Process Innovation Activity in a Mixed Oligopsony: The Role of Marketing Cooperatives." *Journal of Rural Cooperation* 36, 2(2008): 131-156.

Fulton M., K. Giannakas. "The Future of Agricultural Cooperatives." *Annual Review of Resource Economics* 5(2013): 61-91.

_____. "The Value of a Norm: Open Membership and the Horizon Problem in Cooperatives." *Journal of Rural Cooperation* 40, 2(2012): 145-161.

_____. "Inserting GM Products into the Food Chain: The Market and Welfare Effects of Different Labeling and Regulatory Regimes." *American Journal of Agricultural Economics* 86(2004): 42-60.

_____. "Organizational Commitment in a Mixed Oligopoly: Agricultural Cooperatives and Investor-Owned Firms." *American Journal of Agricultural Economics* 83(2001): 1258-1265.

Gabszewicz J., J. Thisse. "Location." In Aumann R., S. Hart (eds.) *Handbook of Game Theory*, Amsterdam: North-Holland, 1992.

Giannakas K. "Coexistence of Genetically Modified, Conventional and Organic Food Products: A Framework and Analysis." In Kalaitzandonakes N. (ed.) *The*

Coexistence of Genetically Modified, Organic and Conventional Foods, Springer Academic Publishers, October 2016, pp. 345-362.

_____. "Consumer Demand in Vertically Differentiated Markets." *Chapter 9* in Lusk J., J. Roosen, J. Shogren (eds.) *Oxford Handbook on the Economics of Food Consumption and Policy*, Oxford University Press, September 2011, pp. 243-259.

_____. "Information Asymmetries and Consumption Decisions in Organic Food Product Markets." *Canadian Journal of Agricultural Economics* 50(2002a): 35-50.

_____. "Infringement of Intellectual Property Rights: Causes and Consequences." *American Journal of Agricultural Economics* 84(2002b): 482-494.

Giannakas K., M. Fulton. "Process Innovation Activity in a Mixed Oligopoly: The Role of Cooperatives." *American Journal of Agricultural Economics* 87(2005): 406-422.

_____. "Consumption Effects of Genetic Modification: What if Consumers are Right?" *Agricultural Economics* 27(2002): 97-109.

Giannakas K., J. Kaplan. "Policy Design and Conservation Compliance on Highly Erodible Lands." *Land Economics* 81(2005): 20-33.

Giannakas K., A. Yiannaka. "Doing Well by Doing Good: Agricultural Biotechnology in the Fight against Hunger." *Agricultural Economics* 49, 6(2018): 725-739.

_____. "Market and Welfare Effects of the Second-Generation, Consumer-Oriented GM Products." *American Journal of Agricultural Economics* 90(2008): 152-171.

_____. "Agricultural Biotechnology and Organic Agriculture: National Organic Standards and Labeling of GM Products." *AgBioForum* 9, 2(2006): 84-93.

_____. "The Market Potential of a New High-Oleic Soybean: An *Ex Ante* Analysis." *AgBioForum* 7, 3(2004): 101-112.

Giannakas K., M. Fulton, J. Sesmero. "Horizon and Free-Rider Problems in Cooperative Organizations." *Journal of Agricultural and Resource Economics* 42, 3(2016): 372-392.

Giannakas K, N. Kalaitzandonakes, A. Magnier, K. Mattas. "Economic Effects of Purity Standards in Biotech Labeling Laws." *Journal of Agricultural & Food Industrial Organization* 9, 1(2011): 1-45.

Holloway G. "The Farm-Retail Price Spread in an Imperfectly Competitive Food Industry." *American Journal of Agricultural Economics* 73(1991): 979-989.

Just R.E., D.L. Hueth. "Welfare Measures in a Multimarket Framework." *The American Economic Review* 69(1979): 947-954.

Just R.E., D.L. Hueth, A. Schmitz. *Applied Welfare Economics*. Edward Elgar, 2008.

Kahneman D., A. Tversky. "Prospect Theory: An Analysis of Decision Under Risk." *Econometrica* 47(1979): 263-291.

Lassoued R., K. Giannakas. "Economic Effects of the Consumer-Oriented GM Products in Markets with a Labeling Regime." *Journal of Agricultural Economics* 61, 3(2010): 499-526.

Mavroutsikos C., K. Giannakas, C. Walters. "Market and Welfare Effects of the Federal Crop Insurance Program." Western Agricultural Economics Association (WAEA) Meeting, Anchorage, Alaska, June 2018.

Meerza S.I.A., K. Giannakas, A. Yiannaka. "Market and Welfare Effects of Food Fraud." *Australian Journal of Agricultural and Resource Economics* (2019, Special Issue): forthcoming.

Meerza S.I.A., K. Giannakas, A. Yiannaka. "Optimal Policy Response to Food Fraud." Agricultural & Applied Economics Association Annual Meeting, Washington D.C., August 2018.

Mérel P.R., R.J. Sexton. "Models of Horizontal Differentiation in Food Markets." *Chapter 10* in Lusk J., J. Roosen, J. Shogren (eds.) *Oxford Handbook on the Economics of Food Consumption and Policy*, Oxford University Press, September 2011, pp. 260-291.

Omidvar V., K. Giannakas. "The Effects of Fair Trade on Coffee Growers: A Framework and Analysis." *Agricultural Economics* 46, S1(2015): 29-39.

Panzar J.C., R.D. Willig. "On the Comparative Statics of a Competitive Industry with Inframarginal Firms." *The American Economic Review* 68(1978): 474-478.

Perloff J.M., A. Golan, L.S. Karp. *Estimating Market Power and Strategies*. Cambridge University Press, 2007.

Plastina A., K. Giannakas, D. Pick. "Market and Welfare Effects of Mandatory Country-Of-Origin-Labeling in the US Specialty Crops Sector." *Southern Economic Journal* 77, 4(2011): 1044-1069.

Plastina A., K. Giannakas. "Market and Welfare Effects of GMO Introduction in Small Open Economies." *AgBioForum* 10, 2(2007): 104-123.

Sexton R.J. "Industrialization and Consolidation in the U.S. Food Sector: Implications for Competition and Welfare." *American Journal of Agricultural Economics* 82, 5(2000): 1087-1104.

Sexton R.J. "Market Power, Misconceptions, and Modern Agricultural Markets." *American Journal of Agricultural Economics* 95(2013): 209-219.

Tirole J. *The Theory of Industrial Organization*. MIT Press, 1988.

Thurman W.N. "Applied General Equilibrium Welfare Analysis." *American Journal of Agricultural Economics* 73 (1991): 1508-1516.

Thurman W.N., M.K. Wohlgenant. "Consistent Estimation of General Equilibrium Welfare Effects." *American Journal of Agricultural Economics* 71(1989): 1041-1045.

Tran V., A. Yiannaka, K. Giannakas. "Market Potential and Economic Impacts of Food Nanotechnology Innovations." *Journal of the Knowledge Economy* (2018): https://doi.org/10.1007/s13132-017-0494-9

_____. "Economic Impacts of Nanofood Labeling." *Journal of Policy Modeling* (2019): forthcoming

Veyssiere L., K. Giannakas. "Strategic Labeling and Trade of GMOs." *Journal of Agricultural & Food Industrial Organization* 4, 1(2006): 1-38.

Waterson M. *Economic Theory of the Industry*. Cambridge University Press, 1984.

Wohlgenant M.K. "Consumer Demand and Welfare in Equilibrium Displacement Models." *Chapter 11* in Lusk J., J. Roosen, J. Shogren (eds.) *Oxford Handbook on the Economics of Food Consumption and Policy*, Oxford University Press, September 2011, pp. 292-318.

About the Author

Dr. Konstantinos "Dinos" Giannakas is the Harold W. Eberhard Distinguished Professor of Agricultural Economics and the Director of the Center for Agricultural & Food Industrial Organization at the University of Nebraska-Lincoln. He holds a Ph.D. from the University of Saskatchewan in Canada, an M.Sc. from the Mediterranean Agronomic Institute of Chania and a B.Sc. from the Aristotle University of Thessaloniki in Greece. He loves living in Lincoln and spending his summers in his native Greece. He is married to Dr. Tala Awada and is the (very) proud father of Ritsa and Christos. His academic interests include the areas of Agricultural & Food Industrial Organization, Regulatory Economics and Policy Analysis, and the Economics of Innovation and Product Differentiation. His non-academic interests include tennis, skiing, opera, poetry, philosophy and orthodoxy, Big Red football and wine, Islay single malts, and Cuban cigars.

About the Book

"Over the past two decades Dinos Giannakas has developed a powerful, integrated framework for modeling markets and policies that explicitly accounts for heterogeneity of producers and consumers. This book presents the framework and illustrates its potential for illuminating analysis of farm and food policy issues in a range of diverse applications. It is a valuable addition to the tool-kit for any applied economist and will serve as a useful resource for teachers and graduate students alike."

Julian Alston (Distinguished Professor, University of California, Davis)

"Dr. Giannakas has provided a valuable resource for those interested in modeling the market behavior of heterogeneous consumers and producers. The simple, yet powerful framework is useful in understanding the potential impacts of new product introductions, labels, taxes, subsidies, and other policies. "

Jayson Lusk (Head and Distinguished Professor, Purdue University)

"Dinos Giannakas has been at the forefront in modeling agent heterogeneity in food markets on both the consumer and producer sides of the market and applying these methods to interesting and important problems. Now he has brought this body of work together and extended it to produce this excellent book. Readers who invest the time and energy to work through this in-depth analysis will benefit greatly from their investment."

Richard Sexton (Distinguished Professor, University of California, Davis)

"Macroeconomic and international economic researchers, among others, have made significant strides in incorporating heterogeneous agents into their models over the past two decades. In this new and challenging text, Dinos Giannakas does an excellent job of accounting for such heterogeneity in the food marketing chain. Drawing on an extensive body of published work, Professor Giannakas provides the reader with a theoretically consistent and compelling framework for analyzing economic interactions and public policy in an important sector of the economy."

Ian Sheldon (Andersons Chair, The Ohio State University)

www.ingramcontent.com/pod-product-compliance
Lightning Source LLC
Chambersburg PA
CBHW051213200326
41519CB00025B/7103